Scandinavian Women's Law in the 21st Century

Ruth Nielsen & Christina D. Tvarnø (eds.)

Scandinavian Women's Law in the 21st Century

Djøf Publishing
2012

Ruth Nielsen & Christina D. Tvarnø (Eds)
Scandinavian Women's Law in the 21st Century

Cover: Bo Helsted
Print and Binding: Ecograf, Højbjerg

Printed in Denmark 2012
ISBN 978-87-574-2567-3

Sold and distributed in Scandinavia by:
DJØF Publishing
Copenhagen, Denmark
Email: forlag@djoef.dk
www.djoef-forlag.dk

Sold and distributed in North America by:
International Specialized Book Services (ISBS)
Portland, USA
Email: orders@isbs.com
www.isbs.com

Sold in all other countries by:
The Oxford Publicity Partnership Ltd
Towcester, UK
Email: djof@oppuk.co.uk
www.oppuk.co.uk

Distributed in all other countries by:
Marston Book Services
Abingdon, Oxon, UK
Email: trade.orders@marston.co.uk
www.marston.co.uk

List of Content

Preface

Thirteen legal and economic scholars, lawyers and an MD have participated in the creation of this anthology regarding Scandinavian women's law in the 21st century. The aim of the book is to set the stage of women's law today (2011) and take a look into the future of women's law.

The anthology was planned at the closing meeting in the Danish Association for Women's Law in fall 2010. All the members of the association present agreed upon the idea of publishing an anthology concerning women's law in the 21st century and to celebrate the over more than 10 years long history of the association's work. The Women's Law Series[1] is funding the publication of this anthology.

The work is now completed with the result of eleven contributions from both scholars and practitioners in Scandinavia.

In Chapter 1 Eva Maria Svensson analyses how the legal discipline regarding women's law has developed and will develop in the future, and she raises the question whether or not there is a future for Scandinavian women's law. Eva Maria Svensson argues that women's law has transformed into a broader field of knowledge and is no longer only a question of legal rules in regard to women but more to the gendered aspects of law and legal scholarship.

Anne Helum defines in Chapter 2 the discipline of women's law and analyses which challenges in a complex social, cultural and legal landscape, women's law is facing. She describes how women's law was introduced as a legal discipline after the introduction of the Convention on the Elimination of All Forms of Discrimination against Women (CEDAW), which was adopted by the UN General Assembly in 1979 and she uses a Norwegian perspective in her analysis.

Chapter 3 contains Ruth Nielsen's analysis of the interaction between EU gender equality and discrimination law and Scandinavian law in this area. Ruth Nielsen asks what is valid law on gender equality at EU level and in

1. Kvinderetlig Skriftserie

Scandinavian law and how EU law and Scandinavian gender equality law are interacting.

Hanne Petersen combines a historical, cultural and gender specific perspective on normative cultures in Chapter 4, when she analyzes the legal, philosophical and literary sources, indigenous myths with a personal and professional experience in her approach. She looks at/focuses on women's law from local, national, regional and global positions in the Nordic and Scandinavian normative cultures when she asks whether or not to set a new agenda on Nordic and indigenous/arctic perspectives of humans and nature.

Agnete Andersen defines in Chapter 5 the concept of "Gender mainstreaming" from a United Nations, EU and Danish perspective and among other things she explains why gender mainstreaming was introduced as a gender equality tool and shows a snapshot of how the development perspectives of the inter-ministerial gender mainstreaming project is to be seen in Denmark today.

In Chapter 6 Susanne Fransson presents results from a wage survey project at the University of Gothenburg in 2002-2006 regarding the Swedish labour market which shows that the average wage differentials between men's and women's wages were 17 per cent and she compares it with the general gender pay gap in the European Union. In addition, the chapter includes an international perspective on the labour market as a whole.

Trine Baumback analyses a specific area of women's law when she in Chapter 7 looks at equality in reality. She discovers that discrimination against women is not identified in the field of criminal law. She defines gender inequality in the field of criminal law and shows that discrimination against women has many faces for example that domestic violence has been seen as a private matter in which the government should not interfere.

In Chapter 8 Pia Deleuran & Bente Holm Nielsen analyse the Woman's Share in the Reproductive Chain and they set up an illustration of a brick in the foundations of women's rights law. In this chapter the authors describe the protection of the dignity of motherhood from a practical and interdisciplinary perspective. They clarify how a superficial understanding of motherhood has consequences, which affect the prevalent perception of women in the world community as well as in Danish society, illustrated with examples from the Danish Act of Parental Responsibility.

Vibeke Strand analyses the legal rules in regard to wearing a hijab in Chapter 9. She describes the balance between an individual and a structural approach towards gender equality. She begins the analysis in the Norwegian debate concerning whether or not wearing the hijab with the police uniform should be allowed. She discusses the individual's protection against discrimination in the Gender Equality Act Section and turns to a brief overview of the status of international human rights conventions in Norwegian law. She also analyses the actual use of the hijab and the legal obligation to protect individuals against discrimination and the complex dilemma that lies in wearing a hijab.

In Chapter 10, Sabine Nielsen and Morten Huse, both economics scholars, analyse the Norwegian legislation on women's quotas in company boards from an economic business case perspective. The authors analyse empirical data from Morten Huse's Norvegian "Value-creating board program" from 2003/04 and 2005/06; a survey sent to CEOs and board members explaining why and how women can be valuable board members and contribute to the work of corporate boards. In this chapter the authors present some of the most important findings as the ratio of women directors and board effectiveness, the importance of board processes, women directors' professional experiences and personal values and equality perception.

In the final chapter of the anthology, Christina D. Tvarnø's analysis concerns women's quotas in company boards. The chapter presents a comparative analysis of the legal rules regarding women quotas on boards in Norway and in France and describes the legal status in Denmark, Great Britain and the EU. The aim is to investigate whether aspects of Norwegian and French law can be useful in regard to establishing legal rules in other countries such as Denmark.

In Scandinavia, women's law was established as a distinct legal discipline in university teaching and legal scholarship in the mid 1970s. The University of Oslo (Norway) played a particularly pioneering role. At that time, there was general terminological agreement: the name of the discipline was kvinnerett in Norwegian, kvinderet in Danish and kvinnorätt in Swedish.

There were Nordic Women's law meetings where kvinnerett/kvinderet/kvinnorätt was discussed in Norwegian/Danish/Swedish. Those languages are so similar that – at least in the generation that started Scandinavian Women's law – Scandinavian women can talk with each other each using their mother tongue without translation. It was well-known in the 1970s that there was something in the Anglo-American world called feminist studies or gender studies but Scandinavian Women's law was rather home-grown and generally not understood as inspired from or similar to the Anglo-American feminist studies.

During the last 40 years, Scandinavian Women's law has been mainstreamed into the general development of European law on gender equality and discrimination. As a consequence many authors today have abandoned the term 'women's law' as outdated. We have chosen to keep the old terminology in the title of this book in order to point to the historical background of present day gender and law studies from Scandinavia. The word 'kvinneret' (women's law) is still used at the University of Oslo in descriptions of the research area, see http://www.jus.uio.no/ior/forskning/omrader/kvinnerett/.

The European Union has pursued a strong gender equality and non-discrimination agenda since the 1970s. Denmark entered the EU 1 January 1973, Sweden and Finland 1 January 1995, Norway is not a member. Scandinavian women's law as developed through the last 40 years and EU gender equality law are thus contemporaries. Because of the direct effect and supremacy of EU law over national law, the interplay between elements of law stemming from EU-level and from national level has been particularly important in the Nordic EU-member states (Denmark, Sweden and Finland).

There is considerable difference between the approach to gender equality law in public international law and EU law. International law takes an asymmetrical approach to the sexes. There is only weak protection for men against discrimination on grounds of their sex while women are covered by a specific convention against discrimination of women (CEDAW). Norwegian women's law seems to put much more emphasis on public international law than the other Nordic countries which put more emphasis on the more far-reaching – and gender-neutral – prohibitions against discrimination in EU law.

In regard to theoretical and methodological choices Scandinavian women's law has always been multi-facetted. The contributions in the present book do not only analyse the subject from a narrow legal dogmatic perspective but also draws in perspectives from international law, comparative law, social science, economics and cultural perspectives.

Ruth Nielsen & Christina D. Tvarnø

Frederiksberg
October 2011

CHAPTER 1

Is there a Future for Scandinavian Women's Law?

By Eva-Maria Svensson, Professor, LLD, Department of Law, School of Business, Economics and Law, University of Gothenburg and Faculty of Law, University of Tromsø

1. Introduction

The theme for this anthology, Scandinavian women's law in the 21st Century, spurs me to ask a question, quite rhetoric I admit; is there a future for Scandinavian women's law? The answer is both no and yes. *No* in the sense that 'scandinavian women's law' as a school of thought already has lost its privilege to define legal scholarship about the consequences of sex/gender in relation to law. Women's law has transformed into a broader field of knowledge, feminist scholarship in law, and is no longer restricted to questions related to the situation of women, but more to the gendered aspects of law and legal scholarship. Nor is it exclusively a Scandinavian discipline anymore. The field is a part of international legal scholarship, usually called feminist legal studies in the sense that there is a need for research on the relationship between law, legal scholarship and sex/gender. The framing as well as the context for the field of knowledge is however different today compared to the situation when women's law was formed as a discipline in Scandinavia.[1]

In this text I will try to explore these two answers, the no and the yes, within three themes, the contemporary status of the field, the need for re-

1. The English concept of Scandinavia includes the Nordic countries Denmark, Finland, Norway and Sweden, and not only Denmark, Norway and Sweden as Scandinavia would be understood in the Scandinavian languages.

search in the field and finally I will conclude some future issues urgent to study. My answer to the question and my conclusion is (not so surprisingly) that women's law, today more accurately labelled as Feminist Legal Studies or Gender Legal Studies, as a *field of knowledge* has without doubt a future in the 21st century.

First some words about the context. The field of knowledge, originally called Women's Law is a critical perspective on law. Women's Law has, at least in Sweden, changed name to gender and law. It is not only a matter of words but also of content. The legislation has changed the knowledge base and has passed the focus on biological sex. We have examples of legislation that are constructed out of the relevance of and taking in consideration the unequal relationship between the sexes; men and women.

At the same time there is an increasing focus on the biological sex and the body. I think of the questioning of women's right to abortion, the discussion about the right to sell one's body (in prostitution, in surrogacy, in the organ business). It may be connected to the questions above as a third step in a process, in which we now again have to deal with issues related to (the biological) sex, but the formal sex neutrality is not a useful strategy here. It is also possible to start in these questions directly.

Law is changing over time and the scholarship studying the relation between sex and law is consequently changing. If the object changes, the research has to change. In the early days of the Women's Law discipline the focus was on women as a group defined out of biology, a group opposite to the group men. This focus correlated to the legal principle of sex neutrality, which was consolidated in the constitutions with some exceptions.

The legislation is (still) generally based on sex, but now as a prohibition to treat someone differently based on the sex of her or his person. As a result of a critique towards the inefficiency (in reaching 'real' neutrality) of (only) formal sex neutrality, possibilities to treat women and men formally different were introduced. Measures like affirmative action and quotas have, however, met resistance in both the EU, its member states and in Norway. Other active measures, such as equality plans, have been criticized as not being efficient enough.

Politics, on the other hand, has over time been more based on gender, i.e. not the biological sex but the living conditions. Gender equality politics aims at giving men and women the same power to take part in the development of the society and in their own lives. Different living conditions are seen as important for the construction of society (at least on a rhetorical level) and are supposed to have influence on the future legislation (as a part of the infrastructure of society). Examples of legislation resulting from this reconsidering of living conditions are the two offenses gross violation of women's integrity and prohibition of purchase of sex, introduced in Sweden in 1998. They are not sex neutral, on the contrary They acknowledge the unequal relationship between women and men, in order to achieve neutral living conditions. Also affirmative action is a measure to obtain neutral living conditions in cases where it is not the case.

2. The contemporary status of the field of knowledge

In a four-volume selection of *Feminist Legal Studies,* edited and published in 2009, Joanne Conaghan presents an extensive body of feminist legal scholarship.[2] The volumes cover 30 years of research on key interventions and developments in feminist legal studies, feminist legal scholars' engagement in liberalism as well as in legal method and reasoning, and contemporary challenges and contestations within the discipline. As a discipline or as a perspective in law, feminist legal studies have developed in different parts of the world, and in different jurisdictions. Conaghan mentions US, Canada, UK, Australia and Norway. Except for Norway, all of the mentioned jurisdictions are situated in English-speaking countries. The majority of the selected works are from English-speaking countries. The main impression of the discipline, as presented in the four volumes, is consequently the predominance of '*Anglo*-inter/national' texts.

According to Anne Bottomley, feminist legal scholarship has become a well-established presence in the academy.[3] There has been a proliferation of texts, journal papers, seminars and courses which evidence its presence. Joanne Conaghan agrees and adds; despite the fact that feminist scholarship in law "...is of fairly recent vintage".[4] Several journals and publishing house series guarantee publications of research are widely spread and read.

Scandinavian Women's Law is not as well-established as Feminist legal studies in the contexts of Bottomley and Conaghan. In a Nordic context the field of knowledge is relatively indistinct, at least when it comes to the situation in the academy as an organization. After 40 years in Scandinavian legal

2. Conaghan, Joanne (ed.) (2009). *Feminist Legal Studies*, Volume I – IV. London: Routledge.
3. Bottomley, Anne (2004). "Shock To Thought: An Encounter (of a third kind) with Legal Feminism". In: *Feminist Legal Studies* (2004) 12: 29-65, p. 29.
4. Conaghan, Joanne (ed.) (2009). *Feminist Legal Studies*, Volume I – IV. London: Routledge.

scholarship there is one organizational unit, namely a section of a department (Oslo). There are very few positions in the field and the competence is often seen as additional to a legal (traditional) discipline, such as criminal law or labour law. Not recognizing the competence as a specific competence but more as supplementary, has consequences in several aspects, as will be explored in this article. On the other hand, as a research fields it has grown extensively since the beginning of the 1970s, in Scandinavia as well as in other parts of the world. When it comes to publications, there are several comprehensive publications about the field of knowledge, among them some in English.[5] An anthology in Scandinavian languages, to be published at the end of 2011, a collaboration among scholars from the four Scandinavian countries Denmark, Finland, Norway and Sweden, has the aim to give an overview of the contemporary status of the knowledge field.[6]

The field of knowledge focusing on the relationship between law, on one hand, and women, men, gender, sexuality on the other, as a specific part of Scandinavian legal scholarship, has been the object for me in three studies in recent years.[7] The three studies are related to each other, the latter are sequels of and further elaborations of the first of the three studies about the boundaries of Scandinavian legal scholarship.[8] The studies fall in a research tradition called Studies of Academic Knowledge.

5. Nousiainen, Kevät, Gunnarsson, Åsa, Lundström, Karin & Niemi-Kiesilainen, Johanna (red.) (2001). *Responsible Selves, Women in the Nordic legal culture.* Dartmouth, Great Britain: Ashgate; Svensson, Eva-Maria, Pylkkänen, Anu & Niemi-Kiesiläinen, Johanna (red.) (2004). *Nordic Equality at a Crossroads. Feminist legal studies coping with difference.* Aldershot: Ashgate; Gunnarsson, Åsa, Svensson, Eva-Maria & Davies, Margaret (red.) (2007). *Exploiting the Limits of Law: A Swedish Feminist Challenge to Pessimism.* Aldershot: Ashgate Publishing.
6. *På vei – Kjønn og rett i Norden*, Eva-Maria Svensson, Ulrika Andersson, Hege Brækhus, Monica Burman, Anne Hellum, Stine Jørgensen & Anu Pylkkänen, (red.). Göteborg: Makadam förlag & bokproduktion AB.
7. Svensson, Eva-Maria (2011). "Formering och transformering av ett kunskapsfält" (Mapping a field of knowledge). In: *På vei – Kjønn og rett i Norden*, Eva-Maria Svensson, Ulrika Andersson, Hege Brækhus, Monica Burman, Anne Hellum, Stine Jørgensen & Anu Pylkkänen, (red.). Göteborg: Makadam förlag & bokproduktion AB; Svensson, Eva-Maria, "Contemporary Swedish Feminist Legal Studies – Five Doctoral Thesis". *NORA* Vol. 17, No. 2, 120-128, June 2009; Svensson, Eva-Maria (2007). "Boundary-work in Legal Scholarship." In: *Exploiting the Limits of Law*, (red.) Åsa Gunnarsson, Eva-Maria Svensson & Margaret Davies, Ashgate.
8. Svensson, Eva-Maria (2007). "Boundary-work in Legal Scholarship." In: *Exploiting the Limits of Law*, (red.) Åsa Gunnarsson, Eva-Maria Svensson & Margaret Davies, Ashgate.

The main purpose was to analyze how the academic discipline is mapped, when it comes to content as well as organization and institutionalization in the academy. The first issue, about the field of knowledge, has to do with which parts of legal scholarship are included as well as which theoretical and methodological tools are used or should be used. The second issue, about the academic discipline, has to do with how the discipline is made visible and is consolidated in legal scholarship and in the university organization.

One problem noticed in the studies is the indistinct status of the field of knowledge, both as a part of legal scholarship as well as in legal education. The reasons for the indistinct status are several and it is complicated to point them out clearly. One problem is the status of legal scholarship in general explored in the text Boundary-work. [9] The purpose of the article was to analyze changes in the field of legal scholarship in order to discuss the position of feminist legal studies within legal scholarship. A presumption was that the boundaries of legal scholarship are determined by the social context and not by an inner logic.

In Nordic legal culture the academic discipline (legal scholarship) has more or less been seen as analogous to its object, the law. As a Finnish legal scholar put it (using the term 'legal science' instead of 'legal scholarship'), 'legal science is not only a scientific but also a legal practice, which participates in the reproduction and modification of the legal order – its own object of research'.[10] Legal scholarship has traditionally been understood as one of the sources of law in the application of law, and not as an independent academic activity. However, its influence as a source of law has been weak.[11] Arguments can only be gathered from inside the system, and the aim of scholarship is to preserve the system. From such a perspective, critical analysis of the boundaries of law and its basic presumptions are problematic. However, legal scholarship, as I claim in the article Boundary-work, like other academic fields, goes through periods of paradigmatic calm supplanted by new thinking, in the wake of revolutions which have varying impacts. Different critical approaches, such as feminist legal studies, have been challenging the boundaries determined by the current law. Legal scholarship is constantly changing and feminist legal studies has an important role in the process of making legal scholarship more distinct and more independent from legal

9. "Boundary-work in Legal Scholarship." In: *Exploiting the Limits of Law*, (red.) Åsa Gunnarsson, Eva-Maria Svensson & Margaret Davies, Ashgate.
10. Tuori, Kaarlo (2002). *Critical legal positivism*. Ashgate, p. 285.
11. Björne, Lars (1991). *Nordisk rättskällelära* (Nordic doctrine of legal sources). Rättshistoriskt bibliotek 46, p. 162.

practice, One consequence could be that legal scholarship is no longer necessarily structured out of legal fields, but out of theoretical approaches.

The name 'women's law' is logic within a system according to which legal scholarship corresponds to the division of 'the law' into separate areas, such as family law and tort law. But 'women's law' has never been comparable to other legal areas. On the contrary, it has been overlapping most legal areas. What is more, 'women's law' primarily associates to the situation for women as a group and consequences of different kinds of law. But the field is more comprehensive. Feminist legal scholarship takes a critical perspective, critical in relation to epistemology as well as practice to both internal and external aspects of law and legal scholarship. 'Women's law' does not cover this comprehensive content.

The name of the field, 'women's law', becomes a problem. But the next problem is; what name is suitable and why is the question of labelling so controversial?[12] Every effort to write about the knowledge field as a part of legal scholarship raises questions about the label. There are several labels in use in both English and in the Scandinavian languages. Scandinavian scholars writing in the field in English translate Scandinavian labels, sometimes randomly chosen, sometimes consciously chosen. There is no consensus about which term to use, neither in the Scandinavian countries, nor internationally. Different names are used in different contexts, indicating more than just a difference in labeling. The question of the label for the field is of course not the cause for the indistinct status, but more a symptom of the same indistinct status. The question of label has consequences of both internal and external kind. I will come back to the question of name, but first some more reflections on the institutional aspects of the field of knowledge.

Women's law as an academic discipline[13] in Law Faculties and Departments around Scandinavian countries is almost non-existing today – if we talk about *women's law* as such. There are hardly any positions in the discipline. Women's law as a subject taught in law programmes has changed its appearance to for example gender and law or discrimination and (gender)

12. Schömer, Eva (2009), "Recension: Åsa Gunnarsson och Eva-Maria Svensson, Genusrättsvetenskap". *Retfaerd* nr. 127 2009/4.

13. I make a distinction between discipline and field of knowledge. A discipline is more of a subject in an academic organizational aspect, taught in a law programme and a subject in which positions are held. A field of knowledge is defined out of epistemological boundaries, more or less restricted. My intention is not to make boundaries which exclude some research, rather it is to be able to talk about a kind of knowledge, losely hold together by a common interest in law and sex/gender.

equality law. The discipline has also been, or at least is supposed to have been mainstreamed into other law disciplines (at least this is the case in Sweden). The status of the discipline as a specific discipline has to some extent changed to be a perspective in other disciplines, sometimes invisible for students, sometimes non-existing.

In Oslo, at the section *Avdeling for kvinnerett, barnerett, likestillings- og diskrimineringsrett* (KVIBALD, in English; Section for women's law, children's law, (gender) equality and discrimination law) the courses offered today are Discrimination and (gender) equality law and Women's Law and Human Rights. At other Law programs there are courses in variations of Law and sex/gender or in Discrimination and (gender) equality law. Sweden is the only of the Scandinavian countries in which it is compulsory to integrate a sex/gender perspective in the law program. According to the Swedish National Agency for Higher Education, the implementation of the obligation is weak.[14]

The presence of textbooks in the field also says something about the status of the field. The purpose of a textbook is to help students learn about something and give an overview of a specific field and some deepening knowledge about central themes and issues in the field. The absence of a textbook makes it harder to reach the knowledge and, on the contrary, the existence of a textbook, makes it easier to reach knowledge. Textbooks in the actual field were produced in the 1970s and 1980s.[15] After almost 20 years without any comprehensive textbook, *Genusrättsvetenskap*, was published in 2009.[16]

When it comes to the status of the research field the situation is more positive. There are approximately 50 researchers active in the field.[17] According

14. *Rapport 2000:8 R Lärosätenas arbete med jämställdhet, studentinflytande samt social och etnisk mångfald.* Högskoleverket.
    Rapport 2000:9 R Goda exempel Hur universitet och högskolor kan arbeta med jämställdhet, studentinflytande och social och etnisk mångfald. Högskoleverket.
    Rapport 2000:1 R Rätt juristutbildning? Högskoleverket.
    Rapport 2007:18 R Utvärdering av juris kandidatutbildningar samt grund- och forskarutbildningar i juridik, rättsvetenskap, handelsrätt och affärsrätt vid svenska universitet och högskolor. Högskoleverket.
15. The most well-known was Dahl, Tove Stang (red.) (1985), *Kvinnerett I.* Oslo: Universitetsforlaget. It was published in English some years later; Dahl, Tove Stang (1988), *Women's law: An Introduction to Feminist Jurisprudence.* Oslo: Norwegian University Press.
16. Gunnarsson, Åsa & Svensson, Eva-Maria (2009). *Genusrättsvetenskap*, (Gender legal studies). Lund: Studentlitteratur.
17. It is not easy to fix a number, partly because of the abscence of specific positions. The number is my estimation based on personal knowledge.

to official databases (containing doctoral thesis), there are 20 doctoral theses in the discipline in Norway and Sweden. I have not been able to find out the situation in Denmark and Finland.[18] The researchers publish extensively, also in English. To publish in English is not very common in legal scholarship in general. The discipline is understood as quite local and primarily of interest within the specific jurisdiction. There are several international collaborations. Research activities of different sorts are organized regularly.

The research is performed under different names, such as gender and legal scholarship, women's law, feminist legal studies, feminist approach to law, sex/gender perspective, feminist legal theory, feminist legal jurisprudence or sex/gender and law. One of the problems with the indistinct name is that it is hard to find research in the field in databases. Not only the names used by researchers vary, but also the classifications or the index entries used in the library systems differ. In the Swedish national library classification system SAB there is *no* index entry for 'women's law', 'gender/feminist legal studies' or similar names, under the index entry for legal scholarship. The only way to find publications in the field is therefore to seek for already known authors or titles, or for the world women, sex/gender and law or other similar words in the title search field. In the Norwegian corresponding system there is an index entry for women's law (kvinnerett) and several for women's law in combination with something else. The system is however not national, every university library has its own variations of the system BIBSYS.

The existence of an index entry is of course important. The possibility to find publications in the field of knowledge is of course relying on the existence of such index entries. Regina Graycar and Jenny Morgan started the second edition of the book; The hidden gender of law[19] with a retrospect to the opening of the first edition published in 1990. It "...opened with the observation that in 1988 the Index to Legal Periodicals had added an index entry for feminist jurisprudence. At that time, this was a landmark: after all, it was only in 1985 that Kathleen Lahey had described feminist legal scholarship as 'an uncatalogued item'.

18. The databases are Minna in Finland, Kilden in Norway and GENA in Sweden. In Denmark there is no specific database with doctoral theses. The database KVINFO contains a lot more, but when searching for women's law and law, 9 hits were found. A search for women's law does not exclude publications that are not in the discipline law.
19. Regina Graycar & Jenny Morgan (2002). *The hidden gender of law*. Sydney: The Federation Press, p. 1.

The name issue is not just about the name. It's about boundary-work. The term boundary-work captures the process of establishing boundaries. Internally it has to do with the work done by scholars aiming to win credibility contests concerning epistemic authority. Externally it is foremost a matter of visibility. An established name is a consequence of an established field of knowledge, but an established name also has consequences for the establishment of the field, and for the visibility of the field.

Other scholars have raised similar questions about the boundary-work related to the process of making a field and the important role the name has in this process. In connection with producing the four-volume anthology of feminist legal scholarship[20] Joanne Conaghan had some doubts about the value and integrity of the project and about how best to tell the 'story' of feminist engagement with law. Despite thinking of it as a pleasurable activity, the selection of scholarly work to be published in an anthology called Feminist Legal Studies has certain impacts. Conaghan was *marking out the field* of feminist legal studies, as she puts it in the article *The Making of a Field or the Building of a Wall? Feminist Legal Studies and Law, Gender and Sexuality.*[21] The business of field-making is, according to Conaghan; "…a far from neutral exercise. To delineate a field, to give it form, content, texture and depth was an active, not a passive interaction with the materials. It entailed the drawing up of boundaries by which the outer reaches of the field could be determined (essentially a process of inclusion and exclusion). It required the static, cartographic representation of a dynamic, multidimensional, spatially and temporally contingent sphere of ongoing intellectual and political engagement. It instituted a normative order, which could then serve as a frame for interpretation and evaluation. Its effect, in other words, was unavoidably prescriptive."[22]

One aspect of the field-making is the process of naming. According to Anne Bottomley, the name-giving process is not innocent and carries very specific messages.[23] An act of naming must be, as Bottomley puts it, backed by evidence of a coherent identity. "Narratives to establish identity usually

20. Conaghan, Joanne (red.) (2009a). *Feminist Legal Studies I-IV.* Series: Critical Concepts in Law, London: Routledge.
21. Conaghan, Joanne (2009b). "The Making of a Field or the Building of a Wall? Feminist Legal Studies and Law, Gender and Sexuality." In: *Feminist Legal Studies* (2009) 17:303-307.
22. A.a. p. 304.
23. Bottomley, Anne (2004). "Shock To Thought: An Encounter (of a third kind) with Legal Feminism". In: *Feminist Legal Studies* (2004) 12: 29-65.

activate three scenarios: an account of origins, a geography of the terrain (premises, principles and methods), and a map for future work. They are generally assertive in their tone and compelling in their arguments – they are stories of arrival. The rhetorical strength of the argument is premised on an assertion that so much has already been achieved that it now demands recognition. Foundations are already well laid; we are now building above ground. To move forward within these terms is therefore to have to accept that the foundations are, indeed, well laid."[24]

As Bottomley points out, there is, however, a problem with this. Such a presentation demands that a coherent account of feminism is presented which will make the best case for inclusion. It is Bottomley's "contention that drawing out these 'communalities' is a dangerous enterprise when they are put to the purpose of constructing an internal coherence (and direction) for 'legal feminism as a whole'. It is this which helps to begin to construct (an) orthodoxy – an act of recognition, by a feminist, of what can be held together within 'the' project, which becomes in effect the claim to an identity."[25]

The question of name-giving, understood as a part of mapping-the-field, has several consequences which have been explored above through some examples.[26] Whether a field of knowledge is distinct or not has internal as well as external aspects. As some Swedish scholars put it, "to be named, is to be…"[27] As a consequence of the forming process, a discipline can become institutionalized in the academy, in publications, in research activities and in a longer perspective be transformed in a way (idealistically) typical for the academy, through critical reflection and internal discussions it can further develop. Individual scholars are made visible in an academic world characterized by an increasing importance of bibliometrics. When applying for research funding, scholars in the field may be valued by other scholars with competence within the field. What is more, a distinct field is easy to find and take part of.

24. A.a. p. 37.
25. A.a. p. 38.
26. Svensson, Eva-Maria (2011). "Formering och transformering av ett kunskapsfält" (Mapping a field of knowledge). In: *På vei – Kjønn og rett i Norden*, Eva-Maria Svensson, Ulrika Andersson, Hege Brækhus, Monica Burman, Anne Hellum, Stine Jørgensen & Anu Pylkkänen, (red.). Göteborg: Makadam förlag & bokproduktion AB.
27. Niskanen, Kirsti & Florin, Christina (red.) (2010). *Föregångarna. Kvinnliga professorer om liv, makt och vetenskap.* (Forerunners. Female professors about life, power and science.) Stockholm: SNS förlag, p. 23.

However, there are also negative aspects of forming a distinct field. The risk of exclusionary practices or the tendency to form a 'school of thought' as a specific body of knowledge is to be taken seriously, as stated by Bottomley.[28] I agree with her that there is a risk, but I don't think forming a specific (dominant and fundamental) school of thought is a necessary consequence of forming a distinct field of knowledge. Considering the distinction between the external and internal aspect, it is easier to see the risk internally, but externally I would say that it is important to form a distinct field and that the positive aspects weigh heavier than the negative. Is it possible to form a field that is pluralistic and varying within the field and distinct in relation to other scholarship and in a broader context? I would say yes.

3. The need for research in the field

Is there a need for feminist/gender legal research in the most gender-equal region of the world and can international feminist legal studies learn something from the Scandinavian? Feminist legal studies are often described as a discipline with a contextual epistemology (theory and practice are interrelated), with a political agenda (to make life better for women), and with an emancipatory interest of knowledge (i.e. a critical and self-reflective approach to knowledge).

This contextual epistemological standpoint could, or perhaps should, imply an extensive awareness of limitations based on the specific context in which the research is performed. Is this the case? Are the consequences of different political and societal contexts taken into account in feminist legal studies? What are the consequences of different jurisdictions? Do the differences affect the notions, the formulation of theories and methods and the use and relevance of them? The explicit assumption of a connection between theory and practice in feminist legal studies, ought to make us to be self-reflective of the contextuality of the discipline's own theories and methods. For example, the distinction between private and public is understood in different ways in different countries. The *welfare state* model is not the same everywhere and *gender equality* as a political goal and a legal principle is understood, expressed and implemented differently in different contexts.

28. Bottomley, Anne (2004). "Shock To Thought: An Encounter (of a third kind) with Legal Feminism". In: *Feminist Legal Studies* (2004) 12: 29-65, p. 39.

I would like to see more reflections of these differences and what impacts they have on the discipline and its notions, theories and methods. The present overweight of studies from the English-speaking world should be challenged from other parts of the world. The relation between the centre and the periphery should be switched in favour of the (until now) periphery. The meaning and consequences of a contextual epistemology should be taken seriously.

In my opinion, there are two political and societal changes that are important: first; the individualisation and the de-powering of the collective democratic political system in favour of the civil society, second; the increasing commodification of human beings. The individualisation is an on-going process that has impacts in different ways. In a Nordic context there has been a shift from redistribution and collective solutions to individual and private solutions when it comes to social security and health care but also education and transportation. The increased discourse of individual human rights is, at least in a Nordic context, not only positive. If at the same time the tax-funded welfare system is decreasing, the result can be to the worse. Pylkkänen has studied this shift in her book; Trapped in Equality.[29] What is more, the political system, supposed to be democratic, looses force in favour of the market and private solutions in the civil society. The need for charity is increasing when the welfare state is dismantled. What are the consequences of these changes? And is it possible to use the different contexts for Scandinavian and English-speaking countries respectively, to reflect on these changes?

In a coming article, Åsa Gunnarsson and I point out some recent measures and tendencies in the Nordic or more precisely; Swedish gender equality policy.[30] Despite being one of the most gender-equal countries, the Swedish gender-equality policies have been criticised for being inefficient and not sufficiently radical. Some areas of society are not even close to achieving gender equality and the main tool, the gender mainstreaming strategy, is criticised as being inadequate. Gender-equality policy is a political field with high ambitions but insufficient implementation. The critique came from among others the non-government organisation Sveriges Kvinnolobby (Swedish Women's Lobby Group, 2010). Despite economic efforts to enforce gender-equality policies under the previous government, the impacts are not impressive.

29. Pylkkänen, Anu, *Trapped in Equality: Women as Legal Persons in the Modernisation of Finnish Law*, Helsinki 2009. Reviewed in Feminist Legal Studies Vol. 18. No. 3, December 2010.
30. Gunnarsson, Åsa & Svensson, Eva-Maria (to be published in 2011/2012). "Gender Equality in Swedish Welfare State Law", In: *feminists@law*.

Gender-equality policies are still based on the objectives formulated in the 1990s, that women and men should have the same power to form society and their own life. Yet, when it comes to the specific measures taken by the Government in recent years, it seems that the question of shared power is transformed into individual behaviour, attitudes and preferences.

One important issue today, highlighted in the article, is the reluctance to take legal measures when it comes to the unequal distribution of power and influence in the market, e.g. the question of business leadership in enterprises. The government still understands the problem as a question which can be solved by begging the enterprises to act differently, and legal measures are avoided. What is more, the earlier focus on structural discriminatory practises in working-life has been replaced by individual choices and strategies, for instance to promote a less gender-divided working life. The same individual ideological framing characterises the parental leave schemes. An equal share among the parents could be a vigorous measure for changing the uneven distribution of care work if equally divided between the parents, but this is controversial. Every proposition to individualise parental leave is understood as a violation of the free will of the families to decide what is best for them.

Another controversial issue, reflected on in the article by Gunnarsson and me, and an issue where Sweden stands out as unique, is the political and legal view on purchase of sex. Swedish policy discourses on prostitution differ from the standpoints of both radical and liberal feminism. Jenny Westerstrand has described the Swedish position as a contextual approach.[31] The focus is on the demand and the view that it is unacceptable to both society and individuals that men should buy sexual services from women and children and the questions of free will and the distinction between forced prostitution and non-forced prostitution have no relevance in the criminalisation of the purchase. In an international setting, the contextual approach seems to be made invisible in favour of the dichotomy between the radical 'victim-focused' approach and the liberal 'sex-worker' approach as well as the distinction between forced prostitution and sex work. In the Swedish context, there is no such distinction; the contextual approach focuses on the demand and the buyer and not on whether or not the 'seller' is forced. The Swedish legislation is questioned, but the recent evaluation of the law showed that it does have an effects on the demand.[32]

31. Westerstrand, Jenny (2008), *Mellan mäns händer. Kvinnors rättssubjektivitet, internationell rätt och diskurser om prostitution och trafficking.* Uppsala: Uppsala universitet.
32. SOU 2010:49.

The question of purchase of sex can be reflected on as part of an increasing commodification of human beings. This process can be seen for example in the discourse of sex-work, surrogacy, cosmetic surgery and commercialism of the human being. To sell and buy a human body or parts of it in several ways is becoming normalized. What are the consequences of this commodification of the human being and what alternatives are there? How can the commodification be challenged from other standpoints than religious or conservative moralism? Another interesting issue is the powerful ideology of motherhood and the desire for the perfect home for young women today. How do these tendencies interact with legal regulations that aim to achieve gender equality, based in individual responsibility?

4. Conclusion – some future issues urgent to study

To sum up, there is a future for the field of knowledge in the 21st century indeed. Not in terms of women's law but as a critical perspective within legal scholarship. Feminist legal studies or gender legal studies are the names I prefer. They signify all that is connected to feminist scholarship, namely an emancipatory purpose, a critical, non-dogmatic approach, a rejection of a distinction between theory and practice and a contextual epistemological standpoint. It also signifies that it is a part of legal scholarship and not (just) a part of the legal system.

I think there is need for more (re)considering of the theoretical and empirical meanings and impacts of notions like not only 'feminist', 'gender', 'gender relations', 'woman', but also 'man' and 'masculinity'. In the Nordic countries, especially in Sweden, the focus has not been on women in the same extent as internationally but on gender equality, or the relationship between women and men. To improve the situation for women it is necessary to include men in the analysis. And what is more, some problems with consequences for women, is better dealt with if the focus is primarily on men. This is the case when it comes to purchase of sex and care work for instance.

The name is important in several aspects and a common name makes it easier to form a distinct field, especially in a knowledge e-based sociological aspect. "To be named is to be…" as the quote said, and it is easier to find research in the field if there are distinct index entries as an example. Forming a distinct field of knowledge does not necessarily mean that a specific school of thought has to dominate the field. A field that is distinct in relation to the world outside can be pluralistic and heterogenic within the field.

Scandinavian feminist legal scholarship and English-spoken feminist legal scholarship have a lot in common, but there are differences depending on context. The different scholarly communities can use the differences to re-think the field, in order to continue to re-make the field to better fit the needs of gendered human beings all over the world.

CHAPTER 2

CEDAW and the discipline of women's law: Continuity and change in the understanding of gender and law[1]

By Anne Hellum, Professor – Department of Public and International Law, University of Oslo

1. CEDAW and the discipline of women's law: challenges in a complex social, cultural and legal landscape

Women's law, which was introduced as a legal discipline at the Faculty of Law at the University of Oslo in 1975, and the Convention on the Elimination of All Forms of Discrimination against Women (CEDAW), which was adopted by the UN General Assembly in 1979, are products of the same era.[2] This is reflected in their common focus on the situation of women and the objective to change the position of women in law and society. To study the relationship between gender and the law on the basis of women's lived reality has been the core of the discipline of women's law. According to Tove Stang Dahl, who was the first professor in women's law at the Faculty of Law in

1. This article is a revised version of Anne Hellum (2011) "Den globale likestillingsnormen: Kontinuitet og endering i forståelsen av rett og kjønn". In I *På vei – Kjønn og rett i Norden.* Eva-Maria Svensson, Ulrika Andersson, Hege Brækhus, Monica Burman, Anne Hellum, Stine Jørgensen & Anu Pylkkänen, (red.)Makadam förlag & bokproduktion AB, Göteborg.
2. *Convention on the Elimination of All Forms of Discrimination against Women*, was adopted by the UN General Assembly in 1979 and entered into force 3 September 19811249. CEDAW and is currently ratified by 186 states. Norway ratified CEDAW 21. May 1981.

Oslo, the overall objective was to describe, understand and improve the position of women in law and society.[3] In the same vein CEDAW has been based on research and documentation describing the actual situation of women in different parts of the world. CEDAW's state reporting and individual complaints procedures are today a global arena where various legal, cultural and social constructions of gender are discussed, negotiated and confronted with a view to achieving substantive gender equality and eliminating discrimination against women.

To describe, understand and change law on the basis of women's lived realities is easier said than done in today's research landscape, where both female gender and the law constitute complex, compound and contested categories. In Norway, like the other Nordic countries, national law is challenged both from above and below. From above it is faced with a growing body of international and regional human rights obligations protecting the rights of minorities, immigrants and refugees. From below an unprecedented cultural and normative diversity, embedded in transnational personal, social and religious relations, challenge the assumption of homogeneity that often underpin both national legislation and the coexisting customary and religious norms of different minority groups.[4] In Norway, like the other Nordic countries, international instruments, such as EU law, the UN Women's Convention and the UN Race Convention, have enhanced women's protection against discrimination on the basis of gender, sexuality, ethnicity, age and disability.[5] Enhanced protection against discrimination applies not only to women from the Nordic majority populations, but also to women from different minority groups in-

3. See Tove Stang Dahl (1987), *Introduction to Women's Law*, Oslo, Norwegian University Press and "Taking Women as a Starting Point: Building Women's Law", *Working Paper in Women's Law* No. 4. University of Oslo.
4. See Anne Hellum, Shaheen Sardar, Ali & Anne, Griffiths (eds.) (2010) *From Transnational Relations to Transnational Laws. Northern European Laws at the Cross Roads*. Aldershot: Ashgate. Regarding the challenges of women's right to equality and non-discrimination associated with religious pluralism, see Anne Hellum & Hege Skjeie (red.) (2008), *Demokrati, religionsfrihet og kvinners menneskerettigheter*. In: "Kvinnerettslig skriftserie" no. 76. Institute of Women's Law. University of Oslo and Stina Solhøy, Vibeke Blaker Strand & Jorunn Økland (2010), "Rettferdighetens grenser – religion, kjønn og homofili". In: *Rettferdighet.* (red.) Beatrice Halsaa and Anne Hellum, Oslo: Universitetsforlaget, p. 103-126.
5. Anne Hellum & Kirsten Ketscher (2008), "Introduksjon til diskriminerings- og likestillingsretten", In: *Diskriminerings- og likestillingsrett.* (red.) Anne Hellum & Kirsten Ketscher, Oslo: Universitetsforlaget, p. 17-30.

cluding immigrants and refugees. [6] Through the Nordic countries' human rights-based foreign aid policy, women's protection against discrimination in post-colonial states with pluralistic legal systems has been placed on the agenda.[7] These legal, political and social globalisation processes challenge established notions about women, gender and the law as coherent and stable categories. To make different groups of women's right to equality and non-discrimination real there is, in the Nordic countries as elsewhere in the world, a need for research examining how gender relations are constructed and re-constructed through interaction between international law, state-law and co-existing social and cultural norms.[8]

6. In recent years, a number of Nordic researchers have concerned themselves with migrant women's protection against discrimination. See Diana Mulinari, Kjerstin Sandell & Eva Schomer (red.) (2003), "*Mer an bara kvinnor och men. Feministiska perspektiv på genus*". Lund; Student literature; Stine Jørgensen (2007) "*Etniske minoritetskvinders sociale rettigheter. Arbeidsmarked, seksualitet og uddannelse".* København: Jurist & Økonomiforbundets Forlag; Rubia Mehdi, Petersen, Hanne, Reenberg Sand, Erik & Gordon Woodman (eds.) (2008), "*Law and Religion in Multicultural Societies".* København: DJØF Publishing. A related theme is the intersectional character of discrimination. See Ruth Nielsen (2009), "Is European Union equality law capable of addressing multiple and intersectional discrimination yet? Precautions against neglecting intersectional cases". In: *European Union Non-Discriminiation Law: Comparative Prespectives on Multidimensional Equality.* Dagmar Shiek, and Victoria Chege (red). London and New York: Routledge Cavendish, s. 31-47. Kevat Nousiainen (2009), "Utility-based equality and disparate diversities: from a Finnish perspective". In: *European Union Non-Discriminiation Law: Comparative Perspectives on Multidimensional Equality.* (eds.) Dagmar Shiek & Victoria Chege, London and New York, Routledge Cavendish, s 185-206.
7. See Ingunn Ikdahl (2011) "Lik rett til å være trygg i sitt hjem. Koner, enker, og andre kvinner i internasjonale menneskerettigheter". In I *På vei – Kjønn og rett i Norden.* Eva-Maria Svensson, Ulrika Andersson, Hege Brækhus, Monica Burman, Anne Hellum, Stine Jørgensen & Anu Pylkkänen, (red.) Makadam förlag & bokproduktion AB, Göteborg and Ingunn Ikdahl (2010). *Securing women's homes. The dynamics of women's human rights at the international level and in Tanzania.* PhD thesis. Faculty of Law. University of Oslo.
8. An-Na'im. A. State responsibility under international human rights law to change religious and customary Laws, in *Human Rights of Women. National and International Perspectives*, edited by Rebecca Cook. Pennsylvania: University of Pennsylvania Press, 1995; Shaheen Sardar Ali (2000). *Gender and Human Rights in Islam and International Law* (Hague/London/Boston: Kluwer Law International; Anne Hellum (1999), *Women's Human Rights and Legal Pluralism in Africa: Mixed Norms and Identities in Infertility Management in Zimbabwe* (Oslo/Harare: TANO/MHOND books), Sally Engle Merry (2006), *Human Rights and Gender Violence* (Chicago: University of Chicago Press; Anne Hellum, Julie Stewart, Shaheen Sardar Ali and

The purpose of this article is to show what kind of knowledge an empirical and women-focused perspective from below and within contributes to the understanding of the increasingly complex relationship between gender and law. To illustrate some lines of development within jurisprudence and international law I have used as my basis for this article the women's law research that began at the Faculty of Law in Oslo in the mid-1970s and the practice of the UN Committee on the Elimination of All Forms of Discrimination Against Women (the CEDAW Committee). The practice of the CEDAW Committee, in terms of general recommendations, concluding comments on state reports and decisions in individual complaints, is used as a window into the development of international law, and particularly the handling of conflicts between various local, national and international gender structures.[9]

This article is divided into five parts. The next part (2) addresses the woman-focused gender research of the 1970s, which achieved great importance both for the field of women's law and CEDAW. Continuity and change in women's law research and the CEDAW Committee's balancing of equality and difference between women is addressed in part three (3). Part four (4) deals with the shift towards a more complex understanding of female gender and protection against discrimination deriving from research focusing on how discrimination is constituted in the intersection of female gender, ethnicity, age and religion. Part five (5) addresses the situation of immigrant women who, because of their complex identities and affiliations, are caught between the national state's law and norms and expectations embedded in family relationships and membership of different ethnic and religious groups. It explores how women's law research and international law deal with situations where several normative systems impact on the construction of gender; what is termed legal pluralism. In the final part (6), attention is focused on the porous nature of international protection against discrimination and especially its ability to respond to new insights and interpretations that are developed through research and action at local, national and global levels.

Amy Tsanga (2007) (eds.), *Human Rights, plural legalities and gendered realities. Paths are made by walking* (Harare: Weaver Press).

9. Anne Hellum (2008), "Kvinnekonvensjonens betydning for det alminnelige kjønnsdiskrimineringsvern". In: *Diskriminerings- og Likestillingsrett.* (red.) Anne Hellum & Kirsten Ketscher, Oslo: Universitetsforlaget, p. 58.

2. CEDAW in the context of the women-focused research of the 1970s

Both the field of women's law and CEDAW were developed in the context of growing international research on women, which accelerated in the 1970s. This research built upon the work of pioneers like Simone de Beauvoir, who emphasised the social character of gender.[10] A common feature of the research of anthropologists, such as Michelle Rosaldo and Loise Lamphere[11], economists, such as Ester Boserup[12] and philosophers and lawyers, such as Alison Jaggar[13], Katharine MacKinnon[14] and Tove Stang Dahl[15] was that it was based on women's situation. The contributions of these pioneers, who hailed from different disciplines, centred all the focus on systematic relationships between skewed gender distribution of political power and economic resources. Gender was analysed as a hierarchical social, political and legal structure that created and maintained a skewed gender distribution of power and resources in all parts of the world. Another common feature was the focus on the social, cultural, political and legal distinctions between public and private spheres, and how it legitimised exploitation and violence against women in the family.

This research, which was concerned about identifying common features of women's position in various parts of the world, created a common framework of understanding as reflected in the CEDAW's definition of the relationship between gender equality and discrimination.[16] In order to create equality, Article 1 of CEDAW forbids all forms of discrimination against women. Here it differs from the gender-neutral bans on discrimination in the UN Convention on Civil and Political Rights (ICCPR) and the UN Covenant on Economic, Social and Cultural Rights (ICESCR) from 1966. Research on women's iden-

10. Simone de Beauvoir (1970), *Det annet kjønn I og II.* Oslo: Pax forlag.
11. Michelle Zimbalist Rosaldo & Loise Lamphere (1974), *Women, Culture and Society.* Stanford: Stanford University Press.
12. Ester Boserup (1970), *Woman's Role in Economic Development.* London: Earthscan.
13. Alison Jaggar (1983), *Feminist Politics and Human Nature.* U.K: Harvester Press.
14. Katharine MacKinnon (1987), "Difference and Dominance on Sex Discrimination". In: *Feminism Unmodified. Discourses on Life and Law.* Harvard University Press.
15. Dahl, Tove Stang (red.) (1985), *Kvinnerett I og Kvinnerett II.* Oslo: Universitetsforlaget.
16. Boserup (1970), Boserup examines here what has happened with women in the process of economic and social growth in the 3rd world. In the foreword of the 1989 edition, Dr. Swasti Mitter says that Boserup's devoted and scholarly works gave inspiration to the UN women's decade between 1975 and 1985.

tification of the skewed gender distribution of power and resources gave rise to a broad international political consensus on strengthening monitoring and implementation of women's protection against gender discrimination. This was one of the reasons that the UN General Assembly in 1979 adopted the Convention on the Elimination of All Forms of Discrimination against Women (CEDAW) with a separate monitoring body, the CEDAW Committee.

Another distinct feature of the Convention, which reflects the 1970s research on women and women's struggles, is its horizontal nature. In light of extensive research, which documented abuses and economic exploitation of women in the family, it makes no exception for private life. In its interpretation of the Convention's ban on discrimination, the CEDAW Committee has regarded violence against women as part of the prohibition against discrimination.[17] Another human rights innovation, which is also reflected in research on women's interpretations of how hierarchical gender relations are created and maintained, is CEDAW's prohibition against structural discrimination in Article 5a. This provision is based on the assumption that discrimination against women, as individuals and as a group, is created and upheld through the gender stereotypes that become established in social, cultural and religious norms, practices and structures. Unlike ICCPR and ICESCR, CEDAW provides no protection for religion and culture. As part of efforts to overcome the social, cultural and religious structures, which create and maintain gender stereotypes, the Convention imposes on member states the obligation to take all measures necessary to:

> "Change men and women's social and cultural behaviour pattern with a view to eliminating prejudice and customary and all other practices which are based on stereotypical male and female roles, or the notion that one of the sexes is the other inferior or superior."[18]

3. Handling similarities and differences between women

CEDAW was drawn up in the context of a global woman-centred research tradition that was concerned with universal aspects of women's subordinate position in different cultures and societies. The principle of equality and non-discrimination is the Convention's cornerstone. It is embedded in the Aristotelian notion of justice prescribing that 'like cases' be treated alike while permitting 'unalike' cases to be treated differently. It is generally agreed that

17. The CEDAW Committee's General recommendation no. 19
18. Jf. CEDAW Article 5a.

equality and difference need to be balanced to achieve substantive equality. Yet in a changing world with increased mobility of people, values and norms, what constitutes permissible and impermissible gender differences constitutes a site of contestation.

3.1. A review of debates regarding similarities and differences

Different views on the equality non-discrimination principle's ability to deal with women's different life situations and life values are expressed in the collective work on the UN's Covenant *The Human Rights of Women.*[19] This book was edited by Canadian human rights professor Rebecca Cook and published in connection with the Beijing conference in 1995. Most of the authors in the book were concerned with the importance of the equality and non-discrimination standard for including various groups of women who, because of legal, cultural and social barriers, had been excluded from access to resources and participation. This view was in line with American feminist and law professor Katharine MacKinnon's scepticism to the difference-oriented stream of feminism that she felt ignored systematic power differences between women and men. In the article, "Difference and Dominance: On Sex Discrimination" she concluded:

> "Seeing sex equality questions as matters of reasonable or unreasonable classification is part of the way male dominance is expressed in law. If you follow my shift in perspective from gender as difference to gender as dominance, gender changes from a distinction that is presumptively suspect. The difference approach tries to map that reality; the dominance approach tries to challenge and change it. In the dominance approach, sex discrimination stops being a question of morality and starts being a question of politics."[20]

Canadian human rights researcher Kathleen Mahoney, on the other hand, was sceptical to CEDAW's equal status approach, because it did not deal with the male norm that lay at the base of the law:

> "...it does not allow for any questioning about the ways in which law has maintained and constructed the disadvantage of women, nor does it allow for an examination of the extent

19. Rebecca Cook (ed.) (1995) "*Human Rights of Women*". University of Pennsylvania Press.
20. MacKinnon (1987), p. 44.

to which the law is male-defined and built on male conceptions of problems and of harms."[21]

African women's rights scholars, such as Adethun Illemoka from Nigeria, pointed out CEDAW's western normative foundation:

"The international women's rights movement, like the international human rights movement, largely projects the concerns of privileged women who are able to make their voices heard. The voices of middle class European and American women, because of their cultural affinity with and the access to power from where the dominant discourse emanates, often is loudest."[22]

In the 1970s and 80s already, Norwegian women's law researchers put the normative premises underlying the equal status approach under scrutiny.[23] The book "*Juss og Juks*", which was the first work on women's law in Norway, criticized the then Government's proposed Gender Equality Act because it ignored the existing social, cultural and economic differences between women and men.[24] The research, which was carried out in this initial phase, compared the gender-neutral laws with women's actual values and life circumstances. By using the women's life circumstances as a basis it showed how the gender-neutral legislation was largely rooted in men's living conditions and life cycle.[25] Many of these studies were based on growing body of empirical studies carried out by women's researchers in the social sciences. A number of women's law scholars were also using the sources of insight about

21. Kathleen Mahoney (1994), "Canadian approaches to equality, rights and gender equality in the courts". In: *Human Rights of Women. National and International Perspectives.* (red.) Rebecca Cook, Pennsylvania: University of Pennsylvania Press, p. 442.
22. Adethun Ilumoka (1994), "African women's economic, social and cultural rights – Toward a relevant theory of practice". In: *Human Rights of Women. National and International Perspectives.* (red.) Rebecca Cook, Pennsylvania: University of Pennsylvania Press, p 320.
23. At the University of Copenhagen seminars in women's law were started in 1979. In accordance with the Introduction in the Yearbook for Women's Law from 1978, the most important sources of inspiration for the field were "the new feminist movement, Marxism and the legal tradition." Indledning av redaktionsudvalget Jytte Lindgård, Ruth Nielsen and Jytte Thorbek (1978).
24. Tove Stang Dahl (et.al) (1975), *"Juss og Juks"*. Oslo: Pax.
25. Contributions from a number of researchers in the field are compiled in Tove Stang Dahl (1987)*An Introduction to Women's Law,* Norwegian University Press, Oslo.

the intersection between life and law that lay in legal aid and legal literacy cases.[26]

The systematic gender differences that the gender neutral welfare legislation, particularly the National Insurance Actgave rise to, was revealed through comparisons between the complex life cycle of women in the intersection between birth, care and paid work and men's linear life cycle as wage earners.[27] Comparisons between different categories of women that did the same work – such as birth and care work, showed how women's rights constituted a status hierarchy where relations established through a work contract were ranked higher than relations based on a marriage contract.[28] In the assessment of the status of house and care work, consideration for equality and consideration for women's equal worth and dignity pulled in different directions. Whether the mutual maintenance obligation in marriage should be done away with on the basis of an equality principle based on the assumption that spouses were and should be financially and socially equal individuals was a site of contestation.[29]

These research contributions provided elements that together formed an empirical and theoretical basis for incorporating knowledge about women's life circumstances into general legal considerations, such as freedom, equality, dignity and integrity. Making a synthesis on the basis of a number of authors' empirical contributions Tove Stang Dahl in *Introduction To Women's Law* placed the emphasis on defining the common features of women's actual and legal situation compared to that of men.[30] In accordance with feminist

26. Vogt, Agnes (1981) "Kvinners rett til fellesboligen ved separasjon og skilsmisse – en undersøkelse av JURK-sakene." In: *Kvinnerettslige studier* 1981 nr. 2 1981. Oslo: Universitetsforlaget; Kirsti Strøm Bull (1982) "Hjemmearbeidets erstatningsrettslige stilling". In: *Tidsskrift for rettsvitenskap* 1982 s 903-936; Anne Hellum and Mariann Fastvold (1987) "We have researched to have women's voices heard". In: *Money and Work in Marriage, Studies in Women's Law* 1985 No. 26. University of Oslo, p. 2-13.
27. Tone Sverdrup (1984) "Folketrygden i kvinneperspektiv". In: *Folketrygden i støpeskjeen.* (red.) Asbjørn Kjønstad, Oslo.
28. Marianne Fastvold (1977) "Fødselsrett og likhet". In: *Kvinnerettslige studier* nr. 2. Institute of Women's Law, University of Oslo.
29. Anne Hellum (1987) "Money and diginity". In Marianne Fastvold and Anne Hellum *Money and Work in Marriage*, In: Studies in Women's Law No. 26 University of Oslo.
30. Dahl (1987) .

cannons of the time, such as Allison Jaggar[31], it was the similarities among women across class and race that were in focus.

3.2. Challenges from the south: similarities and differences

The inherent westernness of this theory was challenged in a meeting with African women lawyers, who in the period 1987-1990 came to the Institute of Women's Law in Oslo to build competence in women's law. The collaboration was part of the emphasis on North-South university cooperation at the University of Oslo and the new focus on women's rights in Norwegian development policy. In 1985 the University of Zimbabwe and the University of Oslo entered into a bilateral agreement in a number of academic areas including law. The reason for the collaboration in the field of law was that as part of efforts to build up a new legal system, the Faculty of Law at the University of Zimbabwe wanted to draw on experiences from the Nordic social democracies. As a step in decolonization of the law, they wanted ideas from the research traditions in human rights, sociology of law and women's law represented by internationally renowned researchers at the Faculty of Law in Oslo, such as Torkel Opsahl, Asbjorn Eide, Vilhelm Aubert, Torstein Eckhoff, Tove Stang Dahl and Thomas Mathiesen.

Mary Maboreke, who was a master's student at the Institute of Women's Law in 1985 and introduced women's law as a legal discipline at the Faculty of Law at the University of Zimbabwe in 1987, gave the following summary of her experience with this collaboration:

> "Starting out from a Norwegian women's law framework, which of course reflects the Norwegian culture, and at the same time being African, made women's law strange and difficult. I can use the considerations of woman's law as an example: equality, justice, self-realisation, self-determination and integrity. I can see that these considerations fit the Norwegian context. A person is a person, and people are evaluated on an individual basis. In an African context this is completely different. I am never just Mary Maboreke, except when I am at work. When I am at home I am the mother of Tachinga, wife of Lawrence, sister of George, etc. These relationships will continue and continue. It is such relationships that give me and other African women an identity".[32]

In a specific and direct manner, this educational and research collaboration brought the ethnocentrist dimension into the Norwegian women's law tradi-

31. Jaggar (1983).
32. Mary Maboreke was interviewed by Else Anette Grannes and Hanne S. Børing (1991) "Så, i hvilken grad kan datteren være annerledes enn sin mor", In: *Hefte for Kritisk Juss* no. 1-2 1991" p. 3-17.

tion. The criticism from the African women's rights lawyers forced us to consider our own research from the outside and increased awareness about our own Norwegian-ness and whiteness. Our African partners were looking for legal theories and concepts that were based on the situation of African women, which at that time did not exist. For me as leader of the cooperation in women's law, it was a challenge to design a research and teaching programme that provided tools for the development of new knowledge. The methodological principle of analysing the law on the basis of women's reality was a fruitful tool, but difficult to put into practice in an African context in Norway. Therefore, we decided to move the program to the University of Zimbabwe, where it would be possible to include field studies as an integral part of teaching.

As part of efforts to teach students and researchers at Master's and PhD level to incorporate different types of empirical data in the description and analysis of African law, after we had moved the program to the Faculty of Law at University of Zimbabwe in 1990, a method project was initiated. This resulted in the book "Pursuing Grounded Theory in Law. South-*North* Perspectives in Developing Women*'s Law."*[33] It was a book co-authored by myself, Julie Stewart and Welshman Ncube from the University of Zimbabwe and Agnete Weis Bentzon and Torben Agersnap from the University of Copenhagen. Our work on the book was based on African teaching and research experiences that came from ongoing Master's and PhD projects at the Women's law Programme at the University of Zimbabwe. Work on the book became an arena for reflection and further development of analysis tools that emanated from the action oriented research carried out by the Women and Law in the Southern Africa Research Project, Norwegian women's law theory, Nordic sociology of law and the legal anthropological tradition of legal pluralism. We enjoyed hearing Agnete Weis Bentzon's experiences from her work on creating a new legal system on Greenland in connection with decolonization and autonomy. She was a member of the Greenland expedition, which had the task of identifying and incorporating the Inuits' living customs into the new common legal system for Danes and Inuits. Her work in this area was an important contribution to Nordic sociology of law and was a methodological source of inspiration in the effort to develop African theory of

33. Agnete Weiz Bentzon et.al. (1998), *Pursuing Grounded Theory in Law. South-North Experiences in Developing Women's Law.* Oslo/Harare: TANO/Mond Books.

women's law, which was based on empirical knowledge about women's circumstances and local law.[34]

Another challenge that arose was to develop an understanding of CEDAW as a tool for change in a pluralistic legal and cultural landscape characterised by rapid and uneven change, with significant differences between women from different races, ethnic groups and classes. In my own PhD work, which was written during this period, comparisons of the situation of different groups of childless women helped provide an understanding of the interaction between CEDAW, which was ratified by Zimbabwe in 1990, the increasingly gender neutral and unified national marriage legislation and the relational and gendered customary laws.[35] The study, which described and analysed the impact of CEDAW on different groups of women, emphasised the importance of focusing on the similarities and differences among women:

> "Identification of similarities between women makes it possible to identify common problems, values and interests in specific location and time frames. Differences are important because they show variation and question the validity of tentative generalisations when it comes to women's common problems, values and interests."[36]

3.3. CEDAW's handling of similarities and differences – what is the trend?

After this glance back in time and space, I will now return to the development of the international equality and non-discrimination norm. How have CEDAW and other international and regional standards responded to the different circumstances and life values of women? Has it, as many difference oriented feminist scholars feared, become a white, western, middle class feminists' stronghold?

A consistent trend in the practice of the CEDAW committee is the strong emphasis on de facto protection against discrimination and thus a convergence in views on what should be treated equally and what should be treated

34. Agnete Weis Bentzon (1968) *Familiens økonomiske administration of ejendelenes tilhørsforhold i de grøndlandske samfund* In: "Nyt Fra Samfundsvidenskaberne no. 11". Agnete Weis Bentzon (1979) Ret og Reformer 1 and Ret og Reformer 2. A sociological study of the Lay Judge System in the Greenlandic transitional society 1951-1976. In: "Nyt Fra Samfundsvidenskaberne".
35. Anne Hellum (1999) *"Women's Human Rights and Legal Pluralism in Africa: Mixed Norms and Identities in Infertility Management in Zimbabwe."* Oslo/Harare: TANO Aschehoug/Mond Books.
36. Ibid p. 426.

differently. For example, the CEDAW Committee stated in General Recommendation No. 25:

> "8. In the Committee's view, a purely formal legal or programmatic approach is not sufficient to achieve women's de facto equality with men, which the Committee interprets as substantive equality. In addition, the Convention requires that women be given an equal start and that they be empowered by an enabling environment to achieve equality of results. It is not enough to guarantee women treatment that is identical to that of men. Rather, biological as well as socially and culturally constructed differences between women and men must be taken into account. Under certain circumstances, non-identical treatment of women and men will be required in order to address such differences. Pursuit of the goal of substantive equality also calls for an effective strategy aimed at overcoming underrepresentation of women and a redistribution of resources and power between men and women."

The jurisprudence of the CEDAW committee has, in the same way as the other human rights treaty bodies – for example the Human Rights Committee and the Committee on Social, Economic and Cultural Rights – moved from a formal to a substantive concept of equality. This is reflected in a discrimination regime that includes both direct and indirect discrimination. The CEDAW Committee states in General Recommendation No. 28 that:

> "...identical or neutral treatment of women and men might constitute discrimination against women if such treatment resulted or had the effect of women being dined the exercise of a right because there was no recognition of the pre-existing gender-based disadvantage and inequality that women face."

This shows a dynamic international legal development, which takes into account the characteristics of women's lives that are different from men's. A key question is how the concept of direct and indirect discrimination has engendered women's civil, political, social and economic rights at international and national level. Sandra Fredman, in her approach to social and economic rights makes a distinction between extending existing rights to women and engendering rights.[37] The concept of "engendered social and economic rights" according to Fredman entails:

> "As a start it is necessary to recognize the distinctive nature of women's experience of poverty and disadvantage. This suggests that it is not sufficient simply to extend socio-economic rights women. Instead, socio-economic rights need to be recast in the light of the

37. Sandra Fredman "Engendering Socio-economic Rights", 25 *South African Journal of Human Rights* 410-11.

demands of substantive gender equality. Substantive gender equality goes beyond treating women in the same way as men and require transformative measures. This in turn entails reconceptualising the rights themselves."

To explore the extent to which the international equality and non-discrimination norm has responded to women's experiences and recast women's rights in the light of the demand of substantive equality I will in the following address the relationship between equal status and equal worth.

3.4. The tension between equal status and equal worth

The relationship between equal status and equal worth has been at the core of the discussion of how 'justified' and 'unjustified' distinctions between the sexes should be drawn without succumbing to either homogenizing universalism or paralyzing cultural relativism since the CEDAW Convention's reception in 1979.

CEDAW is based primarily on a modern gender model that assumes that women and men compete in the same arena. The preamble to the Convention states that:

"The traditional male and female role in society and the family must be changed to achieve full equality between women and men."

According to Article 5 a), the state party's commitment to working to eliminate gender stereotypes is a step in realising the goal that women must have the same access as men to education, employment, health care and politics. The Convention also has an element of equal worth thinking. In the introduction, attention is drawn to the equal worth of women's economic contributions in terms domestic work and care:

"Women's important contributions to family welfare and to the development of society, which so far has not been fully recognised, the social significance of the role of mother and both parents' role in the family and the upbringing of children, and is aware that the role of women in reproduction should not give rise to discrimination, and that fostering responsibility for children must be shared between men and women and society as a whole".

Thus, an inner tension can be sensed between equal status and equal worth and what should be treated equally and what should be treated differently. In the discussion below part time work, *hijab* and *mahr* illustrate the dilemmas and conflicts that the balancing of these principles gives rise to in relation to the demand of substantive equality.

3.5. Adjustment between family and work in labour law and family law: the part-time dilemma

In the Nordic countries many women work part time in order to balance participation in the labour market with caring obligations. The gendered division of paid work and caring work gives rise to a series of challenges and dilemmas regarding the balancing of equality and difference in relation to the goal of substantive equality.

The development in international and national discrimination law reflects how women's reality as part time workers and part time carers has begun to make its mark on the equality and non-discrimination standard. As pointed out by Ruth Nielsen in chapter 3 in this volume the CJEU was, through its case law, in the 1979s 80s and 90s way ahead of the CEDAW Committee in the development of women's protection against direct and indirect discrimination in the labor market. Through a dynamic interpretation of EU-law the CJEU in this period strengthened women's protection against discrimination related to pregnancy and maternity. Through the development of the concept of indirect discrimination the CJEU strengthened the legal position of part time workers who often are women trying to balance paid work and caring work.[38] This body of case law is now codified in the 2002 directive on Equal Treatment for Men and Women and a number of other directives that define direct and indirect discrimination.[39]

Norway is not a member of the EU but has since 1 January 1994 been a member of EFTA and bound by the EEA Agreement.[40] The directive on Equal Treatment for Men and Women, which in accordance with the EEA Agreement is binding for Norway has led to significant improvements in the protection of pregnant women and part-time working women in the Gender Equality Act. Elisabeth Vigerust and Helga Aune's doctoral studies, which examine the protection of pregnant women and part-time working women against discrimination in the labour market, clearly demonstrate that the linear life cycle of male paid workers no longer represents the equality concept's premise provider, neither in international nor Norwegian law.[41]

38. See in particular Case 170/84 Bi*lka* [1986] ECR p. 1607.
39. 2002/73/EC, now repealed and replaced by the Recast Gender Equality Directive 2006/54, Ethnic Equality Directive (2000/43/EC) Article 2, the Employment Framework Directive (2000/78/EC) Article 2 and the Gender Equality (Goods and Service) Directive (2004/113EC) Article 2.
40. http://www.efta.int/eea/eea-agreement.aspx.
41. Elisabeth Vigerust (2008) "Vern mot graviditetsvern i arbeidsforhold". In: *Diskriminerings- og likestillingsrett* (red.) Anne Hellum & Kirsten Ketscher, Oslo: Universi-

Yet in many of the Nordic countries women's equal rights have to a certain extent been promoted through reforms that negatively affect women who are full time or part time home workers from their economic safety net. In Norway women's entry into the labour market was, according to family law professor Tone Sverdrup "to some extent promoted by depriving them of the legal safety net both regarding spousal support and certain social benefits."[42] According to Sverdrup the equal division rule upon divorce was, for example, limited to certain assets in 1991 due to the increasing number of divorces. A spouse may, according to Sverdrup withhold pension rights from division and spousal maintenance is granted only in exceptional cases in Norway. Because 40% of all women are engaged in part-time work, wives earn small pensions, and are thus disadvantaged by these provisions. The sharing of pensions has, according to Sverdrup, been the subject of political and legal dispute for many years:

> "However, proposals for reform have gained little support from the political establishment. The self-sufficiency principle has prevailed in Norway for more than thirty years. The idea is that part-time work should not be favoured indirectly through pension sharing as this could cement gender roles. This policy raises several dilemmas for the legislator. How much account shall be taken of existing inequalities between various groups in society and should legislation be based on the ideal objective or on reality as it is today? Who shall be sacrificed on the altar of equality?"[43]

The economically disadvantaged position of women who have worked part time in order to care for children epitomizes the tension between equal status and equal worth and what constitutes permissible and impermissible difference. Invoking Article 16 of CEDAW the Norwegian NGO shadow report to the CEDAW Committee from 2011 argues that "...the gender-neutral rules governing pension rights after marital breakdown hinders women's financial independence and may thus be discriminating against women in marriage."[44] What the implication of general recommendation no. 21 to Article 16 stating

tetsforlaget, p. 187-210; Helga Aune (2008) "Deltids- og midlertidig ansattes diskrimineringsvern". In: *Diskriminerings- og likestillingsrett* (red.) Anne Hellum & Kirsten Ketscher, Oslo: Universitetsforlaget, p. 239-261.

42. Tone Sverdrup (2012)." Equal rights at all costs". In: Elaine Sutherland (ed.) *The Future of Child and Family Law: International Predictions* (Cambridge University Press, forthcoming 2012).
43. Sverdrup ibid.
44. NGO Shadow Report 2011. Supplementing and Commenting on Norway's 8th Periodic Report. Norway's 8th periodic report is scheduled for review in February 2012. Supplementing and commen

that financial and non-financial contributions, such as housework and care, should be treated equally will hopefully be addressed in the CEDAW Committee's concluding comments to Norway's 8th Periodic Report.[45]

3.6. Between stereotypes and substantive equality: mahr and hijab

The coexistence of gender-neutral legislation and religious norms that create and maintain inequality between women and men is another theme that invites reflection on the balancing of equality and inequality in relation to the goal of substantive equality. For the CEDAW Committee, evaluation of the interaction between modern gender-based marriage legislation and informal marriage norms, which have been based on equal worth, gives rise to dilemmas and conflicts. One example is the CEDAW Committee's evaluation of the Muslim marriage dowry, *mahr* which is a mandatory part of Muslim marriage contracts, and implies that the man is obligated to give the woman a gift, often of a certain value, for their wedding or divorce.[46] According to Article 16 of CEDAW, the question is whether this different gender structure can be combined with the equality principle, which requires that women and men have the same rights and obligations when entering into marriage, during marriage and on divorce. The dilemma is illustrated by the CEDAW Committee's contradictory statements in the concluding comments on state reports from various North African countries. During the committee's 14th session, where Tunisia's periodic report was considered, the following statement emerged from one of the members, Ms. Cartwright, who:

> "...noted that the persistence of the custom of providing a dowry indicated that women were still, to some degree, regarded as a commodity."[47]

At the 27th Session, Committee Member Ms. Manolo commented on the Tunisian report:

> " ...that the continuation of that practice gave the impression that the bride was bought and could be managed like a chattel."[48]

45. The CEDAW Committee's General recommendation no. 21.
46. Lene Løvdahl (2009) "Private International Law, Muslim Laws and Gender Equality". *Kvinnerettslige studier*, no. 79. Oslo: University of Oslo.
47. http://daccessdds.un.org/doc/UNDOC/GEN/N95/801/12/PDF/N9580112.pdf?OpenElement read 10.09.08
48. http://daccessdds.un.org/doc/UNDOC/GEN/N02/426/33/PDF/N0242633.pdf?OpenElement read 10.09.08.

At the 38th Session, the Committed requested Syria to:

> " ...review its existing laws and policies to ensure that women who go to shelters do not forgo other legal rights, such as rights to maintenance and dower."[49]

This example indicates that the Committee sees the need, in certain situations, to take the complementary structure of the Muslim marriage contract into consideration in order to achieve de facto financial equality between women and men in divorce. This means that under certain circumstances, recognition of *mahr* is seen as a necessary measure in order to achieve substantive equality between spouses on an unequal financial footing.

The CEDAW Committee's handling of the *hijab* issue also testifies to the tense relationship between the goal of substantive equality and the demand for the elimination of gender stereotyping practices under Article 5a. The Committee has not made direct statements concerning the relationship between the duty to eliminate gender stereotypes in Article 5a) and gendered religious dress codes such as the hijab.[50] Hijab problems are indirectly addressed in the Committee's concluding comments to countries that have adopted laws prohibiting the use of headscarves in education and employment. In discussing Turkey's state report, the Committee expressed concern about how the law prohibiting the use of religious headdress in the education sector would impact women and girls' right to education and stated:

> " ...The Committee is also concerned about the impact on girls and women of the ban on wearing headscarves in schools and universities."[51]

Based on this, the Committee requested the Turkish government for an ongoing account of the impact the statutory ban has had on women's access to education. In its discussion of France's state report, the CEDAW Committee said in a similar manner that it was:

> "...concerned that the ban should not lead to the denial of the right to education of any girl and their inclusion in all facets of French society."[52]

49. http://daccessdds.un.org/doc/UNDOC/GEN/N07/375/96/PDF/N0737596.pdf?OpenElement read 10.09.08.
50. The complex legal issues that the use of hijab in the police gives rise to in relation to the Norwegian Gender Equality Act, the Norwegian Discrimination Act, the CEDAW and the ECHR are dealt with in Vibeke Blaker Strand's chapter in this book.
51. CEDAW. A/60/38 (Turkey), par. 371 and 372

It is worth noting that in their statements to Turkey and France, the CEDAW Committee did not use Article 5a, which obliges the state parties to take all appropriate measures, but emphasizes consideration for de facto equality as regards education and employment. Instead, the CEDAW Committee considered the cumulative negative effects of legislation, which on paper seeks gender and religious neutrality, but which in practice can have a skewed gender effect as regards Muslim women and girls' social and economic rights. This shows how the committee sought to address the unresolved relationship between the ban on stereotype in Article 5a and the right to substantive equality under Article 1.[53] The Committee's practice may be understood as a tacit acceptance that the hijab can be regarded as a part of the development of intersectional protection against discrimination that takes into account how accumulated disadvantages in the intersection between gender and religion can lead to indirect discrimination against Muslim women and girls.[54]

52. CEDAW/C/FRA/CO/6 (2008) par. 20
53. Anne Hellum (2010), "The global equality standard meets Norwegian sameness". In: *From Transnational Relations to Transnational Laws. Northern European Laws at the Cross Roads*. In Hellum, Anne, Shaheen Sardar, Ali & Anne, Griffiths (eds.). Aldershot: Ashgate. p.71-93
54. Such an interpretation of the relationship between intersectionality and indirect gender discrimination has been used by Titia Loenen (2009) "The headscarf debate: Approaching the intersection of sex, religion, and race under the European Convention on Human Rights and EC Equality Law". In: *European Union Non-Discrimination Law: Comparative Perspectives on Multidimensional Equality*. (red.) Shiek, D & Victoria Chege, London and New York: Routledge Cavendish ; Hege Skjeie (2009), "Multiple equality claims in the practice of the Norwegian anti-discrimination agencies". In: *European Union Non-Discrimination Law: Comparative Perspectives on Multidimensional Equality*. (red.) Shiek, D & Victoria Chege, London and New York: Routledge Cavendish, p.295.305. and Lynn Roseberry (2009) "Religion, ethnicity and gender in the Danish headscarf debate". In: *European Union Non-Discrimination Law: Comparative Perspectives on Multidimensional Equality*. (red.) Shiek, D & Victoria Chege, London and New York: Routledge Cavendish. On the other hand, Kirsten Ketscher has maintained that the hijab constitutes a gender stereotype dress code and that any ban would not constitute discrimination against women neither on the basis of sex, ethnicity or religion. Kirsten Ketscher (2005). "Etnisk ligebehandling, religionsfrihed og ligestilling mellom kvinder og mænd – set I lyset af Føtex-sagen" In *Ugeskrift for Retsvæsen*.

4. Towards a complex gender discrimination notion – intersectionality

In the 1980s and 90s, strong criticism of equality-focused feminism emerged. In their research, researchers who concerned themselves with black American women, third world women and lesbians and transgender women showed that female gender was not a homogeneous but a complex category that was closely related to a woman's sexuality, race and class.[55] This research concluded that understanding of gender that was based on comparisons between women and men was not representative of all women, but primarily concerned heterosexual, Western, white middle class women. It was black American women's rights lawyer Kimberle Crenshaw, who on the basis of the relationship between gender and race in the United States transcended the dichotomous debate with difference-oriented feminists on one side and equal status oriented feminists on the other. With the concept of intersectionality, she launched a legal theory where the relationship between gender and race was not seen as a question of whether black women had more in common with white women or black men, but how discrimination on the basis of gender and race work together, without the unfavourable result being attributed to any single form of discrimination.[56]

4.1. Multiple discrimination in CEDAW

Although the wording of CEDAW does not use terms such as intersectionality or multiple discrimination, the preamble to the Convention takes into account that the position of women in law and society is not only related to gender but also disability, race and class. The parties to the Conventions expressed in the preamble:

> ". ..concern over the fact that women in poor conditions have minimal access to food, health care, education, training and employment, and to having other needs taken care of."

55. C. Mohanty (1988), "Under Western Eyes: feminist Scholarship and Colonial Discources". *Feminist Review* 30; J. Butler (1999) "*Gender Trouble: Feminism and the Subversion of Identity*". London and New York: Routledge.
56. Kimberlé W. Crenshaw (2004), "Demarginalising the intersection of race and sex: A black feminist critique of anti-discrimination doctrine, feminist theory and anti-racist politics". In: *Anti-Discrimination Law, International Library of Essays in Law and Legal Theory, Second Series.* (red.) Christopher. McCrudden, Dartmouth: Ashgate, p. 479 – 507.

It is interesting to note how through its jurisprudence, the CEDAW committee has gradually developed a nuanced and complex understanding of female gender. General recommendation no. 18 emphasises the special vulnerability of women with disabilities and urges state parties to submit information on measures adopted to promote their right to education, employment, health and political participation. In general recommendation No. 25, where the Committee deals with measures to promote de facto equality, they emphasise the need for measures that concern multiple discrimination:

"Certain groups of women, in addition to suffering from discrimination directed at them as women, may also suffer from multiple forms of discrimination based on additional grounds such as race, ethnic or religious identity, disability, age, class caste or other factors. Such discrimination may affect these groups of women primarily, or to a different degree or in different ways than men. States parties must take specific temporary measures to eliminate such multiple forms of discrimination against women and its compounded negative effect on them."[57]

The same applies to General Recommendation no. 26 regarding female migrant workers, where Article 14 emphasises the complex nature of discrimination:

Moreover, women migrant workers often experience intersecting forms of discrimination, suffering not only sex- and gender-based discrimination, but also xenophobia and racism. Discrimination based on race, ethnicity, cultural particularities, nationality, language, religion or other status may be expressed in sex- and gender-specific ways.[58]

In recent years, the CEDAW Committee has paid particular attention to the situation of refugee, immigrant and minority women in the Nordic countries. In its concluding comments to Norway's 5th, 6th and 7th periodic reports, the Committee has asked Norway to explain what is being done to ensure immigrant and refugee women the same social and economic rights as ethnic Norwegian women.[59] As part of the efforts to identify discrimination against women, which can be attributed to the interaction between various types of discrimination, the CEDAW Committee has requested Norway to present sta-

57. CEDAW Committee's General Recommendation no. 25, Article 7
58. CEDAW Committee's General Recommendation No. 26, Article 14
59. The CEDAW Committee's comments on Norway's 5th-6th periodic reports and the CEDAW Committee's comments on Norway's 7th periodic report.

tistics that shed light on abuse, education, political and employment participation on the basis of women's age and ethnic background.[60]

4.2. Women as a cross-cutting category of anti-discrimination law

A challenge for today's research and teaching in women's law is how to recast the concept of equality and non-discrimination in the light of the complex nature of the female gender. The actual legal position of girls, older women, women with disabilities or women in various religious communities is often affected by multiple interacting forms of discrimination. In practice, women's multiple and complex identities mean that the various types of discrimination interact, overlap or collide. This requires complex and compound considerations in relation to anti-discrimination law. In Norwegian women's law, where equality and anti-discrimination law is a key area, the cross-cutting nature of the gender perspective is emphasised.[61] This is a perspective that cuts across different types of discrimination, such as ethnicity, sexuality, disability and age. [62]This is because women constitute the largest population group and are part of all the different groups that are protected by the different types of discrimination set out in the anti-discrimination legislation.[63]

5. Complex female identities and complex legal status

Increased migration has led to major social and cultural changes, such as a growing religious and cultural pluralism. This means that the law in the Nordic countries no longer works in a homogeneous cultural context but interacts with a multiplicity of social and cultural norms. In Norway, where the official legal system basically does not recognise other legal systems than Norwegian state law, in practice, the formal national law operates side by side and in interaction with various informal norms that operate on the ground.[64] This situ-

60. The CEDAW Committee's comments on Norway's 7th periodic report, Articles 20, 23 and 26.
61. Today, equality and anti-discrimination law is an optional subject in the Master's programme at the Faculty of Law in Oslo.
62. Vibeke Blaker Strand's doctoral thesis *Diskrimineringsvernets rekkevidde i mote med religionsutøvelse, Universitetet I Oslo oktober 2011* develops an approach that transverses discrimination on the ground of gender, sexuality and religion.
63. Hellum, Anne & Kirsten Ketscher (red.) (2008), p. 18.
64. Anne Hellum (2006), "Menneskerettigheter, pluralisme, kompleksitet og integrasjon". In: *Festskrift til Carl August Fleischer* (ed..) Aslak Syse m.fl, Oslo: Universitetsforlaget, p.225-247.

ation is described in legal anthropology as the law's semi-autonomy or legal pluralism.[65]

Many immigrant women are caught between national law and the norms and expectations largely followed by members of ethnic or religious groups to which their families and local communities belong. A challenge for contemporary women's law research is to gain a better understanding of the relationship between women's multiple identities, rights awareness and rights realisation. As highlighted in American legal anthropologist Sally Engle Merry's groundbreaking research into violence against women, there is a huge gap between knowledge of rights and the realisation of rights, which is due to women's complex and multiple identities and affiliations.[66]

As Tina Storsletten Nordström's research on immigrant women's right to legal information shows women's enhanced protection against discrimination under Norwegian and international law has to a limited extent benefited women from different ethnic minorities and immigrants.[67] The main beneficiaries of the Norwegian Gender Equality Act law are middle class women that are working full time. The CEDAW Committee's approach to immigrant women's right to information about their rights emphasises the importance of making protection against discrimination available to women who in practice have to negotiate their rights under state law with coexisting social and moral norms. Like other UN Committees, the CEDAW Committee has emphasised the authorities' responsibility to inform immigrant women about their rights. As part of efforts to make the information about rights understandable, relevant and acceptable to different groups of women, the importance of both linguistic and cultural translation is emphasised.[68] In this way, the CEDAW

65. Sally Falk Moore (1978), *Law as Process*. London: Routledge; John Griffiths (1986) "What is Legal Pluralism?" In: *Journal of Legal Pluralism* nr. 24, s. 1–55; Anne Griffiths (2002) "Legal pluralism". In: *An Introduction to Law and Social Theory.* (ed.) R. Banakar & M. Travers, Oxford: Hart Publishing, p. 289–310.
66. Sally Engle Merry (2006), *"Human Rights and Gender Violenc*e". Chicago: University of Chicago Press.
67. Tina Storsletten Nordstrøm (2011). "Rettighetsinformasjon og rettshjelp: virkemidler for å skape et reelt diskrimineringsvern for innvandrerkvinner". In: I *På vei – Kjønn og rett i Norden.* Eva-Maria Svensson, Ulrika Andersson, Hege Brækhus, Monica Burman, Anne Hellum, Stine Jørgensen & Anu Pylkkänen, (red.) Makadam förlag & bokproduktion AB, Göteborg
68. About the human rights requirement that legal information shall be accessible and understandable, see Tina Storsletten Nordstrøm (2010), "Innvandrerkvinners rett til rettighetsinformasjon: Hva gjøres og hva krever FNs kvinnekonvensjon?" In: *Kritisk Juss* nr.2 2010, published by Rettspolitisk Forening, Fagbokforlaget, Bergen.

Committee takes into account a situation where different normative traditions co-exist, legal pluralism.

The Special Rapporteur on violence against women has highlighted the weakness of one-dimensional, legalistic approaches. In her discussion of measures in relation to crimes of honour, she is as critical to:

> The arrogant gaze of critical outsiders' who suggest simplistic legalistic solutions.

In her view, rights must be communicated and implemented in a way that takes into consideration how women's identity has been socially rooted:

> Where international attention and leverage are rooted in culturally-sensitive strategies and locally supported, they can give strong underpinning to our situation-specific approaches and interventions on the ground.[69]

In the context of the new multicultural Scandinavia, post-colonial research into women and law from immigrant women's background countries in Africa and Asia is highly relevant. A central theme of this research is the relationship between women's multiple identities, legal pluralism and the realization of human rights. In their approach to information on rights, African and Pakistani researchers have been concerned that women are not only individuals but are also part of family and kinship relationships that place strong normative constraints on women's choices.[70] They have emphasized the importance of not only informing the woman, but also her family and community on the rights and obligations of family members. This research emphasizes the importance of a methodical approach that takes into account that women are not only citizens with individual rights but are also part of the family relations, which in practice may be decisive for their access to resources in terms of property, education and work.

In the light of experience acquired in cooperation with women's law researchers in Pakistan and Africa, I and other women's law researchers in Oslo became interested in the interaction between Norwegian law and informal religious and social norms. In the research project "From formal to real rights" concerning immigrant women's protection against discrimination, we

69. Radika Coomaraswamy (2005), "Preface: Violence against women and crimes of honour". In: *'Honour' Crimes, Paradigms, and Violence against Women* .(red.) Lynn Welchman & Sara Hossain, London: Zed Books, xiii.
70. Amy Tsanga (2007) "Legal literacy in plural legal contexts", In: *Human Rights, plural legalities and gendered realities. Paths are made by walking.* (red.) Anne Hellum (et.al.), Harare: Weaver Press, p. 407-437.

have taken a practice-oriented approach to this topic. In cooperation with the student legal aid initiative "Legal Advice for Women" (JURK) and immigrant organisations, we have studied how information about human rights, as laid down in Norwegian law, can be communicated in a way that makes it accessible and understandable for women from different religious and ethnic groups.[71] Through insight into the work of organisations that provide immigrant women from the Pakistani community with information on rights, advice and guidance, we have gradually begun to gain knowledge about how, in order to achieve their rights, women manoeuvre between the various legal, religious and social norms.[72]

In collaboration with Professor Shaheen Sardar Ali, who is an expert on women's human rights and Islam, a comparative information strategy, including Norwegian state-law, Pakistani state-law and Islam was initiated. In this pilot project Norwegian, Pakistani and Islamic law were integrated into the communication of women's rights. The request came from various Pakistani women's groups in Oslo who felt a need to understand the relationship between Norwegian, Pakistani and religious norms. These women's groups, who repeatedly invited JURK to provide training in Norwegian law, see it as a problem that women themselves and many in their local community, consider Norwegian law to be in conflict with Islam.

On this basis, we have arranged information meetings where JURK has given a presentation of women's rights under Norwegian law followed by a review of Pakistani law and Islam. To translate between Norwegian law and Islam, Shaheen Sardar Ali usually begins here lecture by stressing that under international Islamic law, Muslims shall obey the law in the country in which they live:

> As citizens of Norway, the UK etc. we are duty bound to obey the laws of the country that has offered us citizenship, this is what Islam demands of us. So long as the laws of our acquired countries do not contradict the main pillars of our faith, such as saying prayers, fasting during Ramadan, haj, zakat and so on.[73]

71. Tina Storsletten Nordstrøm (2011)
72. Anne Hellum & Farhat Taj (2010). "Taking what law where and to whom". In: *From Transnational Relations to Transnational Laws. Northern European Laws at the Cross Roads.* (red.) Anne Hellum, Shaheen Sardar Ali & Anne Griffiths. Aldershot: Ashgate, p. 93-117.
73. Shaheen Sardar Ali (2000). *Gender and Human Rights in Islam and International Law.* Hague/London/Boston: Kluwer Law International.

Shaheen Sardar Ali, who has helped develop a liberal, feminist interpretation of Islamic teachings, often has an opinion that differs from that of the local Imams in Oslo. In her handling of controversial issues, such as the right to divorce, she emphasizes similarities between Norwegian and Islamic law. For example, she argues that the principle of justice, which is found in both Norwegian law and Islam, does prevent the man from divorcing his wife through so-called triple talaq:

> Islam is justice. Three instant verbal talaq is not justice to woman. I want to tell you this method of talaq is nowhere in Quran. I request all you sisters to please read Quran carefully so that you know that this method of divorce is not in Quran.[74]

The potential of this approach can be illustrated through the following comments from one of the women who attended one of the meetings:

> As Muslims we believe we have to be accountable and answerable to God on the Day of Judgement about what we do in this world. We follow the Norwegian law to get social benefits or some relief, like divorce or to have our human rights protected. But it would psychologically very difficult to follow the law if we know that the law violates Islam. We think we get benefits from the Norwegian law, but at the same time make our life hereafter very difficult. We then think it is better to not follow the Norwegian law because Norwegian law is only for this worldly life which is short and rather make sure to protect ourselves from perpetual punishments on the day of judgements. Dr Shaheen's lectures and our discussions with her beautifully convince us that going by the Norwegian law is not a violation of Islam. This is such relief in terms of concerns about the life hereafter.[75]

The women we have been in contact with through this legal information project have all expressed a strong desire to assert their rights under Norwegian law. Many of them find that Norwegian legal practitioners, lawyers and public employees do not understand the normative cross pressure they are living under as women, muslims and immigrants. Therefore, experience so far provides a basis for believing that the insight into the relationship between women's multiple identities, legal pluralism, human rights awareness and rights realization is of importance for making women's human rights real.

74. Ali (2000).
75. Field notes, Farhat Taj 24 March 2009.

6. The porous and reflexive nature of equality and protection against discrimination

As this review shows, women's law research has moved from a position that emphasises the similarities in the situation of women compared with that of men to a position that examines the similarities and differences amongwomen. Based on the situation of different categories of women, many of today's women's law researchers are concerned about what should be treated equally and what should be treated differently to achieve substantive equality, not only between women and men, but also among different groups of women. There has also been a move from an understanding of female gender as a uniform size to a complex and compound category. There is increasing focus on women's compound and complex identities as individuals and members of various religious and ethnic groups and how an intersectional protection against discrimination can be developed in response. In order to develop measures that address the complex legal relationships to which women's complex identities and affiliations give rise, the interaction between national law and religious and social norms, the importance of legal pluralism has grown.

The CEDAW Committee has become a global arena where the line between what should be treated equally and what should be treated differently is under constant negotiation and contestation. The need to achieve substantive equality as regards education, employment and livelihood is given considerable weight in assessing what should be treated equally and what should be treated differently. The question whether pension sharing, *hijab* or *mahr* should be prohibited to promote gender equality epitomizes the unresolved relationship between equality and difference. The Committee's silence regarding these issues reflect a rather unclear relationship between the balancing of women's right to substantive equality and women's protection against gender stereotypes. In recent years, the Committee has devoted greater attention to the cumulative negative impact of discrimination in the intersection among gender, ethnicity, age and other types of discrimination. This once again demonstrates how there has been a change in the Committee's understanding of the female gender from a homogenous to a complex and diverse category. On several occasions, for example, on the right to legal information, the Committee has stressed the importance of measures to enhance women's protection against discrimination taking into account social and cultural circumstances.

All in all, these examples illustrate the open and porous nature of the international protection against discrimination and its ability to respond to new insights and interpretations that are developed through the incorporation of women's realities as well as research and action at local, national and global levels[76] This dynamic feature is a factor which on the one hand helps to strengthen gender equality and the legitimacy of protection against gender discrimination in relation individual women, women's organisations and women's law researchers in different parts of the world. On the other hand, the open and reflexive nature of the processes also give rise to opposition from many states who claim that through their dynamic style of interpretation, international legal bodies are instrumental in weakening of national sovereignty and undermining democratic legislative processes.[77]

In the dynamic processes that are outlined here, the equality and anti-discrimination standard of international law represents continuity with change. With its uncovering of inequality and complexity, the perspective from below and within challenges notions on what female gender is, as well as what should be treated equally and what should be treated differently. The interaction between these perspectives creates a dynamism that constitutes both continuity and change in jurisprudence and legal development.

Bibliography

Ali, Shaheen, Sardar (2000). *Gender and Human Rights in Islam and International Law.* Hague/London/Boston: Kluwer Law International.

Aune Helga (2008). "Deltids- og midlertidig ansattes diskrimineringsvern". In Hellum, Anne and Kirsten Ketscher (eds.). *Diskrimineringsrett.* Oslo: Universitetsforlaget.

Beauvoir, Simone de (1970). *Det annet kjønn I og II.* Oslo: Pax forlag.

Bentzon, Agnete Weis (1968). *Familiens økonomiske administration of ejendelenes tilhørsforhold i de grønlandske samfund.* Nyt Fra Samfundsvidenskaberne nr. 11. Tøløse: Midtsjællands bogtrykkeri.

Bentzon, Agnete Weis, Anne Hellum Julie Stewart, Welshman Ncube and Torben Agersnap (1998). *Pursuing Grounded Theory in Law. South-North Experiences in Developing Women's Law.* Oslo/Harare: TANO/Mond Books.

Boserup, Ester (1970). *Woman's Role in Economic Development* . London: Earthscan

Bull, Kirsti, Strøm (1982). "Hjemmearbeidets erstatningsrettslige stilling". In *Tidsskrift for rettvitenskap* p. 903- 36.

Butler, J. (1999). *Gender Trouble: Feminism and the Subversion of Identity.* London and New York: Routledge .

76. This feature is highlighted in Ingunn Ikdahl (2010), *Securing Women's homes. The dynamics of women's human rights at the international level and in Tanzania.* PhD thesis. Faculty of Law. University of Oslo.
77. For example, refer to Hege Skjeie (2006) "Menneskerettighetene – en trussel mot demokratiet?" In: *Kønsrelationer. Om magt og mangfoldighed.* (red.) A.D. Christensen & A Bochorst, Aalborg Universitetsforlag, p. 111-131.

Børing, Hanne S. and Anette Grannes (1991). "Så, i hvilken grad kan datteren være annerledes enn sin mor" Mary Maboreke interviewed by Hanne S.Børing and Anette Grannes. In topic number *Kvinner, rett og utvikling i sørlige og østlige Afrika. Hefte for Kristisk Juss*. Nr. 1 1991. Oslo: Rettspolitisk forening.

Cook, Rebecca (ed.) (1995). *Human Rights of Women*. University of Pensylvania Press.

Cook, Rebecca and Cusak, Simone (eds.) (2010). *Gender Stereotyping*. Pennsylvania: University of Pennsylvania Press.

Coomaraswamy, Radika (2005). "Preface: Violence against women and crimes of honour" in *'Honour' Crimes, Paradigms, and Violence against Women*, Lynn Welchman and Sara Hossain. (eds). London: Zed Books.

Crenshaw, Kimberle (2004). "Demarginalizing the intersection of race and sex: A black feminist critique of anti-discrimination doctrine, feminist theory and anti-racist politics". I *Anti-Discrimination Law, International Library of Essays in Law and Legal Theory, Second Series*. Christopher. McCrudden (ed). Dartmouth: Ashgate.

Dahl, Tove Stang, Kjersti Graver, Anne Hellum and Anne Robberstad (1976). *Juss og Juks. En arbeidsbok i likestilling*. Oslo: Pax forlag.

Dahl, Tove Stang (1987). *An introduction to Women's law*. Oslo: Norwegian University Press.

Dahl, Tove Stang (1986). "Taking Women as Starting Point: Building Women's Law", *Working Paper in Women's Law* No. 4. University of Oslo.

Fastvold, Marianne (1977). "Fødselsrett og likhet", *Kvinnerettslige studier* nr. 2. Institute of Women's Law. University of Oslo.

Fastvold, Marianne and Anne Hellum and (1987) ."We have researched to have women's voices heard". In:*Money and Work in Marriage*, *Studies in Women's Law* 1985 No. 26. University of Oslo, p. 2-13.

Fredman, Sandra (2009) "Engendering Socio-economic Rights". 25 South African Journal of Human Rights 410-11

Griffiths, Anne (2002). "Legal pluralism" In *An Introduction to Law and Social Theory*,edited by R. Banakar and M. Travers. Oxford: Hart Publishing, 289–310.

Griffiths, John (1986). "What is Legal Pluralism?". In *Journal of Legal Pluralism* 24: 1–55.

Hellum, Anne (1987)."Money and diginity". In Marianne Fastvold and Anne Hellum *Money and Work in Marriage*. In Studies in Women's Law No. 26 University of Oslo.

Hellum, Anne (1999). Women's Human Rights and Legal Pluralism in Africa: Mixed Norms and Identities in Infertility Management in Zimbabwe. Oslo/Harare: TANO Aschehoug/ Mond Books.

Hellum, Anne (2006). "Menneskerettigheter, pluralisme, kompleksitet og integrasjon". *In Festskrift til Carl August Fleischer* (Syse, Aslak et al eds.). Oslo: Universitetsforlaget.

Hellum, Anne, Shaheen Sardar Ali, Julie Stewart and Amy Tsanga (eds.). (2007). "Introduction". In *Human Rights, plural legalities and gendered realities. Paths are made by walking*. Harare: Weaver Press.

Hellum, Anne and Kirsten Ketscher (eds.) (2008). *Diskrimineringsrett*. Oslo: Universitetsforlaget.

Hellum, Anne and Hege Skjeie (eds.) (2008). *Demokrati, religionsfrihet og kvinners menneskerettigheter*. Kvinnerettslig skriftserie no. 76. Institute of Women's Law. University of Oslo.

Hellum, Anne (2010). "The global equality standard meets Norwegian sameness". *From Transnational Relations to Transnational Laws. Northern European Laws at the Cross*

Roads. I Hellum, Anne, Shaheen Sardar, Ali & Anne, Griffiths (eds). Aldershot: Ashgate

Hellum, Anne and Farhat Taj (2010). "Taking what law where and to whom". In *From Transnational Relations to Transnational Laws. Northern European Laws at the Cross Roads*. Hellum, Anne, Shaheen Sardar, Ali & Anne Griffiths (eds). Aldershot: Ashgate.

Ikdahl, Ingunn (2011). "Lik rett til å være trygg i sitt hjem. Koner, enker, og andre kvinner i internasjonale menneskerettigheter". In *På vei – Kjønn og rett i Norden*. Eva-Maria Svensson, Ulrika Andersson, Hege Brækhus, Monica Burman, Anne Hellum, Stine Jørgensen & Anu Pylkkänen, (red.) Makadam förlag & bokproduktion AB, Göteborg

Ikdahl, Ingunn (2010). *Securing women's homes. The dynamics of women's human rights at the international level and in Tanzania*. PhD thesis. Faculty of Law. University of Oslo.

Ilumoka, Adethun (1994). "African women's economic, social and cultural rights – Toward a relevant theory of practice". *In Human Rights of Women. National and International Perspectives*. Rebecca Cook (red). Pennsylvania: University of Pennsylvania Press.

Jaggar, Allison M. (1983). *Feminist Politics and Human Nature*. U.K: Harvester Press.

Jørgensen, Stine (2007). *Etniske minoritetskvinders sociale rettigheter. Arbeidsmarked, seskualitet og uddannelse*. København: Jurist & Økonomiforbundets Forlag.

Ketscher, Kirsten (2005). "Etnisk ligebehandling, religionsfrihed og ligestilling mellom kvinder og mænd – set I lyset af Føtex-sagen". In *Ugeskrift for Retsvæsen*.

Ketscher, Kirsten (2007). "Cultural Rights and Religious Rights", In Titia Loenen (red) *Religious Pluralism and Human Rights in Europe. Where to Draw the Line*? Internsentia.

Løvdahl, Lene (2009). "Private International Law, Muslim Laws and Gender Equality". Masters thesis, Faculty of Law. *Studies in Women's Law*. No. 79. Oslo: University of Oslo.

Mahoney, Kathelin (1994). "Canadian approaches to equality, rights and gender equity in the courts". I *Human Rights of Women. National and International Perspectives*. Rebecca Cook (red). Pennsylvania: University of Pennsylvania Press.

MacKinnon, Cataharine A. (1984)"Difference and Dominance on Sex Discrimination". *I Feminism Unmodified. Discourses on Life and Law*. Harvard University Press.

Mehdi, Rubya (red) (2007). *Integration og Retsudvikling*. København. Jurist- og økonomforbundets Forlag.

Mehdi, Rubya, Petersen,Hanne, Reenberg Sand, Erik and Gordon Woodman (eds.) (2008) *Law and Religion in Multicultural Societies*. København: DJØF Publishing.

Merry, Sally, Engle (2006). *Human Rights and Gender Violence*. Chicago: University of Chicago Press.

Mohanty, C. (1988). "Under Western Eues: feminist Scholarship and Colonial Discourses". *Feminist Review* 30.

Moore, Sally, Falk (1978). *Law as Process*. London: Routledge.

Mulinari, Diana, Sandell, Kerstin og Schomer, Eva (red.) (2003). *Mer an bara kvinnor och men. Feministiska perspektiv på genus*. Lund: Studentlitteratur.

Nielsen, Ruth, Jytte Lindgård og Jytte Thorbek (1979) *Årbog for kvinderet 1978*. Kvinderetlig skriftserie. København. Jurist- og Økonomforbundets forlag.

Nielsen, Ruth (2009). "Is European Union equality law capable of addressing multiple and intersectional discrimination yet? Precautions against neglecting intersectional cases". In *European Union Non-Discrimination Law: Comparative Perspectives on Multidi-*

mensional Equality. Shiek, Dagmar and Victoria Chege (red). London and New York: Routledge Cavendish.

Nordstrøm, Tina Storsletten (2011). "Rettighetsinformasjon og rettshjelp: virkemidler for å skape et reelt diskrimineringsvern for innvandrerkvinner". In *På vei – Kjønn og rett i Norden*. Eva-Maria Svensson, Ulrika Andersson, Hege Brækhus, Monica Burman, Anne Hellum, Stine Jørgensen & Anu Pylkkänen, (red.) Makadam förlag & bokproduktion AB, Göteborg

Nordstrøm, Tina Storsletten, "Innvandrerkvinners rett til rettighetsinformasjon: Hva gjøres og hva krever FNs kvinnekonvensjon?", *Kritisk Juss* no.2 2010, Published by Rettspolitisk Forening, Fagbokforlaget, Bergen.

Nousiainen, Kevat (2009). "Utility-based equality and disparate diversities: from a Finnish perspective". *In European Union Non-Discrimination LAW: Comparative Perspectives on Multidimensional Equality*. Shiek, Dagmar and Victoria Chege (eds.). London and New York: Routledge Cavendish.

Petersen, Hanne (1991). *Informel ret på kvindearbejdsplasser*. København: Akademisk forlag.

Rosaldo, Michelle Zimbalist and Lamphere, Louise (1974). *Women, Culture and Society*. Stanford: Stanford University Press.

Skjeie, Hege (2009). "Multiple equality claims in the practice of the Norwegian anti-discrimination agencies". In *European Union Non-Discrimination Law Comparative-Perspectives on Multidimensional Equality*. Shiek, D and Victoria Chege (red). London and New York: Routledge Cavendish.

Skjeie, Hege (2006). "Menneskerettighetene – en trussel mot demokratiet?", In (red.) Christensen, A.D. og Bochorst, A. *Kønsrelationer. Om magt og mangfoldighed*. Aalborg Universitetsforlag.

Strand, Vibeke Blaker. (2011) *Diskrimineringsvernets rekkevidde i mote med religionsutøvelse*, PhD thesis University of Oslo oktober 2011.

Solhøy, Stina Hansen, Vibeke Blaker Strand og Jorunn Økland (2010). "Rettferdighetens grenser – religion, kjønn og homofili". In Halsaa, Beatrice og Hellum, Anne (red.) *Rettferdighet*. Oslo: Universitetsforlaget.

Sverdrup, Tone (1984). "Folketrygden i kvinneperspektiv". In Asbjørn Kjønstad (red) *Folketrygden i støpeskjeen*. Oslo.

Sverdrup, Tone (2012)." Equal rights at all costs". In Elaine Sutherland (ed.*) The Future of Child and Family Law: International Predictions* (Cambridge University Press, forthcoming 2012).

Tsanga, Amy (2007). "Legal literacy in plural legal contexts", In *Human Rights, plural legalities and gendered realities. Paths are made by walking*, Hellum, Anne, Julie Stewart, Shaheen S. Ali and Amy Tsanga (eds.) Harare: Weaver Press.

Vigerust, Elisabeth (2008). "Vern mot graviditetsvern i arbeidsforhold". In Hellum, Anne and Kirsten Ketscher (red) *Diskrimineringsret*t. Oslo: Universitetsforlaget.

Vogt, Agnes (1981). Kvinners rett til fellesboligen ved separasjon og skilsmisse – en undersøkelse av JURK-sakene. *Kvinnerettslige studier* 1981 no.2 1981. Oslo: Universitetsforlaget.

CHAPTER 3

The Impact of EU Law on Scandinavian Law in Matters of Gender Equality

By Ruth Nielsen, Professor, dr. jur, Law Department, Copenhagen Business School

1. Introduction

This chapter consists of a legal dogmatic analysis of the interplay between EU gender equality and discrimination law and Scandinavian law in this area. The main question I look into is 'what is valid law on gender equality' at EU level and in Scandinavian law and how are EU law and Scandinavian gender equality law interacting. This question is studied in an evolutionary perspective with a view to highlighting the main changes in EU law and Scandinavian law that has occurred since the inception of the European Union in the middle of the 20th century. This analysis primarily builds on already existing literature in Scandinavia – most of which is written in Danish, Swedish or Norwegian.[1] In the last parts of the article I discuss the development in the law in a methodological and theoretical perspective.[2]

1. In Scandinavia most academics from Denmark, Sweden and Norway understand the languages of the other Scandinavian countries. Nordic meetings are typically held in those three languages without translation. Finnish is very different but many Finns are very good at Swedish. Finland is bi-lingual (Finnish and Swedish) in regard to law. All Finnish legislation exists both in Finnish and Swedish, see http://www.finlex.fi/fi/.
2. The questions examined in the last part of the article are by and large the same as the questions examined in the current research project 'Towards a European Legal Meth-

Gender discrimination law is one of the oldest and most developed parts of EU labour law.[3] The period from the inception of EU to present day can in regard to gender equality law be divided into the following phases:

- From the Rome Treaty to the Amsterdam Treaty (1958-1999)
- From the Amsterdam Treaty to the Lisbon Treaty (1999-2009)
- After the Lisbon Treaty came into force (since 01/12/2009)

Until 1 May 1999 (the coming into force of the Treaty of Amsterdam), there were only explicit EU legislation on non-discrimination on grounds of nationality and sex, and as far as gender was concerned, mainly in employment and occupation. Anti-discrimination law thus started historically as an appendix to the internal market regulation and the prevention of competition. In the 35 years from the adoption of the EC-Treaty in 1957 to the Maastricht Treaty in 1992, there was virtually no change in the EU's formal goals as formulated in the former Article 2 EC. By the Maastricht Treaty, which entered into force 1.11.1993, the European Union (EU) was created and the purpose as defined in the former Article 2 EC changed (significantly). In the following years, the constitutional and fundamental rights dimension of gender equality has been developed intensively.

The CJEU has played an important role in the field of equal treatment between men and women, in particular in the period from the 1970s to the 1990s.[4] Since 2000 the EU legislator has played the leading role in the development both by adopting a number of directives and by means of soft law, except perhaps in regard to fundamental rights where the CJEU is still very active and where the basic treaties have been changed.

od – Synthesis or Fragmentation' carried out from 2010-2012 in collaboration between CBS (Copenhagen Business School) and the University of Copenhagen, see for a description of that project http://www.cbs.dk/Forskning/Institutter-centre/-Institutter/LAW/Menu/Forskningsprojekter#ELM1

3. See for a critical analysis in a comparative perspective of the law in this field Roseberry, Lynn: The Limits of Employment Discrimination Law in the United States and European Community, Copenhagen 1999 and Beryl Philine ter Haar, Paul Copeland: What are the Future Prospects for the European Social Model? An Analysis of EU Equal Opportunities and Employment Policy, European Law Journal 2010 p. 273. See on EU labour law generally Barnard, Catherine: EC Employment Law, Oxford 2006 and Nielsen, Ruth: EU Labour Law, Copenhagen 2011.
4. See Kilpatrick, Claire: Gender Equality: A Fundamental Dialogue in Sciarra, Silvana (ed.), Labour law in the courts – National judges and the European Court of Justice, Oxford, 2001.

2. From the Rome Treaty to the Amsterdam Treaty (1958-1999)

2.1. EU level

In 1957, the then EC-Treaty contained only one single provision (Article 119 EEC, now Article 157 TFEU) on gender discrimination, namely the principle of equal pay between men and women for work of equal value. The equal pay provision in Article 119 EEC was inserted in the Treaty on the demand of France, which believed that there were stricter rules on equal pay in France than in some of the other original Member States of the EU and wanted a uniform level of equal pay protection in order to protect businesses established in France against distortion of competition.

In the first years nothing happened, but the EU has pursued a strong non-discrimination agenda since the mid-1970s and has, at EU level, given high priority to anti-discrimination. Since the mid-1970s, a number of directives prohibiting sex discrimination have been adopted.[5] Most of them were repealed and replaced by the recast directive on gender equality in employment in 2006.[6]

The three *Defrenne* Cases[7] dealt with various aspects of the original equal pay provision in the Treaty. In *Defrenne-I* the Court held that a retirement pension established within the framework of a social security scheme laid down by legislation falls outside the scope of the equal pay provision in the Treaty.

In *Defrenne-II*, the CJEU held that Art. 119 EEC (now Article 157 TFEU) had direct effect as binding for private employers and that the equal pay provision in the Treaty not only had the original economic aim of securing equal competition between employers established in different Member States, but had a double aim, both economic and social.

In *Defrenne-III*, Defrenne – a female air hostess – tried to rely on the equal pay provision in the Treaty against a sex discriminatory dismissal practice of her employer, the referring court asked whether the principle of equal pay laid down by Article 119 EEC may be interpreted as requiring general equality of working conditions for men and women, so that the insertion into the contract of employment of an air hostess of a clause bringing the contract to an end when she reaches the age of 40 years, it being established that no

5. See in particular the Equal Pay Directive (75/117/EEC) and the Equal Treatment Directive (76/207/EEC).
6. 2006/54/EC.
7. Case 80/70 *Defrenne-I* [1971] ECR p. 445; Case 43/75 *Defrenne-II* [1976] ECR p. 455; and Case 149/77 *Defrenne-III* [1978] ECR p. 1365.

such limit is attached to the contract of male cabin attendants who carry out the same work, constitutes discrimination prohibited by the said provision. The CJEU held that the equal pay provision should not be applied to dismissal on grounds of sex.

The referring court also asked whether, apart from the specific provisions of Article 119 EEC, Community law contained any general principle prohibiting discrimination based on sex as regards the conditions of employment and working conditions of men and women. The CJEU replied that the principle of non-discrimination on grounds of sex was a fundamental right, but since the *Defrenne-III* Case was about a problem (dismissal) that at the material time of the case was outside the scope of EU law, EU law on fundamental rights could not be relied upon; see the following citation from the CJEU's answer:[8]

> "The court has repeatedly stated that respect for fundamental personal human rights is one of the general principles of community law, the observance of which it has a duty to ensure.
>
> 27. There can be no doubt that the elimination of discrimination based on sex forms part of those fundamental rights…
>
> 30. On the other hand, as regards the relationships of employer and employee which are subject to national law, the community had not, at the time of the events now before the Belgian courts, assumed any responsibility for supervising and guaranteeing the observance of the principle of equality between men and women in working conditions other than remuneration ."

In the infringement case against Denmark on grounds of the first Danish Equal pay Act,[9] the CJEU struck down a traditional element in the Nordic legislative practice, see below in section 5, namely the reliance on preparatory works of statutory laws, as insufficient in connection with implementation of the Equal pay Directive. The CJEU held that Denmark had failed to fulfill its obligations under the EEC-Treaty by placing part of the Directive's provisions in the preparatory works of the Danish Equal pay Act. It argued that the principles of legal certainty and the protection of individuals require an unequivocal wording which would give the persons concerned a clear and precise understanding of their rights and obligations and would enable the courts to ensure that those rights and obligations are observed.

The *Deutsche Telekom* Cases on equal pay were about violations by a German employer (Deutsche Telekom) of the equal pay principle by exclud-

8. Para. 26.
9. Case 143/83 *Commission* v *Denmark*, [1985] ECR p. 427.

ing German part-time workers from pension schemes.[10] Because most part-time workers in Germany are women, such exclusion is indirect sex discrimination in violation of the equal pay rules in both EU law and national German law. The German rules apply to periods from the coming into force of the German *Grundgesetz* in 1949. Article 157 TFEU (ext art. 119 EC and 141 EC) is only directly applicable against employers in regard to equal pay in periods after 8 April 1976; see *Defrenne-II.*[11] In *Barber*, a special time limitation at 17 May 1990 was fixed for pension matters.[12] The workers in the *Deutsche Telekom* Cases claimed equal pay for periods for which they had such a claim under German law but not under EU law. The employer Deutsche Telekom asserted that EU law on equal pay – Article 157 TFEU – should be interpreted as a maximum provision in order to protect German employers from distortion of competition by being treated by stricter equal pay standards than employers which were established in other EU countries. Deutsche Telekom did therefore not accept that it should respect the equal pay principle in pension matters for periods before 17 May 1990. As appears from the above, German law was more favourable for discriminated women than EU law, *i.e.* their fundamental right not to be discriminated against was better protected by German law than by EU law.

The CJEU held that the equal pay provision in Article 157 TFEU [then Article 119 EC] does not preclude provisions of a Member State which lay down a principle of equal treatment by virtue of which part-time workers are entitled to retroactive membership of an occupational pension scheme and to receive a pension under that scheme, notwithstanding the risk of distortions of competition between economic operators of the various Member States to the detriment of employers established in the first Member State. The application of national law cannot be held to be contrary to the principle of non-discrimination on grounds of nationality merely because other Member States allegedly apply less strict rules. Moreover, the economic aim pursued by Article 157 TFEU [then Article 119 EC], namely the elimination of distortions of competition between undertakings established in different Member States, is secondary to its social aim, which constitutes the expression of a fundamental human right not to be discriminated against on grounds of sex.

Since 1984, the Commission has been assisted by the European Network of Legal Experts in the field of Gender Equality in order to help monitor the

10. Case C-50/96 *Schröder* [2000] ECR p. I-743; Case C-270/97 *Sievers* [2000] ECR p. I-929; and Joined cases C-234/96 and C-235/96 *Vick et al* [2000] ECR p. I-799.
11. Case 43/75 *Defrenne-II* [1976] ECR p. 455.
12. Case 262/88 *Barber* [1990] ECR p. I-1889.

implementation of the EU *acquis* related to the principle of equal treatment between women and men in the EU countries and to develop new legal initiatives in this specific field. The network is appointed following a call for tender, which is normally issued every three years. The current network consists of independent experts – academics and practitioners – from the 27 EU countries, EFTA countries (Liechtenstein, Norway and Iceland) and candidate countries (Croatia, FYR Macedonia and Turkey).[13]

2.2. National level

The Nordic labour relations model is marked by a preference for collective bargaining over statutory regulation.[14] Norway is not a member of the EU but has since 1 January 1994 been a member of EFTA and bound by the EEA Agreement.[15] The Agreement on the European Economic Area (EEA) brings together the 27 EU Member States and the three EEA EFTA States — Iceland, Liechtenstein and Norway — in a single market. The EEA Agreement provides for the inclusion of EU legislation covering the free movement of goods, services, persons and capital — throughout the 30 EEA States. In addition, the Agreement covers cooperation in other important areas such as research and development, education, social policy, the environment, consumer protection, tourism and culture, collectively known as "flanking and horizontal" policies. The Agreement guarantees equal rights and obligations within the Internal Market for citizens and economic operators in the EEA. Sweden and Finland were members of EFTA in 1994. From 1 January 1995 they became members of the EU.

At national level there was well-developed equality legislation in Norway, Finland and Sweden before they were confronted with EU law in the area in 1994. Norwegian equality legislation[16] dates back to the 1970s. The Norwegian equality Act (likestillingslov) which entered into force 15 March 1979 applies to sex discrimination in all areas of society except internal affairs of

13. See the publications from the Commission's Network of legal experts on the gender equality directives at http://ec.europa.eu/justice/gender-equality/tools/legal-experts/-index_en.htm.
14. Niklas Bruun, Boel Flodgren, Håkan Hydén, Marit Halvorsen and Ruth Nielsen: The Nordic Labour Relations Model, Dartmouth 1992 and Ruth Nielsen; Europeanization of Nordic Labour Law, in Scandinavian Studies in Law Volume 43, Stability and Change in Nordic Labour Law, Stockholm 2002 p. 37, available at http://www.scandinavianlaw.se/.
15. http://www.efta.int/eea/eea-agreement.aspx.
16. See Hellum, Anne og Kirsten Ketscher (red.): Diskriminerings- og likestillingsrett, Oslo 2008.

religious communities. In family life and other purely private matters it is not enforced by the special enforcement units (Ombudsman and complaints board). In Sweden, the Jämställdhetslagen (gender equality Act) which entered into force 1 January 1980 consisted in three parts:

- A prohibition on sex discrimination
- An obligation for individual employers to actively promote equality
- Rules on the establishment of a monitoring / support agency (Jämställdhetsombudsmannen) and a complaints board regarding the active duties of the Act (but not on the discrimination ban)

Jämställdhetslagen was subsequently amended several times and 1 January 2009 repealed and replaced by the more general discrimination Act (diskrimineringslag).[17] In Finland, there has also been an equality Act since 1986. Since their EU membership Sweden and Finland have adapted their national gender equality law to EU law. [18]

Denmark became a member of the EU 1 January 1973. At that time, the protection against discrimination was very weak in Danish law. There was, for example, no equal pay or equal treatment legislation relating to any ground of discrimination. Equal pay for men and women was provided for in some but not all collective agreements. It was lawful for an employer to dismiss a pregnant woman on grounds of pregnancy. Denmark has adopted the implementation legislation required by the EU since the 1970s. In addition gender equality law is the area that has been most intensely integrated into national litigation.

The enforcement system in Danish labour law/gender equality law is divided into a part where claims are based on parliamentary legislation or individual contracts and a collective labour law part where claims are based on a collective agreement (social partner legislation). If the matter is governed by a provision in a collective agreement, a case can be brought before an industrial arbitration tribunal or the Labour Court by the trade union which is party to the collective agreement. Individual workers cannot bring a case before industrial arbitrations/the Labour Court, but must leave that to the trade union which is party to the collective agreement. Claims based on parliamentary

17. SFS 2008:567, available in Swedish at http://www.riksdagen.se/webbnav/index.-aspx?nid=3911&bet=2008:567.
18. Roseberry, Lynn: Equal Rights and Discrimination Law, in Scandinavian Studies in Law Volume 43, Stability and Change in Nordic Labour Law, Stockholm 2002 p. 215, available at http://www.scandinavianlaw.se/.

legislation or individual contracts can be brought by the individual workers/employees concerned before the ordinary courts. In practice that is most often done by the trade union of which the worker/employee is a member on behalf of and with the consent of the individual worker/employee.[19] Most trade unions pay the cost of the cases (as part of the service they offer their members in return for the membership fees) and handle the cases on behalf of their members if they so wish. If the individual worker/employee can afford it and so wishes, he or she can bring the case on his/her own without asking the trade union. If a case is covered by a collective agreement and the trade union which is party to the collective agreement chooses to pursue the case through the collective labour law system (*i.e.* the Labour Court or arbitration tribunals), the case cannot be brought before the ordinary courts. Discrimination claims that can be brought before the ordinary courts can also be brought before the Equality Complaints Board, which treats the case free of charge, *i.e.* paid by the tax-payers. After the case has been decided by the Complaints Board, it may be brought before the ordinary courts if one of the parties is unwilling to accept the ruling of the Complaints Board.

The burden of proof provisions in the underlying EU directives[20] have been implemented in Denmark and are used in both the collective labour law part of the enforcement system and by the ordinary courts.

Danish trade unions in the Confederation of Trade Unions (Danish LO) were unwilling to invoke EU law before Danish courts and industrial tribunals until the mid 1980s even though they lost equal pay cases in Danish industrial arbitration tribunals, in particular the *Vejle Amts Folkeblad*[21] and the *Danfoss-I* cases,[22] on grounds of provisions in collective agreements which were rather obviously in contravention of the underlying EU rules prohibiting indirect sex discrimination and consequently invalid, had EU law been

19. In a comparative perspective the level of unionization, i.e. the proportion of the workforce that is member of a trade union, is high in Denmark; around 75-80 %.
20. See Article 8 in the Ethnic Equality Directive (2000/43/EC), Article 10 in the Employment Framework Directive (2000/78), Article 9 in the Gender Equality (Goods and Service) Directive (2004/113EC) and Article 19 in the Recast Gender Equality (Employment and Occupation) Directive (2006/54/EC).
21. HK v Dansk Arbejdsgiverforening/Danske Dagblades Forenings Forhandlingsorganisation for Vejle Amts Folkeblad, Arbitral Award of 11.2.1985. Summary in Danish in Andersen, Agnete, Ruth Nielsen og Kirsten Precht: Ligestillingslovene med kommentarer, Kbhvn. 2010.
22. In Denmark Danfoss-I: HK v DA for Danfoss A/S, Arbitral Award of 16.4.1985. Summary in Danish in Andersen, Agnete, Ruth Nielsen og Kirsten Precht: Ligestillingslovene med kommentarer, Kbhvn. 2010.

properly applied.[23] By the mid-1980s, a trade union with more than 80 % women members broke the consensus about abstaining from using EU law and brought the Danfoss case,[24] in which it demanded that questions should be referred to the CJEU to test the compatibility of the Danish judicial practice with EU law. The outcome was that the earlier Danish practice was overturned. This case marked a breakthrough in Danish trade union attitudes to support claims based on EU law. Since Danfoss, EU law has successfully been invoked against Danish law in a number of cases. In Danfoss, the CJEU ruled that where an undertaking applies a pay system which is characterized by a total lack of transparency, the burden of proof is on the employer to show that his wage practice is not discriminatory where a female worker establishes, by comparison with a relatively large number of employees, that the average pay of female workers is lower than that of male workers. Sophisticated statistical calculations are thus unnecessary to shift the burden of proof. A calculation of average pay is sufficient. This judgment not only changed Danish law but also paved the way for a further development of EU law. The ECJ's ruling in Danfoss was codified in the Burden of Proof Directive, which is now repealed and replaced by the recast Directive on Gender Equality in the labour market.[25]

The majority of cases in Denmark related to equal treatment are about pregnancy, maternity, paternity and parental leave. In Pedersen,[26] the ECJ struck down the pregnancy provisions of the Danish Salaried Employees Act and the Danish practice of granting only benefit (and not full pay) as compensation for absence from work due to pregnancy-related illness in situations when absence from work due to other illnesses resulted in an entitlement to full pay. It also found that it is contrary to the Equal treatment Di-

23. See for details Nielsen, Ruth, Equality in Law between Men and Women in the European Community. Denmark, The Hague, 1995. See also Roseberry, Lynn: Equal Rights and Discrimination Law, in Scandinavian Studies in Law Volume 43, Stability and Change in Nordic Labour Law, Stockholm 2002 p. 215.
24. Case C-109/88 Handels-og-Kontorfunktionærernes Forbund i Danmark v Dansk Arbejdsgiverforening (acting for Danfoss) [1989] ECR 3199. The Danish arbitral award in the case, in Denmark, usually called Danfoss-II: HK v DA for Danfoss A/S, Arbitral Award of 22. 10.1991. Summary in Danish in Andersen, Agnete, Ruth Nielsen og Kirsten Precht: Ligestillingslovene med kommentarer, Kbhvn. 2010.
25. 2006/54/EC.
26. Case C-66/96 Høj Pedersen and others v Fællesforening for Danmarks Brugsforeninger (FDB) and others [1998] ECR I-7327.

rective and the Pregnancy Directive[27] for national legislation to provide that an employer may send home a woman who is pregnant, although not unfit for work, without paying her salary in full when he considers that he cannot provide work for her. Following this judgment the Danish Salaried Employees Act was amended in 1999 thus changing the legal position for the future.

3. From the Amsterdam Treaty to the Lisbon Treaty (1999-2009)

The adoption of the Treaty of Amsterdam 1997, [which entered into force on 1 May 1999], marked a turning point in the development of EU discrimination law. The Treaty of Amsterdam introduced important innovations. In the (Amsterdam) Treaty, there were five provisions that explicitly focused on gender equality: Article 2 EC on gender equality as an objective for the Community, Art. 3(2) EC on gender mainstreaming, Article 13 EC, which gave the community a legal basis to unanimously adopt legislation prohibiting discrimination because of sex, race and ethnic origin, religion, sexual orientation, age and disability in all areas covered by EU competence, Article 137 EC, which gave the community a legal basis for a qualified majority to adopt minimum directives on gender equality in occupation and Article 141 EC on equal pay and equal treatment, which contained a directly enforceable right to equal pay and provided a legal basis for a qualified majority to adopt legislation (regulations, directives, etc.) on gender equality in employment.

On the basis of Article 13 EC a number of directives[28] prohibiting discrimination because of sex, race and ethnic origin, religion, sexual orientation, age and disability in all areas covered by EU competence were adopted. Gender equality in employment is still – also after the adoption of the Amsterdam Treaty – governed by directives adopted on the legal bases found in the employment parts of the Treaties.

27. Directives 76/207/EEC on Equal Treatment [now repealed and replaced by the Recast Directive 2006/54/EC] and 92/85/EEC (the Pregnancy Directive).
28. See the Ethnic Equality Directive (2000/43/EC), the Employment Framework Directive (2000/78) and the Gender Equality (Goods and Service) Directive (2004/113EC). On 2.7.2008 the Commission put forward proposals for a new (horizontal) directive on equal treatment irrespective of religion or belief, disability, age or sexual orientation outside the workplace.

3.1. Basic concepts

One of the innovations in discrimination law delivered by the CJEU is the evolution of the concept of indirect discrimination.[29] Since the adoption of the Amsterdam Treaty the case law of the CJEU on basic concepts has been codified in the Article 19 (formerly 13)-directives and since 2002 in a directive on Equal Treatment for men and women[30] Since 2000, the central discrimination concepts are laid down in the respective directives and are often the subject of further interpretation by the CJEU. The following concepts are used in all the equality directives:[31]

- Direct discrimination occurs '(...) where one person is treated less favourably on grounds of sex or one of the other protected grounds than another is, has been or would be treated in a comparable situation.'
- Indirect discrimination occurs '(...) where an apparently neutral provision, criterion or practice would put persons of one sex or a person affected by one of the other protected grounds at a particular disadvantage compared with persons of other groups, unless that provision, criterion or practice is objectively justified by a legitimate aim, and the means of achieving that aim are appropriate and necessary.'
- Instruction to discriminate on grounds of a person's sex or one of the other protected grounds is in EU law equated with discrimination.
- Harassment occurs '(...) where unwanted conduct related to the sex, ethnic origin, age, etc. of a person occurs with the purpose or effect of violating the dignity of a person, and of creating an intimidating, hostile, degrading, humiliating or offensive environment.'
- Sexual harassment occurs '(...) where any form of unwanted verbal, nonverbal or physical conduct of a sexual nature occurs, with the purpose or effect of violating the dignity of a person, in particular when creating an intimidating, hostile, degrading, humiliating or offensive environment.'

As a rule, direct discrimination is prohibited unless a specific exception applies, such as that the sex of the person concerned is a determining factor for

29. See in particular Case 170/84 Bilka [1986] ECR p. 1607.
30. 2002/73/EC, now repealed and replaced by the Recast directive 2006/54.
31. See the Ethnic Equality Directive (2000/43/EC) Article 2, the Employment Framework Directive (2000/78/EC) Article 2, the Recast Gender Equality (Employment and Occupation) Directive (2006/54/EC) Article 2, and the Gender Equality (Goods and Service) Directive (2004/113EC) Article 2.

the job, for example a male character in a film has to be a man. Indirect discrimination is prohibited, unless it is objectively justified.

Indirect discrimination is concerned with the effects of a certain treatment and takes into account everyday social realities. For instance, less favourable treatment of part-time workers will often amount to indirect discrimination against women because most part-time employees are women. Compared to the case of direct discrimination, the possibilities for justification of indirect discrimination are much broader. The current definition of indirect discrimination was first laid down in the Ethnic Equality Directive. In the proposal for that directive,[32] the Commission refers to the definition developed in ECJ in *Flynn*.[33] In the directives that are adopted after 2000, indirect discrimination is defined as occurring where an apparently neutral provision, criterion or practice would put persons of one sex or a person affected by one of the other protected grounds (ethnicity, age, religion, sexual orientation or disability) at a particular disadvantage compared with persons of other groups, unless that provision, criterion or practice is objectively justified by a legitimate aim, and the means of achieving that aim are appropriate and necessary. Indirect discrimination is concerned with the effects of a certain treatment and takes into account everyday social realities. For instance, less favourable treatment of part-time workers will often amount to indirect discrimination against women because most part-time employees in some (but not all) EU countries are women. Compared to the case of direct discrimination, the possibilities for justification of indirect discrimination are much broader. The justification possibility is designed in the same way as the principle of proportionality and like that principle provides a scope for taking diversity between the Member States into account.

Harassment and sexual harassment include the violation of a person's dignity and the creation of an intimidating, hostile, degrading, humiliating or offensive environment. The main difference is that in case of harassment on grounds of a person's sex, the person is ill-treated because he or she is a woman or a man. In the case of sexual harassment, it rather involves a person being subject to unwelcome sexual advances or, for instance, that the behaviour of the perpetrator aims at obtaining sexual favours. The prohibition against harassment on grounds of sex has an equivalent in prohibitions against harassment on grounds of racial or ethnic origin, religion or belief, disability, age or sexual orientation.

32. COM (99)566.
33. Case C-237/94 *Flynn* [1996] ECR p. I-2617.

The measures permitted as positive action provisions aim at eliminating or counteracting the detrimental effects on an underrepresented sex, often women/ethnic groups etc. which arise from existing attitudes, behaviour and structures based on the idea of a traditional division of roles in society.

3.2. The fundamental rights approach in EU gender equality law

Within the different forms of political democracy that are practiced at national level in the EU, a distinction can be drawn between, on the one hand, majoritarian, parliamentary democracy, which is used in Denmark and the other Nordic countries and the UK and, on the other hand, constitutional democracy.[34] As Føllesdal states:[35]

> "Nordic public debates have tended to conflate legitimacy and majoritarian parliamentarianism. Parliament is seen as the site of legitimacy, as the privileged arena for the expression of the general will. There are no Constitutional Courts, and the constitutions and constitutional conventions leave great scope to parliamentary discretion. Thus it is for the Parliaments themselves to decide whether legislation is within the bounds of the constitution."

In the Nordic countries it is customary to state that it is the legislator that makes, through adopting and amending laws, all important decisions on policies and principles. The role of courts of law is seen as implementing the will of the legislator. Within EU law the situation is different as the normative framework of EU law is incomplete as a legal system and as the Court of Justice of the European Union (CJEU) consequently has a strong position in the development of the law and in securing coherence in law.

A main feature of the development from the Nordic/Danish welfare state as it was on 1 January 1973, when Denmark entered the EC to the multi-level European Social Model, as it is anno 2011, is the shift from a non-constitutional to a constitutional approach to fundamental social rights and

34. See Marlene Wind, Dorte Sindbjerg Martinsen and Gabriel Pons Rotger: The Uneven Legal Push for Europe – Questioning Variation when National Courts go to Europe, European Union Politics No 4, 2008. See also Marlene Wind's description of her research interests at her website http://www.cep.polsci.ku.dk/forskere/mwi/ where she writes: 'Jeg skelner her imellem 'majoritarian democracy' som vi kender fra Danmark og i nordiske lande, hvor det parlamentariske flertal står i centrum og så det 'konstitutionelle demokrati' i det meste af det øvrige Europa, hvor man lægger stor vægt på domstolskontrol med lovgivningsmagten. Min tese er at vores demokratiform med 'ingen over eller ved siden af Folketinget' ikke passer særlig godt med den form man finder i EU og i resten af Europa.'
35. Føllesdal, Andreas: Rawls in the Nordic Countries, European Journal of Political Theory 2002 p. 181.

non-discrimination. For countries like Denmark with a strong tradition of majoritarian, parliamentary democracy and no constitutional courts, the EU development results in a pressure to accept constitutional review of legislation by courts such as the CJEU.

Originally – when the EC was founded in the 1950's – EC law was mainly of an economic character. The EU only later developed into a more political union and now seems to be in the process of developing into a kind of constitutional democracy. In the proposal for the directive on Equal treatment between women and men in the access to and supply of goods and services the Commission thus stated:[36]

> "Equal treatment between women and men and non-discrimination on grounds of sex are fundamental principles of Community law. The European Union's approach to equality has developed considerably over time, so that the original emphasis on equal pay and on avoiding distortions of competition between Member States has been replaced by a concern for equality as a fundamental right."

After the adoption in 2000 of the Charter of Fundamental Rights of the European Union, it has become usual in academic literature to talk about (the) constitutionalisation of the EU.[37]

The distinction between constitutional democracy and majoritarian, parliamentary democracy is linked to the distinction between the monist and dualist approach to the relationship between international and national law, see below in section 5.

4. After the Lisbon Treaty came into force (since 01/12 2009)

The Lisbon Treaty strengthens the rules on gender equality. There are several provisions in the basic treaties on this issue. It also elevates the EU Charter of

36. COM(2003)657 p. 2.
37. There is an abundant academic literature on constitutionalisation of the EU, see among many Beate Rudolf: European Union, International Journal of Constitutional Law 2003 p. 135, Gráinne de Búrca and Jo Beatrix Aschenbrenner: The Development of European Constitutionalism and the Role of The EU Charter of Fundamental Rights, Columbia Journal of European Law 2003 p. 355, Udo Di Fabio: A European Charter: Towards a Constitution for the Union, Columbia Journal of European Law 2001 p. 159, Koen Lenaerts and Eddy de Smijter: A "Bill of Rights" for the European Union, Common Market Law Review 2001 p. 273 and Ingolf Pernice: Integrating the Charter of Fundamental Rights into the Constitution of the European Union: Practical and Theoretical Propositions, Columbia Journal of European Law 2003 p. 5.

Fundamental Rights to Treaty rank. This means that the question of whether equality directives have direct horizontal effect as binding for private employers and other private entities now becomes less important since the ban on discrimination in Article 21 of the Charter of Fundamental Rights, as discussed below – at least in relation to the protection criteria; sex, ethnicity, religion, age, disability, sexual orientation, is likely to have direct horizontal effect.

4.1. The EU-Treaty (TEU)

TEU contains comprehensive provisions on the values, objectives, principles and framework for institutional operation in the EU. According to Article 2 TEU, the EU is founded on the values of respect for human dignity, freedom, democracy, equality, rule of law and respect for human rights including the rights of persons belonging to minorities. This is common to Member States in a society in with pluralism, non-discrimination, tolerance, justice, solidarity and equality between women and men. According to art. 3 TEU, the EU's goal is to promote peace, its values and people's welfare. EU creates a single market and work for the sustainable development of Europe based on balanced economic growth and price stability. The Union shall establish an internal market. It shall work for the sustainable development of Europe based on balanced economic growth and price stability, a highly competitive *social market economy* (my emphasis) aiming at full employment and social progress, and a high level of protection and improvement of the quality of the environment. Although the term 'social market economy' is new in the EU Treaty after its amendment by the Lisbon Treaty, the view that the Treaty's rules on anti-discrimination has a double – both economic and social purpose – is not new, see the judgment in the Defrenne-II case cited above. After the adoption of the Lisbon Treaty substantially revised Article 6 TEU. The most important change relates to the legal status of the Charter. Article 6 TEU now reads:

1. The Union recognises the rights, freedoms and principles set out in the Charter of Fundamental Rights of the European Union of 7 December 2000, as adapted at Strasbourg, on 12 December 2007, which shall have the same legal value as the Treaties.

   The provisions of the Charter shall not extend in any way the competences of the Union as defined in the Treaties.

   The rights, freedoms and principles in the Charter shall be interpreted in accordance with the general provisions in Title VII of the Charter governing its interpretation and application and with due regard to the explanations referred to in the Charter, that set out the sources of those provisions.

2. The Union shall accede to the European Convention for the Protection of Human Rights and Fundamental Freedoms. Such accession shall not affect the Union's competences as defined in the Treaties.
3. Fundamental rights, as guaranteed by the European Convention for the Protection of Human Rights and Fundamental Freedoms and as they result from the constitutional traditions common to the Member States, shall constitute general principles of the Union's law.

Article 51 of the Charter stipulates that the provisions of the Charter are addressed to the institutions, bodies and organs of the EU with due regard for the principle of subsidiarity and to the Member States only when they are implementing Union law. The question whether the EU can accede to the ECHR was answered in the negative in 1996.[38] As appears from the above, the amended Article 6(2) TEU provides that the Union shall accede to the ECHR. The new Article 6(3) TEU builds on the existing Article 6(2) EU which has been used extensively by the CJEU in developing its fundamental rights jurisprudence. Article 6(3) TEU provides that Fundamental rights, as guaranteed by the ECHR and as they result from the constitutional traditions common to the Member States, shall constitute general principles of EU law. See on the Charter below in section 4.3.

4.2. The FEU-Treaty (TFEU)

With the adoption of the Lisbon Treaty, goal provisions were removed from TFEU. All goal provisions are now placed in TEU, see above. Except for renumbering, there are only few significant changes on equality in TFEU.

Article 3(2) which incorporated the requirement of mainstreaming gender equality in the EU is now found in Article 8 TFEU. Article 13 EC which is the legal basis for an expanded anti-discrimination regime prohibiting discrimination not only on grounds of nationality and gender but also on grounds of ethnic origin, religion, age, handicap and sexual orientation is replaced by Articles 10 TFEU and Article 19 TFEU with a nearly identical content. Article 137 EC is now Article 153 TFEU and the equal pay provision – originally Article 119 EEC, later Article 141 EC – is now placed in Article 157 TFEU with somewhat the same content as it had when it was Article 141 EC, see the following:

38. Opinion 2/94 [1996] I-1759.

Article 157 (ex Article 141 TEC)

1. Each Member State shall ensure that the principle of equal pay for male and female workers for equal work or work of equal value is applied.
2. For the purpose of this Article, 'pay' means the ordinary basic or minimum wage or salary and any other consideration, whether in cash or in kind, which the worker receives directly or indirectly, in respect of his employment, from his employer.
   Equal pay without discrimination based on sex means:
   (a) that pay for the same work at piece rates shall be calculated on the basis of the same unit of measurement; EN 30.3.2010 Official Journal of the European Union C 83/117
   (b) that pay for work at time rates shall be the same for the same job.
3. The European Parliament and the Council, acting in accordance with the ordinary legislative procedure, and after consulting the Economic and Social Committee, shall adopt measures to ensure the application of the principle of equal opportunities and equal treatment of men and women in matters of employment and occupation, including the principle of equal pay for equal work or work of equal value.
4. With a view to ensuring full equality in practice between men and women in working life, the principle of equal treatment shall not prevent any Member State from maintaining or adopting measures providing for specific advantages in order to make it easier for the underrepresented sex to pursue a vocational activity or to prevent or compensate for disadvantages in professional careers.

4.3. The Charter of Fundamental Rights

In 1999, when the European Council decided to draw up a Charter of Fundamental Rights of the European Union it adopted some broad guidelines on what the Charter should contain. It declared (emphasis added):[39]

39. Conclusions of the presidency of the European Council of Cologne (3 and 4 June 1999) on the drawing up of a Charter of Fundamental Rights of the European Union, Annex 4 p. 43, available at http://www.consilium.europa.eu/ueDocs/newsWord/-en/ec/57886.doc. See on the background of the Charter de Búrca, Gráinne: The drafting of the European Union Charter of fundamental rights, European Law Review 2001 p. 126, Lammy Betten: The EU Charter of Fundamental Rights: a Trojan Horse or a Mouse?, International Journal of Comparative Labour Law and Industrial Relations 2001 p. 151, Deirdre Curtin: The EU Human Rights Charter and the Union Legal Order: the 'Banns' before the Marriage?, in D O' Keeffe and A. Bavasso (eds.), Liber Amicorum in honour of Lord Slynn of Hadley: Judicial review in European Union Law, Kluwer 2000, Engel, Christoph: The European Charter of Fundamental Rights: A Changed Political Opportunity Structure and its Normative Consequences, European Law Journal 2001 p. 151 and Fredman, Sandra, Christopher McCrudden and Mark Freedland: An EU Charter of Fundamental Rights, Public Law 2000 p. 178.

"The European Council believes that this Charter should contain the fundamental rights and freedoms as well as basic procedural rights guaranteed by the *European Convention for the Protection of Human Rights* and Fundamental Freedoms and derived from the *constitutional traditions common to the Member States*, as general principles of Community law. The Charter should also include the *fundamental rights that pertain only to the Union's citizens*. In drawing up such a Charter account should furthermore be taken of *economic and social rights as contained in the European Social Charter and the Community Charter of the Fundamental Social Rights of Workers* (Article 136 TEC), insofar as they do not merely establish objectives for action by the Union."

There are seven chapters in the Charter: Title I. Dignity;[40] Title II. Freedoms;[41] Title III. Equality; [42] Title IV. Solidarity;[43] Title V. Citizens' Rights;[44] Title VI. Justice[45] and Title VII. General Provisions. The Charter contains 50 rights, freedoms and principles without identifying which of its provisions are rights, which are freedoms and which are principles.

Article 53 of the Charter provides on the level of protection that nothing in the Charter shall be interpreted as restricting or adversely affecting human

40. This title includes: human dignity, right to life, right to integrity of the person, prohibition of torture and inhuman or degrading treatment or punishment and prohibition of slavery and forced labour.
41. This title includes: right to liberty and security, respect for private and family life, protection of personal data, right to marry and right to found a family, freedom of thought, conscience and religion, freedom of expression and information, freedom of assembly and of association, freedom of the arts and sciences, right to education, freedom to choose an occupation and right to engage in work, freedom to conduct a business, right to property, right to asylum and protection in the event of removal, expulsion or extradition.
42. This title includes: equality before the law, non-discrimination, cultural, religious and linguistic diversity, equality between men and women, the rights of the child, the rights of the elderly and integration of persons with disabilities.
43. This title includes: workers' right to information and consultationwithin the undertaking, right of collective bargaining and action, right of access to placement services, protection in the event of unjustified dismissal, fair and just working conditions, prohibition of child labour and protection of young people at work, family and professional life, social security and social assistance, health care, access to services of general economic interest, environmental protection and consumer protection.
44. This title includes: right to vote and to stand as a candidate at elections to the European Parliament, right to vote and to stand as a candidate at municipal elections, right to good administration, right of access to documents, ombudsman, right to petition, freedom of movement and of residence and diplomatic and consular protection.
45. This title includes: right to an effective remedy and to a fair trial, presumption of innocence and right of defence, principles of legality and proportionality of criminal offences and penalties and the right not to be tried or punished twice in criminal proceedings for the same criminal offence.

rights and fundamental freedoms as recognised, in their respective fields of application, by EU law and international law and by the Member States' constitutions. The Charter does thus not lower the already existing level of protection. In EU labour law there are more extensive rights on a number of issues covered by the solidarity provisions in the Charter.[46]

All EU-countries are members of the United Nations, ILO and the Council of Europe. Compared to the ECHR[47] the Charter goes much further in protecting economic and social rights.

The content of the solidarity provisions in the Charter draws heavily on the Council of Europe Revised Social Charter from 1996 to which there are many references in the Explanatory remarks. All 27 EU Member States are signatories to the Revised Social Charter but twelve[48] of them have not ratified this convention and have consequently never been bound by it under public international law.

Eight ILO-Conventions have been identified by the ILO's Governing Body as being fundamental to the rights of people at work, irrespective of levels of development of individual member states. They are grouped into four categories:

1) Freedom of Association[49]
2) Abolition of Forced Labour[50]

46. See on the Charter and the gender equality *acquis* Sophia Koukoulis-Spiliotopoulos: The Lisbon Treaty and the Charter of Fundamental Rights: maintaining and developing the acquis in gender equality, European Gender Equality Law Review 2008-1, available at http://ec.europa.eu/justice/gender-equality/files/egelr2008-1_en.pdf.
47. The ECHR offers some protection of economic and social rights. In Airey v Ireland (Application no. 6289/73, judgment of 9 October 1979), the ECtHR stated (emphasis added): Whilst the Convention sets forth what are essentially civil and political rights, many of them have implications of a social or economic nature. The Court therefore considers, like the Commission, that *the mere fact that an interpretation of the Convention may extend into the sphere of social and economic rights should not be a decisive factor against such an interpretation; there is no water-tight division separating that sphere from the field covered by the Convention.*
48. Austria, Czech Republic, Denmark, Germany, Greece, Hungary, Latvia, Luxembourg, Poland, Slovakia, Spain and the United Kingdom.
49. Convention no 87, Freedom of Association and Protection of the Right to Organise Convention, 1948 and convention no 98, Right to Organise and Collective Bargaining Convention, 1949.
50. Convention no 29, Forced Labour Convention, 1930 and convention no 105, Abolition of Forced Labour Convention, 1957.

3) Equality[51]
4) Elimination of Child Labour[52]

There is generally only scant reference to ILO conventions in EU law. That has been criticized in the literature.[53] In the Charter on Fundamental Rights and the explanations referred to in the Charter that set out the sources of its provisions there is no explicit reference to ILO conventions.

Fundamental rights are binding on the institutions of the EU in the exercise of their powers. Decisions have been struck down by the ECJ in staff cases for non-compliance with fundamental rights, see above on the *Dunnett* and *Maurissen* cases.

According to Article 51 of the Charter it is in addition to the institutions, bodies, offices and agencies of the Union also addressed to the Member States but only when they are implementing Union law. In the Explanations to Article 51 it is stated (emphasis added) that:

> "As regards the Member States, it follows unambiguously from the case-law of the Court of Justice that the requirement to respect fundamental rights defined in the context of the Union is only binding on the Member States when they act *in the scope of Union law* (judgment of 13 July 1989, Case 5/88 Wachauf [1989] ECR 2609; judgment of 18 June 1991, Case C-260/89 ERT [1991] ECR I-2925; judgment of 18 December 1997, Case C-309/96 Annibaldi [1997] ECR I-7493)."

In its case law, the ECJ has required Member States to respect the fundamental rights not only when they transpose an EU rule into national law but also when they take measures that may hinder the free movement of persons, services and capital.

Article 45 TFEU and 157 TFEU give rise to direct effects both in the vertical relationship against the Member States and in horizontal relationships against private employers and organizations. It is generally a condition for direct effect that the provision at issue is sufficiently precise. Some of the provisions in the Charter are reasonably precise. That is, of relevance to gender equality, in particular the case with Article 20 on Equality before the law and

51. Convention no 100, Equal Remuneration Convention, 1951 and convention no 111, Discrimination (employment and Occupation) Convention, 1958.
52. Convention no138, Minimum Age Convention, 1973 and convention no 182, Worst Forms of Child Labour Convention, 1999.
53. O'Higgins, Paul: Some problems of enforcement of rights under the Community Charter of Fundamental Social Rights of Workers in Vogel-Polsky, Eliane (ed.): Quel avenir pour l'Europe sociale: 1992 et après?, Bruxelles 1992 p. 73.

the prohibition against discrimination in Article 21. In my view, these provisions have direct effect. Article 20 on Equality before the law reads:

"Everyone is equal before the law.
Article 21 on Non-discrimination reads:

1. Any discrimination based on any ground such as sex, race, colour, ethnic or social origin, genetic features, language, religion or belief, political or any other opinion, membership of a national minority, property, birth, disability, age or sexual orientation shall be prohibited.
2. Within the scope of application of the Treaties and without prejudice to any of their specific provisions, any discrimination on grounds of nationality shall be prohibited."

5. Changes in the sources of law

5.1. The decreasing role of preparatory works of national legislation

Historical or subjective interpretation refers to interpretations where the interpreter looks for the (subjective) intention of the historical legislator, *i.e.* the author of the provision (Treaty provision, secondary legislation or national legislation) under interpretation. In historical interpretation considerable weight is often put on the preparatory works (*travaux préparatoires).* The relative importance of literal and historical interpretation depends on the drafting traditions in the legal system under interpretation, in particular whether it uses preambles in its legislation. Nordic legislation, for example, usually does not have preambles. Statements that are placed in the preambles in EU legislation are in Nordic legislation found in the preparatory works. Historical interpretation is therefore traditionally more important when interpreting national law in these countries than when interpreting EU law, where a literal interpretation of the preambles will often show views that could only be found by historical interpretation of the preparatory works in Nordic law. The CJEU applies mainly[54] what can be called an objective method of interpretation, which gives the judge the primary role as interpreter and provides wider scope for judicial creativity than an interpretation bound by the subjective legislative intention. The CJEU is a prime example of a Court that has exercised its freedom of interpretation under the objective method to develop

54. See Ulla Neergaard and Ruth Nielsen: Where Did the Spirit and Its Friends Go? On the European Legal Method(s) and the Interpretational Style of the Court of Justice of the European Union in in Ulla Neergaard, Ruth Nielsen and Lynn M. Roseberry (eds.): European Legal Method – Paradoxes and Revitalisation, Copenhagen 2011.

a purposive construction of EU law favouring integration to a high degree, using a wide variety of sources of law. The CJEU thus practices a constructive, creative, non-hierarchical doctrine of the sources of law based on objective interpretation.

In the Nordic countries, preparatory works have traditionally played a predominant role in the interpretation of statutory provisions. In the Nordic tradition on how to draft legislation, there are typically no preambles to the legislative texts. Material that in legal systems, which use preambles to legislative texts (as for example the EU legislator does) will be placed in the preambles, will in the Nordic countries most often be found in the preparatory works, which thus to some extent are functionally equivalent to preambles.

The influx of EU law into Nordic law reduces the significance of national preparatory works since Nordic enactments implementing EU law must be interpreted in accordance with the underlying EU provisions, no matter how the drafters of the implementing legislation think they should be interpreted. This change in the Nordic sources of law because of EU integration is generally recognized. In the preparatory works to the Swedish Accession to the EU, there is thus an extensive discussion of this shift in the traditional pattern of the Swedish sources of law.[55]

The importance of preparatory works has been particularly strong in Finland, Norway and Sweden. Denmark has occupied a medium position. In doctrinal writing and case law, Nordic lawyers often quote the preparatory works, for example the explanatory memorandum, but they do not regard them as binding. Preparation of legislation in some areas of Nordic law, e.g. contract legislation, has to a very high degree taken place in Nordic collaboration so that preference for a subjective method of interpretation will favour Nordic uniformity in contract law while a shift towards objective, purposive interpretation may disintegrate the Nordic legal unity.

The Nordic legislators' habit of placing some rules or observations about the law in the preparatory works of statutes and the importance attached to preparatory works as a source of law has given rise to two infringement cases brought by the Commission against Denmark and Sweden in connection with implementation of directives.

55. Regeringens Proposition 1994/95:19, Sveriges medlemskap i Europeiska Unionen, Del 1. In Case C-478/99 *Commission* v. *Sweden* [2002] ECR I-4147 on the implementation of the Unfair Contract Terms Directive (93/13/EEC) the Swedish government did, however, defend the important role preparatory work for a law as a source of law in the Nordic countries, see below.

In *Commission* v. *Denmark*[56] on the implementation of the Equal Pay Directive from 1975, the Commission claimed that Denmark had failed to implement the Equal Pay Directive[57] correctly because Denmark had chosen not to fully follow the wording of the Directive which required employers to pay men and women equal pay for the same work and for work to which equal value is attributed. The implemented Danish Act explicitly mentioned only equal pay for the same work not equal pay for work of equal value. Denmark argued that it followed *inter alia* from the preparatory works to the Equal Pay Act that the expression 'same work ' would be interpreted in such a broad sense that it also covered 'work to which equal value is attributed'. Denmark lost the case. The CJEU held:

> "11 In this case it appears that the wording of the Danish law does not fulfil those conditions inasmuch as it sets out the principle of equal pay without speaking of work of equal value, thus restricting the scope of the principle. The fact that in the preamble (emphasis added)[58] to the draft law the government stated that the expression 'same work ' was interpreted in Denmark in so broad a sense that the addition of the expression 'work to which equal value is attributed' would not entail any real extension is not sufficient to ensure that the persons concerned are adequately informed."

In this case mention of the correct rule in the explanatory memorandum to the Equal Pay Bill was thus not accepted as sufficient for correct implementation.

In *Commission* v. *Sweden,*[59] the Commission claimed that the ECJ should declare that Sweden had failed to fulfill its obligations under the Directive on unfair terms in consumer contracts.[60] The parties were in dispute as to whether it was necessary to implement through a provision of law the 'indicative, non-exhaustive' list in the annex to the Directive of terms that may be regarded as unfair. The Swedish Government took the view that it is sufficient for the list to be reproduced in the explanatory note to the implementing

56. Case 143/83 *Commission* v. *Denmark* [1985] ECR 427.
57. 75/117/EEC. Now repealed by 2006/54/EC.
58. In the Danish version of the judgment: 'bemærkningerne til lovforslaget', in the French version 'l 'exposé des motifs du projet de loi'. Usually the Danish words 'bemærkninger til lovforslaget' are translated into 'the explanatory memorandum to the draft Act' or 'preparatory works to the Act'. The English word 'preamble' is practically always translated into 'præambel' in Danish. It is, as mentioned above, not a part of the Danish legislative drafting tradition to use preambles (præambler) in Danish legislation. There is no preamble – and there has never been any – in the Danish Equal Pay Act.
59. Case C-478/99 *Commission* v. *Sweden* [2002] ECR I-4147.
60. 93/13/EEC.

law. Finland and Denmark, which have not incorporated the text into their legislation either, supported the position of the Swedish Government. According to the Opinion of the Advocate General, the Swedish government argued ((emphasis added)):

"that the issue of the list in the Annex to the Directive was discussed in depth during the preparation of lagen 1994:1512. Eventually, the Swedish legislature chose not to incorporate the list in the legislation, but to reproduce its contents in the explanatory note in order to facilitate the application of the law. According to the Swedish Government, this is the usual legislative technique in Sweden and legislative texts generally do not contain lists of examples.

50. An individual who wishes to know which terms may be unfair and for that purpose consults lagen 1994:1512 and lagen 1994:1513 will find in both a reference to the explanatory note. (30) In that note the list in the Annex to the Directive is reproduced in its entirety. The note also contains a commentary which clarifies the scope and significance of the list. (31) The explanatory note is published officially and can also be consulted free of charge on the internet.

51. According to long-established legal tradition in Sweden, in common with all the Nordic countries, the preparatory work is an important instrument in the interpretation of laws. After the text of the law, it constitutes one of the most important sources for the interpretation and application of that law. (32) According to the Swedish Government, most of the terms referred to in the Annex to the Directive (to be precise 14 out of 17) have already been declared to be unfair in Swedish case-law and the Marknadsdomstolen (Market Court) made express reference to the list in a judgment delivered in 1997."

The Advocate general stated (emphasis added):[61]

"The Commission claims that the importance of the preparatory work has declined as a result of Sweden's accession to the European Union, but the Swedish Government contests that assertion. It is possible that the preparatory work for a law is still an important source of law in the Nordic countries."

The CJEU did not express any opinion on the Nordic doctrine of the sources of law. It held that:

"22. Inasmuch as the list contained in the annex to the Directive is of indicative and illustrative value, it constitutes a source of information both for the national authorities responsible for applying the implementing measures and for individuals affected by those measures. As noted by the Advocate General in paragraph 48 of his Opinion, Member States must therefore, in order to achieve the result sought by the Directive, choose a form and method of implementation that offer a sufficient guarantee that the public can obtain knowledge of it.

61. In footnote 32 to his opinion.

23. In the present case, the Annex to the Directive has been reproduced in its entirety in the preparatory work for the law implementing the Directive. The Swedish Government has claimed that, according to a legal tradition that is well established in Sweden and common to the Nordic countries, preparatory work constitutes an important aid to interpreting legislation. It has also stated that such preparatory work may easily be consulted and that, in addition, information concerning terms that are considered or may be considered to be unfair is provided to the public by various means. The Commission has not disputed those statements but has confined itself to maintaining that those factors cannot compensate for the fact that the list in the annex to the Directive is not an integral part of the provisions implementing the Directive."

Scandinavian Legal Realism adopted a pluralistic approach to the sources of law, accepting a number of different legal actors and phenomena as capable of creating valid law. This is true even if the concept of law is primarily defined by reference to the judges. This theory also leaves ample scope for judicial creativity.

5.2. Public International Law. Monist and/or dualist theory

In its pure form, the monist approach to the relationship between international and national law considers the rules of international law to be part of the domestic legal system and requires the courts to apply them directly. Conflicts between international law and rules of domestic origin may in a monist system be solved in various ways, for example by giving priority to international law, to the domestic rules, to the domestic rules of a certain rank, etc. Under EU law, international treaties entered into by the EU form part of EU law without any incorporation being necessary. EU law is thus based on the monist approach.

The Scandinavian countries, on the other hand, have traditionally followed the dualist approach according to which international law is a separate legal system, not directly applicable in national courts. This means that conflicts between international and domestic law can in principle not arise before national courts, which are not allowed to apply international law directly but have a duty to interpret national law in accordance with international law if that is possible. In order for treaties ratified by 'dualist' states to become part of national law, they must be incorporated by national legislation of some kind. In most cases the Scandinavian courts will be able to interpret domestic law so as to comply with the country's international obligations, but on a few occasions the principled dualist approach has been upheld by the courts.

The dualist attitude was for example confirmed by the Swedish Labour Court (Arbetsdomstolen) in the case *Svenska Lokmannaförbundet* v *The State* in 1972.[62] The Labour Court held that such international instruments could only become 'valid Swedish law' through Swedish legislation, although they could shed light on the meaning of existing Swedish statutes 'which can be assumed to be compatible with our country's international commitments'.[63] The dualist attitude was also confirmed by a judgment from the Norwegian Supreme Court from May 1997.[64] The Court held that if a particular Norwegian Act prohibiting strikes was inconsistent with ILO Conventions 87 and 98, the Norwegian Act would override international law.

Due to a preference for collective bargaining over statutory regulation,[65] the Nordic (parliamentary) legislators have been somewhat reluctant to fulfil international obligations fully in the field of labour law. Until 1996, it was for example still arguable that Danish private employers under domestic Danish law were legally free to take racist employment decisions, though Denmark ratified the United Nations Convention on the Elimination of All Forms of Racial Discrimination in 1971.

Membership of the EU places the Nordic countries in a double context. The Nordic member states are now both 'monists' as EU states and 'dualist' as individual nation-states. This new context incites a shift in approach from the dualist to the monist theory. In respect of public international law, the traditional Scandinavian preference for the dualist theory is being softened and a more mixed monist and dualist approach is being developed.

6. Shift in basic theories (natural law or legal positivism)

I use the term Scandinavian Legal Realism in a broad sense[66] as a reference to the Nordic variant of legal positivism. As Austin stated nearly 200 years ago:[67]

62. Arbetsdomstolens Domar 1972, no. 5.
63. See further Bogdan, Michael: Comparative Law Stockholm, 1992.
64. Norsk Rettstidende 1997,580. The Court stated (in Norwegian): 'selv i tilfelle streikeforbudet skulle ha vært i strid med folkerettslige bestemmelser om vern av retten til streik, ville det følge av norsk rett at den provisoriske anordning om tvungen lønnsnemnd var gyldig'.
65. Bruun et al: The Nordic Labour Relations Model, Dartmouth 1992.
66. See for a similar broad approach Spaak, Torben: Legal Positivism, Law's Normativity, and the Normative Force of Legal Justification, Ratio Juris 2003 p. 469, who states: 'Legal positivism is a general and descriptive theory about law of the type advanced by scholars like John Austin (1954), Hans Kelsen (1945, 1960), Alf Ross

"The existence of the law is one thing; its merit or demerit is another. Whether it be or not is one enquiry; whether it be or be not conformable to an assumed standard, is a different enquiry. A law, which actually exists, is a law, though we happen to dislike it, or though it vary from the text, by which we regulate our approbation and disapprobation."

Scandinavian legal realism dates back to the period before the creation of EU and was originally closely linked to the Scandinavian legal context, including the traditional Nordic doctrine of the sources of law. It may therefore be asked whether it is simply an outdated theory today (2011) and whether it is too closely bound to a Scandinavian context to be of any relevance for the study of EU law and its interface with national law.

In the Nordic countries, Scandinavian Legal Realism has influenced legal thinking and legal education since the early twentieth century. The first generation of Scandinavian legal realists tried to eliminate all metaphysical, ideological, and normative elements from the scientific study of the legal order. According to its research programme legal science should be a descriptive (as opposed to normative) science about norms, not a science/scholarship/-policy/axiology that expressed itself in norms.

In my view, Scandinavian Legal Realism can be updated to provide theoretical and conceptual tools that can facilitate a dogmatic examination of EU law, the law of EU Member States within the scope of application of EU law and the mutual embeddedness of EU law and the national law of Member States of the EU.[68] One of the problems in applying Scandinavian Legal Re-

(1959), H. L. A. Hart (1961, 1982), Joseph Raz (1979, chap. 3; 1985), and Neil MacCormick and Ota Weinberger (1986), not a theory telling the judge how he should decide hard cases or when civil disobedience is justified.' Other authors focus on the features of the differences between Scandinavian legal realism and the theories of Kelsen or Hart; see for example McCormack, Geoffrey: Scandinavian Realism. The Juridical Review 1970 p. 33.

67. Austin, John: The province of jurisprudence determined, (first edition 1832), 5. edition 1885, edited by Wilfrid Rumble, Cambridge, 1995, p. 157.
68. See Nielsen, Ruth: Scandinavian Legal Realism and EU Law in Ulla Neergaard, Ruth Nielsen and Lynn M. Roseberry (eds.): The Role of Courts in Developing a European Social Model – Theoretical and Methodological Perspectives, Copenhagen 2009, Nielsen, Ruth: Nordic Sources of Law in a European Environment in Cameron, Iain and Alessandro Simoni (eds.): Dealing With Integration: Perspectives from Seminars on European Law 1996-1998 (Skrifter Från Juridiska Fakulteten i Uppsala, 52), Uppsala 1996 where I tentatively concluded: 'scandinavian Legal realism has traditionally adopted a pluralistic approach to the sources of law accepting a number of different legal actors and phenomena as capable of creating valid law... These qualities enable Scandinavian Legal Realism, in a modernised form, to provide a suitable framework

alism to EU law is that the CJEU differs from Scandinavian court and maybe is less positivistic in its approach. In a general textbook on EU law that for a number of years was the leading Scandinavian textbook on EU law, Gulmann and Hagel-Sørensen state that:[69]

> "Seen from a Nordic legal positivist perspective the CJEU's case law contains clear natural law elements."

That was probably not meant as a compliment. In the Nordic legal positivist tradition, leading writers – as for example Alf Ross – have expressed strong criticism of natural law. A main point in this criticism was that any view can be defended by natural law arguments. Ross thus wrote:[70]

> "Like a harlot, natural law is at the disposal of everyone."

The Lisbon Treaty can be seen as a present day natural law codification of fundamental rights. After this codification a positivist approach to EU law will probably be more relevant.

7. EU law and the law of its member states as one big system

There has been much debate in later years on pluralism and diversity in EU law.[71] The development of the EU legal order has given rise to much debate about constitutional pluralism.[72] In that context one can discuss various possible ways of understanding the character of and relations between legal systems in the European Union, in particular, whether there is one EU legal sys-

for understanding and predicting developments in European Union law in general.' In the present paper, I will expand on this conclusion.

69. Translated by Neergaard and Nielsen. See the Danish original Gulmann, Claus and Karsten Hagel-Sørensen: EU-ret, Copenhagen 1995, p. 155, note 22. The original reads: „Set fra en nordisk, retspositivistisk synsvinkel indeholder EF-Domstolens praksis klare naturretlige elementer".
70. See Ross, Alf: On Law and Justice, London 1958 (English translation of Ret og Retfærdighed, Copenhagen1953), p. 261. The Danish original reads: „Som en skøge er naturretten til rådighed for enhver", Ret og Retfærdighed, p. 343.
71. There is abundant literature; see for example Modéer, Kjell-Åke: The Historical Roots of European Legal Culture, JFT (Tidskrift utgiven av Juridiska Föreningen i Finland) 2010, p. 493.
72. See Walker, Neil: The Idea of Constitutional Pluralism, Modern Law Review 2002, p. 317.

tem distinct from and in addition to the national legal systems (the 27+1 model), or whether it is better to conceive of EU law merely as an aspect of Member States' legal systems (the 27 model), or whether we should think of there being but one single EU legal system of which Member States' "national legal systems" are in some sense sub-systems (the one Big system model).[73] In my view European gender equality law should be seen as one big system comprising both sources of law stemming from the EU level and from the national level.

73. See Dickson, Julie: How Many Legal Systems? Some Puzzles Regarding the Identity Conditions of, and Relations Between, Legal Systems in the European Union, http://papers.ssrn.com/sol3/papers.cfm?abstract_id=1279612 (University of Oxford Legal Research Paper Series, Paper No 40/2008). See also Hesselink, Martijn: The Common Frame of Reference as a source of European private law, Tulane Law Review, 2009, p. 919 and Hesselink, Martijn W.: Methodology and Theoretical Disagreement in Ulla Neergaard, Ruth Nielsen and Lynn M. Roseberry (efternavne efterstillede)(eds.): European Legal Method – Paradoxes and Revitalisation, Copenhagen 2011. See also Nielsen, Ruth (efternavn forstillet) og Christina D. Tvarnø(efternavn efterstillet): Retskilder og Retsteorier, Kbhvn. 2011.

CHAPTER 4

Normative Cultures and Gender Cultures

Nordic and indigenous/arctic perspectives of humans and nature – a new agenda?

By Hanne Petersen, professor of legal cultures, Law Faculty University of Copenhagen

> *"for the first time in his life (it) had evoked in the man the overpowering feeling that were he to shoot this animal he would be committing murder"* [1]

> *"Here is a paradox. Over the last thirty or forty years, we have invested an enormous amount of thought, emotion, treasure, and blood in what we call human values, human rights, the defence of human dignity and of human life. Over the same period, quietly but devastatingly, science and philosophy have combined to undermine our traditional concept of humankind. In consequence, the coherence of our understanding of what it means to be human is now in peril."* [2]

1. Introduction

In this article I will combine historical, cultural and gender perspectives on normative cultures – which include both state legal culture, religious norms and indigenous legal culture. I will draw on legal, philosophical and literary

1. Peter Høeg, *The Woman and the Ape*, 1996, p.13-14.
2. Felipe Fernández-Armesto, *So You Think You're Human? A Brief History of Humanking.* Oxford University Press, 2004, p.1.

sources, indigenous myths as well as personal and professional experience. I am approaching the overall topic and issues from local, national, regional and global positions, which are interlinked. Nordic and Scandinavian normative cultures are not only modern majority state legal cultures, although these have been very influential – very much so also for Nordic/Scandinavian women's law in the 20st century. The 21st century context is (perhaps) more global and more diverse, more complex and more confused, and its normative cultures are (perhaps) less hierarchically organized. The relations between humans and nature and especially interspecies relations between humans and animals, which are the starting point of my reflections here, may seem odd and outrageous from a 20th century perspective, although interest has been growing. My inspiration for dealing with this topic comes from my experience of living and teaching in the Arctic for about a decade. During my studies for this and other presentations, I am increasingly becoming convinced that these relations will constitute huge future challenges. I think Scandinavian women's law may have the possibility to contribute to these challenges given that it opens up for other agendas than the ones which dominated the 20th century.

2. Nordic legal culture – an androcentric, anthropocentric and eurocentric heritage

During the last millennium Nordic legal cultures have been strongly influenced by Christian monotheism first as state supportive Catholicism later transformed into Lutheranism and later again Lutheran secularism[3] supplemented by modern confidence in science. In the Nordic countries many people consider themselves secular, but this secularity can be considered a special Nordic version of secularism.[4]

The political cultures and regimes have changed/moved from elected monarchs through absolutist monarchs to democracies. Democracies in the form of constitutional monarchies still play an important symbolic role in

3. This is a term used by Anders Berg Sørensen in his article "The Politics of Lutheran Secularism: Reiterating Secularism in the Wake of the Cartoon Crisis" in Christoffersen et al (eds) *Religion in the 21st Century Challenges and Transformations*, Ashgate 2010, p. 207.
4. Sven-Eric Liedman, Intellectual Challenges from Religion, "in Christoffersen et al (eds) *Religion in the 21st Century.Challenges and Transformations*, Ashgate 2010, p. 51

Norway, Denmark and Sweden. The subsequent legal cultures have been closely linked to the religious/secular and political regimes.

In the Middle Ages, Catholic Margrethe I (1353-1412) gradually expanded her rule on behalf of her son and fosterson from Denmark to Norway and Sweden. She ruled all of these countries together during the period from 1389-1412. Under her leadership the Kalmar Union was established from 1397 strengthening the three countries against the Hanseatic League. Sweden left the union after half a century, but the union between Denmark and Norway lasted as a personal union until 1814 – in Norway sometimes described as the "400 years night." This explains the still very strong linguistic and cultural links between the two countries.

Lutheranism was introduced in Denmark and Norway by King Christian II in 1536 under the principle of *cuius regio, eius religio*, which meant that the king's belief decided the belief of his subjects in the population.[5] The king's subjects had to be Protestant believers and follow church discipline. Danes and Norwegian became forced Protestants for the next 300 years. As a general rule no other religions were allowed. Protestantism and Protestant values became a strongly integrated part of legal culture, not least after the establishment of Absolutist rule and hereditary monarchy from 1660 – which in Denmark lasted until 1849.

Sweden repealed Canonical Law from 1536, and gradually established an Evangelical-Lutheran Church. Traces of this regime still exist in the close relations between church and state in the Nordic countries – traces which have only been gradually disconnected. At the beginning of the 21st century Sweden was the first to undergo a formal process of separation from the state in the year 2000!

Although Denmark has been a monarchy since the turn of the first millennium, it was only at the end of this millennium that a female ruler, Queen Margrethe II (born 1940) took over after her father in the beginning of 1972. This was also the year when a Danish referendum with a rather narrow vote decided that Denmark should become a member of the European Economic Community. This had required a legislative change which took place in 1953, when Denmark experienced its latest constitutional change allowing for decolonization of Greenland within the realm and access to the EEC without the burdensome and formally very difficult process of constitutional change.

5. This principle meaning "Whose realm, his religion" followed the religious disruption of Europe which took place after the Reformation in 1517.

Norway has only been an independent state since 1905. In 1814 after the Napoleonic wars, where Denmark had sided with the losing emperor Napoleon, the absolutist King Frederik VI was forced to turn over Norway to Sweden by a treaty signed in Kiel, then part of the small Danish empire. The union between Norway and Sweden lasted for almost a century. Norway had opted for a monarchy and not a republic, when it managed to accept a constitution in 1814, even if its ideals were France and the United States, who had recently become republics. During the years of foreign rule the Norwegian church played an important role in securing Norwegian language, culture and administrative tradition. The Norwegian Church has thus had an even more important political role than is the case in the other Nordic countries. Norway was the centre for the development of Women's Law from 1975 and the first Nordic country to get a female prime minister, Gro Harlem Brundtland who served three periods (1981, 1986-89, 1990-96).

In Sweden female succession had been accepted already in 1608. In 1632 the very young Kristina (1626-1689) who was born during the 30 years war in Europe (1618-1648) formally became ruler of the country after the death of her father and until her abdication in 1654 at the age of 27. After that she moved to Southern Europe, where she was an important cultural figure in Rome until her death. She converted to Catholicism in 1656, which at the time was almost considered an act of treason.[6] In spite of Sweden's strong record on equality issues it has not yet had a female prime minister.

Denmark got its first female prime minister in September 2011 – ninety-six years after women first got the vote in the country in 1915.

This brief Nordic political history demonstrates both the well known *androcentric* and the perhaps somewhat less recognized Christian/Lutheran influence on Nordic culture in general and not least Nordic legal culture.[7] The understanding of the *anthropocentric* aspects of Western and Nordic legal culture and their links to monotheisms is more recent.

The end of the 19th and the most of the 20th century has been strongly influenced by secularism in the Nordic countries. The turn of the century has been characterized as 'post-secularist' not least due to the increasing influence of and anxiety about Muslim monotheism in Europe and particularly in

6. Marie Louise Renata Rodén, Drottning Kristina – Visionär i nytt ljus, from http://www.kungarochdrottningar.se/stormaktstiden/drottning-kristina/ (last accessed October 10, 2011).

7. See also writings by Anu Pylkkänen, Feminism and the Challenge to Religious Truths on Marriage. The Case of Nordic Protestantism. In Lisbet Christoffersen et al(eds.). *Law & Religion in the 21st Century – Nordic Perspectives.*

Denmark and Norway. Both Islam and Christianity are successor cultures to Judaism. These monotheistic normative cultures are both androcentric and anthropocentric, and operate within a combined gender and species hierarchy, where the (male) God/Father is placed in the sky on top of the hierarchy, followed by human men, human women and at the bottom by animals. Monotheism thus guarantees not only male superiority in gender relations but also the superiority of the human species in relation to other species. These relations are described in the story from Genesis about God's creation of the world:

> "And God said, Let the earth bring forth the living creature after his kind, cattle, and creeping thing, and beast of the earth after his kind: and it was so.
>
> And God made the beast of the earth after his kind, and cattle after their kind, and every thing that creepeth upon the earth after his kind: and God saw that *it was* good.
>
> And God said, Let us make man in our image, after our likeness: and let them have dominion over the fish of the sea, and over the fowl of the air, and over the cattle, and over all the earth, and over every creeping thing that creepeth upon the earth.
>
> So God created man in his *own* image, in the image of God created he him; male and female created he them. And God blessed them, and God said unto them, Be fruitful, and multiply, and replenish the earth, and subdue it: and have dominion over the fish of the sea, and over the fowl of the air, and over every living thing that moveth upon the earth."[8]

The gender and species hierarchy has subordinated women to men and animals to humans. The Jewish-Algerian-French philosopher Jacques Derrida has on several occasion written on these issues and in his important article *"Force of Law: The Mystical Foundation of Authority"* first published in English (and French) in Cardozo Law Review in 1999, he described western culture as *carnophallogocentric,*[9] and wrote that.

> "... there was a time, not long ago and not yet over, in which "we, men" meant "we adult white male Europeans, carnivorous and capable of sacrifice." In the space in which I'm situating these remarks of reconstituting this discourse one would not speak of injustice toward an animal, even less toward a vegetable or a stone... There have been, there are still, many "subjects" among mankind who are not recognized as subjects and who receive this animal treatment... What we confusedly call "animal", the living thing as living and nothing else, is not a subject of the law or of law *(droit).* The opposition between just and unjust has no meaning in this case...

8. Genesis 1, vs. 24-28, The Holy Bible, King James Version, http://www.bartleby.com-/108/01/1.html#26 (last visited 20092011).
9. I first wrote about this article and concept in an article entitled "Ægte eller uægte orden" in a Festschrift for Henrik Zahle, *Retlig Polycentri*, (eds. Peter Blume & Hanne Petersen), 1993, Akademisk Forlag, Copenhagen, pp.93-114.

> In our culture, carnivorous sacrifice is fundamental, dominant, regulated by the highest industrial technology, as is biological experimentation on animals – so vital to our modernity…"
>
> If we wish to speak of injustice, of violence or of a lack of respect toward what we still so confusedly call animals – the question is more topical than ever, and so I include in it, in the name of deconstruction, a set of questions on carno-phallogocentrism – we must reconsider in its totality the metaphysico-anthropocentric axiomatic that dominate in the West, the thought of just and unjust."[10]

Meat, the male phallus, and the word have been and to an overwhelming degree still are at the centre of Western and Nordic (legal) culture.

Denmark is an agricultural society, with an industrialized meat production with a yearly stock of 13,2 million pigs and turning out 28,5 million pigs per year for slaughtering and exportation. Meat is (still) considered prestigious food. There is a well-known gendered pattern in meat consumption with men generally consuming the highest amount of meat. Pig meat has both strong cultural and religious significance, and the eating of especially pig meat has been one of the centres of attention in the religious conflict between Christian and Muslim world views again in the first decade of the 21st century. The issue of economic support to agriculture is at the heart of European Union policy and legislation. A future changing perception of animals would constitute a considerable challenge to this industrial way of life and food production – and probably also to contemporary masculinity.

The gendered consumption pattern of meat is something politicians and legislators have so far not felt inclined to address. I remember a television interview with Swedish politician and former candidate for Prime Minister, Mona Sahlin in December 2006, where she was willing to speak about restrictions on the use of cars, but absolutely refused to discuss political consequences of the detrimental environmental effects of meat production and consumption. Awareness about gendered health patterns seems to be on the move, however.[11]

The male phallus and its (dys)function has also been at the centre of interest since the turn of the 21st century. The quality of semen has fallen in many Western countries including the Nordic countries, and this has been a source

10. This quote is from Jacques Derrida, Force of Law: The "Mystical Foundation of Authority" (translated by Mary Quaintance) in *Cardozo Law Review* 1990, Vol. 11, pp. 951 & 953 (the article is bilingual).
11. In 2011 the University of Lund appointed a medical guest professor, Diana Krause, as part of the university's equality programme. She gave a lecture on "Sex, hormones and the brain circulation", at the 'Hedda-day' in May 2011.

of worry. Environmental pollution has been mentioned as a cause, as has stress and life style.[12] The capacity of erection also seems to have decreased – leading to hype in the sale of Viagra and other compensatory drug – probably greatly contributing both to the profits of the medical industry and to the feeling of insecurity among men.[13]

The dominance of the word – especially the written word – is significant in Western culture not least in legal culture. Until the IT-revolution especially Nordic legal culture had a strong focus on written law – especially state produced law and in spite of the Nordic countries, and especially Finland, having been at the forefront of development and use of IT-technology the consequences for legal culture seem understudied.

The late Swedish professor, Anna Christensen, once wrote that law – 'juridik' – considers theology as a poorer cousin from the countryside.[14] The IT-revolution with its undermining of vertical communication may leave lawyers in the position which theologians had to face at the beginning of the secular era. Male, human and verbal superiority in the formulation and interpretation of norms in a broad sense may be on a downward turn.

In "*The Animal That Therefore I am (More to Follow)*" Derrida again discusses the relation between human and animal, the animal looking at man, man being naked before the animal – which cannot be naked, or cannot feel its own nudity, because there is no nudity "in nature".[15] The communication between man and animal and of animal response raises the issue of what response means, and thus of the role of the word.[16] Derrida claims that philosophers (he names Descartes, Kant, Heidegger, Lacan and Levinas) have not ever been seen by an animal:

> "*The experience of the seeing animal, of the animal that looks at them, has not been taken into account in the philosophical or theoretical architecture of their discourse.*"[17]

12. In Denmark prof.em. Niels Erik Skakkebæk has been working on issues of male infertility and its causes since his dissertation published in 1972.
13. The drug popularly known as Viagra was marketed in 1998, and the sales have soared since then http://en.wikipedia.org/wiki/Sildenafil (last accessed October 13, 2011).
14. I have in vain sought to find the source for this quote. My search led me to a revisit of Anna Christensen's very important article, Kvinnorätten och lagpositivismen in *Retfærd*, no. 33, 1986.
15. Jacques Derrida, "The Animal That Therefore I Am (More to Follow)". In Critical Inquiry, Vol.28, No.2. (Winter 2002), pp.369-418, here from p-373.
16. Derrida, ibid. p.378.
17. Derrida, ibid. p.383.

Man claims his superiority over "what is called animal life", Derrida writes, and this superiority is an inherent element also of Western legal culture.

"The animal is a word, it is an appellation that men have instituted, a name they have given themselves the right and the authority to give to another living creature [à l'autre vivant]."[18]

Derrida invents a new word, *animot:*

"**Ecce Animot**. *Neither a species nor a gender nor an individual, it is an irreducible living multiplicity of mortals, and rather than a double clone or a portmanteau word, a sort of monstrous hybrid, a chimera waiting to be put to death by its Bellerophon.'*

Who or what was the Chimera?
Chimera was, as we know, the name of a flame-spitting monster. Her monstrousness derived precisely from the multiplicity of animals, of **animot**, *in her (head and chest of a lion, entrails of a goat, tail of a dragon).*"[19]

The Western view of hierarchical relations between gender and species has been dominant for the last millennium, and it has influenced these relations also in the Nordic countries.

But it is by no way sure, that these relations will continue to be dominant forever. And the Nordic countries, as well as other Western countries, include normative cultures with a different understanding of gender and species relations.

3. Inuit, Sami and indigenous legal cultures

"The Aboriginal world view holds that human beings are the least powerful and least important elements in creation. They cannot influence events, and are disrespectful if they try. Human interests are not to be placed above those of any other part of creation. Regarding the relative hierarchy and importance of beings in creation therefore, Aboriginal and Western traditions are diametrically opposed."[20]

18. Derrida, ibid.p.392.
19. Derrida, ibid. p.409.
20. Murray Sinclair, "Aboriginal Peoples and Euro-Canadians: Two World View. In John H. Hyden (ed): Aboriginal Self-Government in Canada. Current Trends and Issues. Purich Publishing. Saskatoon, Saskatchewan, Canada, 1994.

This is a quote from Canada's first aboriginal judge, Murray Sinclair from a book published in 1994. In my experience this is a view that is shared by the aboriginal or indigenous populations with close links to the Nordic countries, that is the Inuit in Greenland, and the Sami, who have historically lived in transnational communities crossing the boundaries of Norway, Sweden, Finland and Russia/The Soviet Union.

During my four years (1995-1999) of staying and working at the University of Greenland; Ilisimatusarfik in Nuuk, gender relations puzzled me a lot. On the surface it looked as if the gender pattern was very similar to the Danish-European hierarchical pattern, but something felt different. When Inuits in Canada worked to establish Nunavut as a more independent entity, and to set up an Inuit-parliament, the male spokesmen and central actors were clearly in favour of a parliament with gender parity. This suggestion was defeated at a referendum of the Inuit population.[21] When one of the male spokespersons introduced the work at Ilisimatusarfik in the late 90s, he said that he was sure that future generations of women would not accept not to be represented in the parliament.

The activities in Nunavut led to attempts to establish a women's party in Greenland. They were not successful, but they led to a considerable increase in the number of female candidates and members of the Greenlandic parliament – members who were especially concerned about issues of importance for children, health, families and 'close' relations. Today the Greenlandic parliament has the highest proportion of female members in government amongst the Nordic countries.[22]

3.1. Mating and mythology[23]

Another thing which puzzled me very much during my stay and studies in Greenland were some of the Greenlandic myths collected by the explorer

21. Jens Dahl, Kønskvotering i Nunavut. In *Tidsskriftet Grønland,* no.1-2, 1998.
22. Four out of nine members of the Greenlandic government, Naalakkersuisut, are women in 2011. See also. Anne Mette Klausen, Danmark – kolonimagt eller partner? *NIKK,* Nov. 2010, http://www.nikk.no/Danmark+-+kolonimagt+eller+partner%3F.b-7C_wlfOYQ.ips (last accessed, October 10, 2011.
23. I have been presenting this part of the article as lectures in 2011. The first from August 2011 was given in the framework of an international summer school on *Gender and Body Dynamics in the 21st century. New turns in Theory, Methodology, and Case studies.* Here my title was "Mating and Mythology. Human-Animal Relations". The second presentation took place in Tromsø, Norway in September 2011 at a ph.d.-seminar on Gender Arctic Discourses, and here my title was "Normative Cultures and Gender Cultures – Arctic and Greenlandic".

Knud Rasmussen around the beginning of the 20th century. Knud Rasmussen, who had grown up in Greenland and spoke the local language, was of mixed Greenlandic Danish origin, his mother being herself a daughter of a mixed marriage.

During the summers of the late 90s, I was fortunate to be able to participate in a couple of boat trips along the widespread Greenlandic coastline, where the population lives. At that time the Greenlandic High Court went sailing from place to place in the summertime when the weather permitted travel in order to decide appeal cases in small towns, settlements and locations. During these long trips, which lasted for several weeks, I had plenty of time to read all three volumes of these myths and legends.

Some of the myths which seemed extraordinarily puzzling were the myths dealing with interrelations including inter-marriage between humans and animals, as well as species of animals. The first of the volumes deals with myths from East Greenland, which had only been Christianized around the beginning of the 20th century included several of these stories, with the following titles:

- The raven which took a wild goose for wife
- The unclean woman who visited bears in human form
- The woman who married a fox
- The woman who married a shrimp
- The raven and the diver
- The raven which proposed to the sparrow
- The woman who took a big worm for husband when worms had faces like humans
- The man who took a fox for wife

The raven would take a wild goose for his wife with considerable costs, as he could not swim, and thus could not survive the long flights, which the geese were able to undertake. The unclean woman would visit bears that had taken human form – and intermarried with walrus and fox. A demanding woman would marry a fox, who later would be criticized heavily by his parents-in-law for not contributing with food to the household. A woman, who did not want to marry, became married to a shrimp, who was also scolded as a useless son-in-law. He however – as the fox – finally turned out to be a very hard-working and valuable spouse. Another raven would propose to a sparrow. The woman who would take a big worm for husband at the time, when worms had faces like humans, was forced by the big and strong worm to accept him, and the worm threatened her not to leave him. She bore him twins with human faces but bodies as worms. A man would take a fox for his wife, but unfortunately loose her, when he accepted the custom of interchanging wives with another man.[24]

It has taken me a very long time to realize that these stories are probably related to the quote by judge Sinclair, and that a non-hierarchical view of interrelations between species will also influence the norms and ways of cultures..

The very important Arctic myth, Nerrivik, also called The Mother of the Sea, deals with the survival of humans and their interdependence – and intermarriage – with animals – probably signifying divine or spiritual powers. I have discussed this myth in another context:[25]

"NERRIVIK[26]
A bird once wished to marry a woman. He got himself a fine sealskin coat, and having weak eyes, made spectacles out of a walrus tusk, for he was greatly set upon looking as nice as possible. Then he set off, in the shape of a man and coming to a village, took a wife, and brought her home.

Now he began to go out catching fish, which he called seal, and brought home to his wife.

Once it happened that he lost his spectacles, and his wife, seeing his bad eyes, burst out weeping, because he was so ugly.

But her husband only laughed. "Oho, so you saw my eyes? Hahaha!" And he put on his spectacles again.

Then her brothers, who longed for their sister, came out one day to visit her. And her husband being out hunting, they took her away with them. The husband was greatly distressed when he came home and found her gone, and thinking someone must have carried her off, he set out in pursuit. He swung his wings with mighty force, and raised a violent storm, for he was a great wizard.

When the storm came up, the boat began to take in water, and the wind grew fiercer, as he doubled the beating of his wings. The waves rose white with foam, and the boat was near turning over. And when those in the boat began to suspect that the woman was the

24. Knud Rasmussen, Myter og Sagn fra Grønland. Vol. I Østgrønlændere, Dyrefabler, pp.132-155, Gyldendalske Boghandel, Nordisk Forlag, København, Kristiania, Berlin, London, 1921.
25. See Chapter 10 "The Case Studies Revisited" by Fred Bosselman, Hanne Petersen and Peter Ørebech in Ørebech et al. *The Role of Customary Law and Sustainable Development,* Cambridge University Press, 2005, pp.424-428.
26. This is a very short version taken from Knud Rasmussen's collections of myths and legends from Greenland. This specific myth is printed in the third volume which contains myth from the Cape York district and from Northern Greenland. Knud Rasmussen, Myter og Sagn fra Grønland. (Gyldendalske Boghhandel, Nordisk Forlag 1925). The translation is taken from "Eskimo Folk-tales" collected by Knud Rasmussen and selected and translated by W. Worster. (1921) Published by Gyldendal, Copenhagen & Christiania.

cause of the storm, they took her up and cast her into the sea. She tried to grasp the side of the boat, but then her grandfather sprang up and cut off her hand.

And so she was drowned. But at the bottom of the sea, she became Nerrivik, the ruler over all the creatures in the sea. And when men catch no seal, then the wizards go down to Nerrivik. Having but one hand, she cannot comb her hair, and this they do for her, and she, by way of thanks, sends seal and other creatures forth to men.

That is the story of the ruler of the sea. And men call her Nerrivik[27] because she gives them food."[28]

Mircea Eliade, writes that in many societies myth "supplies models for human behaviour and, by that very fact, gives meaning and value to life".[29] He continues:

"Myths are the most general and effective means of awakening and maintaining consciousness of another world, a beyond, whether it be the divine world or the world of ancestors. This "other world" represents a superhuman "transcendent" plane, the plane of **absolute realities**. *It is the experience of the sacred – that is, an encounter with a transhuman reality – which gives birth to the idea that something* **really exists**, *that hence there are absolute* values, *capable of guiding man, and giving a meaning to human existence. It is then, through the experience of the sacred that the ideas of* **reality, truth** *and* **significance** *first dawn, to be later elaborated and systematized by metaphysical speculation"*[30]

Myths are embodied in customs, and myths are concerned about values, which are capable of guiding humans and giving meaning to human existence. The last decade has witnessed a lot of discussion about ethics and law, and the values underlying Western legal thought can no longer be taken for granted as universal. The discussion about sustainability is amongst others a discussion about the necessity of broadening the value base of western and international rule-making. Sustainability may be understood as a standard for decision-making. Standards are thus an expression of values, which may be used to guide people in situations of insecurity and uncertainty.

27. Literally "Meat Dish."
28. Knud Rasmussen records the myth as "Told by Aisivik from Agpat."
29. Mircea Eliade, *Myth and Reality*, Harper Torchbooks, New York 1974, p.2. (emphasis in original).
30. Mircea Eliade, *Myth and Reality*, Harper Torchbooks, New York 1974, p.139.

3.2. Climate change and indigenous action – protecting Mother Earth[31]

On April 22 in 2009 President Evo Morales Ayma of the 'Plurinational state of Bolivia' suggested that the UN decide on a Mother Earth Day. The proposal was accepted, and April 22 was chosen. On the same occasion the president suggested that the UN should adopt a Universal Declaration of the Mother Earth Rights. The adoption of a UN Declaration on the Rights of Indigenous Peoples (2007) took about two decades. It may thus be expected that preparatory work for this new declaration may take considerable time, and be part of a global awareness raising process and shift in understanding of relations between human and non-human gender and nature. Morales has claimed that where the 20th century was the century of Human Rights, the 21st century will be the century of rights of nature.

This process with its origin in an indigenous colonized culture may turn out to demonstrate cultural and historical perceptions of and challenges to both gender and nature. Morales spoke on this proposal at COP15 in Copenhagen in December 2009.

Indigenous peoples have always been dependent upon and thus concerned with their environment. In the year 2000 The UN set up a special forum called the Permanent Forum of Indigenous Issues (PFII). This is an advisory body to the Economic and Social Council, with a mandate to discuss indigenous issues related to economic and social development, culture, the environment, education, health and human rights. This is a challenge to the international legal culture, which has until very recently primarily been state oriented and state dominated.

The PFII has been concerned about climate change since it was established. In 2004 a report called *Impacts of a Warming Arctic* was released. The *Arctic Climate Impact Assessment* (ACIA) was probably the first major study to describe the ongoing climate change in the Arctic and its consequences: rising temperatures, loss of sea ice, unprecedented melting of the Greenlandic ice sheet, and many impacts on ecosystems, animals, and people. This project was guided by the intergovernmental Arctic Council and the non-governmental International Arctic Science Committee.[32]

In March 2008 the female Chairperson of PFII, Victoria Tauli-Corpuz from the Phillipines and Aqqaluk Lynge from Greenland submitted a report

31. This part of the paper was originally presented in another version at a Workshop on GENDER, POWER AND CLIMATE CHANGE at the University of Lund, March 18-19, 2010.
32. The report can be downloaded from this website http://www.acia.uaf.edu/ (last accessed October 15, 2011).

to the UN ECO-SOC entitled *"Impact of Climate Change Mitigation Measures on Indigenous Peoples and on Their Territories and Lands"* for the 7th Session to take place in New York from April 21 – 2 May 2008.[33]

In 2006 Evo Morales had become what has been said to be the first fully indigenous person to be elected president of Bolivia, and in December 2009 his presidency was renewed with a backing of 63% of votes. This gives an indigenous representative a voice in the community of *states* constituted by the UN, something which is a further challenge to the 'monopoly' representation of hegemonic Western masculinity in the state and state fora.[34]

In a publication from 2008 (published by the Ministry of Foreign Affairs and Cults of Bolivia) entitled *"The 10 Commandments to save the planet, humankind and life"* Morales describes the aspirations of 'the indigenous people of the planet'

> "We, the indigenous people of the planet, have felt and always practiced great respect to Mother Earth. For us, Mother Earth is Life itself, and for that reason we have lived during thousands and thousands of years in harmony with nature.
>
> Today our Mother Earth is seriously ill. Planet Earth has fever. We have never seen before how snow-capped peaks and glaciers disappear. We have never seen before how thousands of animal species and plants disappear. We have never witnessed before so many social and environmental disasters, each time much stronger and more frequent.
>
> We are in a moment of history in which we must make decisions, before nature makes them for us. If the temperature of the planet continues rising and we don't do something about it, the impact of climate change may have fatal consequences for the planet, humankind and life.
>
> We don't have much time. We must act quickly. This millennium that has just begun must be the Millennium of Life, the Millenium of Hope, the Millennium of Harmony between human beings and nature.
>
> For that reason I propose these 10 commandments to save the planet, humankind and life."[35]

These 'commandments' are in abbreviated form:

33. Impact of Climate Change Mitigation Measures on Indigenous Peoples and on Their Territories and Lands, UN E/C.19/2008/1, March 19, 2008 http://daccess-dds-ny.un.org/doc/UNDOC/GEN/N08/277/65/PDF/N0827765.pdf?OpenElement (last accessed Oct. 10, 2011).
34. See R. W. Connell, Masculiniites Polity Press, 2010 (2nd edition, 5th reprint) for a discussion of the history, forms and dynamics of masculinity and for a discussion on the concept of 'hegemonic masculinity'.
35. Evo Morales Ayma (2008): The 10 commandments to save the planet, humankind and life. First edition, Ministry of Foreing Affairs and Cults, Printed in Bolivia (24 pages).

1. To end with Capitalism
2. Renounce war
3. A world without imperialism or colonialism
4. Water as a right for all living beings
5. Clean and environmentally friendly sources of energy
6. Respect for Mother Earth
7. Basic services as a human right
8. Consume just what is necessary and prioritize the consumption of local production
9. Respect for cultural and economic diversity
10. To live well

When on April 22, 2009 President Evo Morales Ayma suggested to begin the work for a *Universal Declaration of the Rights of Mother Earth*, he described it as containing four important rights.

1. The right to life. What does it mean for planet Earth to have the right to exist?
2. The Earth's right to regenerate its bio-capacity.
3. The right to a clean life.
4. The right to harmony and balance of all, between all and for all.[36]

The work for this declaration continues both on state levels, on UN level, and on the level of what could be called global civil society. The Secretariat of the UN Permanent Forum on Indigenous Issues was informed by the Permanent Mission of Bolivia to the United Nations that the Peoples' World Conference on Climate Change and the Rights of Mother Earth was to be held from 20 to 22 April 2010 in the city of Cochabamba, Bolivia. This event was attended by 30.000 people from about 100 countries.[37]

At a side-event at COP15 in Copenhagen in December 2009, Bolivian ambassador Pablo Solon and South African environmental lawyer and author of a book on "Wild Law", Cormac Cullinan presented the Bolivian policy using the analogy of slavery and criticizing the fact that Earth herself is treated

36. Message of the President of the Plurinational State of Bolivia Evo Morales Ayma in the United Nations General Assembly who declared April 22 to be International Day of Mother Earth: Towards a Universal Declaration of the Mother Earth Rights, New York April 22, 2009 (4 pages).
37. http://en.wikipedia.org/wiki/World_People's_Conference_on_Climate_Change (last accessed October 10, 2011).

as property. In a 'statement' in Huffington Post on December 29 2009, they elaborated further on this together in the light of the passing of a UN General Assembly resolution on December 22, 2009 which put the issue of Mother Earth rights as an item on the UN agenda.

> "So what would rights for nature look like? One of the most important implications is that it would enable legal systems to maintain vital ecological balances by balancing human rights against the rights of other members of the Earth community. Presently many environmentally harmful human activities (including those that cause climate change) are completely lawful. Most legal systems define everything that is not a human being or a corporation, as property. Just as slave laws, which turned humans into property, entrenched an exploitative relationship between the two, our legal systems have entrenched an exploitative and inherently damaging relationship between ourselves and Earth. Even most environmental laws do little more than regulate the rate at which environmental destruction may take place." [38]

The conflict between protection of the environment and the earth and (modern) values of equality and development are common to the indigenous cultures of the world. On August 15, 2011 representatives of three indigenous groups and their supporters began a 375-mile trek from Trinidad in the Bolivian lowlands to the highland capital of La Paz, to protest the government's plan to build a highway through their ancestral homeland known as the TIPNIS. The march demonstrates the increasingly conflictive relationship between Morales and the social movements that brought him to power. End of September, 2011 Pablo Solon criticized "President and Brother Evo Morales" in a statement called "There must be coherence between what we do and what we say."

> "Since 2006, Bolivia has shown leadership to the world on how to tackle the most profound challenges of our time. We have achieved the approval of the Human Right to Water and Sanitation in the United Nations and promoted a vision for society based on Vivir Bien (Living Well) rather than consuming more. However there must be coherence between what we do and what we say. One cannot speak of defending Mother Earth and at the same time promote the construction of a road that will harm Mother Earth, doesn't respect indigenous rights and violates human rights in an "unforgiveable" way."[39]

38. Pablo Solon and Cormac Cullinan: We must support a Universal Declaration of the Rights of Mother Earth http://www.huffingtonpost.com/pablo-erick-solon-romero-oroza/why-even-a-successful-agr_b_406547.html (posted December 29, 2009 – last accessed Oct. 10, 2011).
39. Pablo Solon, http://pwccc.wordpress.com/ (last accessed Oct. 10,.2011).

This statement demonstrates both value conflicts and meeting between different normative cultures – but also developments of cultures of diplomacy of importance for other players in world society.

4. Nordic women's law and action – combining equality and sustainability?

Nordic women's law has generally been focusing strongly on issues of gender equality for decades[40] and less on issues of sustainability.[41] But Nordic political cultures and Nordic female politicians have played and still play an influential role in relation to issues of sustainability.

From 1980-1996 Vigdis Finnbogadottir was Iceland's first female president and head of state, and one of the world's first elected female heads of state. She is now involved with UNESCO, and is described on the organization's homepage as follows:

"She has actively participated in the UNESCO Panel on Information and Communication and she presides over UNESCO's World Commission on the Ethics of Scientific Knowledge and Technology. H.E. Vigdís Finnbogadóttir works to bring countries together in all domains, especially concerning women's rights, ecology and education, and has always made every effort to spread these values among the young."[42]

During the 1980s Gro Harlem Brundtland's name became known through the Brundtland Commission and its 1987 report on Sustainable Development, Our Common Future. The commission coined an often-quoted definition of

40. See for instance Eva Maria Svensson, Any Pylkkänen, Johanna Niemi-Kiesiläinen (eds), *Nordic Equality at a Crossroads, Feminist Legal Studies Coping with Difference*, Ashgate 2003.
41. In the research project on polycentric law and pluralistic values in the early 90s (led by Henrik Zahle, Kirsten Ketscher and myself) we published a special issue of *RETFÆRD* on" Law and Ecology" (1994). Related to the research project I wrote an article "Bæredygtighed, børn og badevand. Feministiske og økologiske perspektiver på retlig tænkning" in *RETFÆRD* no. 60/1993 P.15-30. After Henrik Zahle's death in 2006, I published another article, Gender and Environmental Law and Justice: Thoughts on Sustainable Masculinities. In Jonas Ebbeson & Phoebe N. Okowa (eds): Environmental Law and Justice in Context, Cambridge University Press 2009, 98-113. Minna Gillberg's dissertation from 1999 *From Green Image to Green Practice. Normative action and selfregulation.* Lund: Lund University Press deals with environmental issues but hardly with gender issues.
42. http://portal.unesco.org/en/ev.php-URL_ID=8297&URL_DO=DO_TOPIC&URL_-SECTION=201.html (last accessed Oct. 10, 2011).

sustainable development as development that "meets the needs of the present without compromising the ability of *future generations* to meet their own needs." (italics here). In 1998 Brundtland became Director General of the WHO. In 2007 UN Secretary General Ban Ki-moon appointed her as Special Envoy on Climate Change.

From 1999-2004 the Swedish Social Democratic politician, Margot Wahlström was Environment Commissioner in the European Union. She had earlier been Minister for Consumer Affairs, Women and Youth in 1988–1991, Minister for Culture in 1994–1996 and Minister for Social Affairs in 1996–1998 in the Swedish Government.

In November 2007 Connie Hedegaard became Danish minister of a newly established Ministry on Climate and Energy Affairs, Klima- og Energiministeriet. The background was described amongst others as the need to create a more sustainable society, and to secure that Denmark in the long run would become 100% independent of fossil fuel. Another reason was of course the need to strengthen the administrative support of Denmark's role as chair of COP15 in December 2009.

COP 15 was widely regarded as a failure, In my opinion, however, having had the opportunity to be an observer during the formal and informal events, the expectations and ideas of the media and political system in relation to the summit were strongly influenced by views dominated by a Euro-American-centric framework of legal positivism, which saw a full, final and binding legal instrument in the form of a treaty as the only measure for a 'real' success of the summit. There was little understanding of the value of – and the time requirements needed for – the unfolding of a global process of awareness change in relation to climate change, sustainable lifestyles and necessary self restrictions – not least among the affluent parts of the world's populations.

In December 2009 Connie Hedegaard was appointed EU Commissioner for Climate Action for the new EU Commission starting February 2010. Her successor, Lykke Friis, was elected in December 2009, and at a change of Danish government in February 2010, she was also given the area of Equality. For some this combination seems awkward, but the career paths of other national female leaders have often combined equality issues and other substantial issues – not least climate, as probably Brundtland's career demonstrates most clearly. After the 2011 elections Denmark got a male minister of climate, another male minister of church affairs and equality – the first 'non-ethnic' Dane to become a minister, and a young female minister; Ida Auken (from the Socialist People's Party and a niece of Svend Auken) as minister of the environment.

5. Cultural metamorphoses – a new agenda?

The Myth of the Sea Mother from the Arctic is a story about metamorphosis of humans and animals, about relations between humans and animals – as relations of both love and dependence, and about violent sacrifice of humans to nature for the purpose of both peaceful conditions and survival. Sacrifice from latin *sacri-ficare* means to make holy. The woman in the story, who has married an animal with supernatural force, is sacrificed – made holy – in order to establish a proper relationship with nature – mediated through shamanic visits. In the contemporary versions of the myth this is understood as a need for respect for nature. If humans do not treat (marine and other) animals well and pollute their living conditions, then the Sea Mother will withhold the animals until practices have changed. – This is a message very similar to the attempts to protect Mother Earth originating amongst the indigenous peoples of Latin America.

Colonial powers have always considered themselves superior to the 'primitive' indigenous cultures of the world – be they Inuit, Sami or Indians from Latin America. We may however now enter a period, where there is more willingness to listen to these other voices, and to learn from these other normative cultures also in the formerly dominant Euro-American legal cultures, to which the Nordic legal cultures belong.

Not least the growing influence of Asian normative cultures can be expected to educate Western (legal) cultures about different views of both relations between gender and species in this century. Buddhists and Hindus have a very different view of animals than the Western view, and Chinese understandings of the relations between male and female gender do not necessarily see them as dichotomous as Western legal culture has traditionally done.

Chinese (American) (legal) philosopher Tu Wei Ming, who is regarded as a neo-Confucian mentioned Western anthropocentrism in passing in a key note address at a global conference of the IVR (the International Association for Legal Philosophy) held in Beijing in 2009:

"The Enlightenment mentality, **anthropocentrism to the core**, *is rooted in secularity. Indeed, the secular age was a tremendously complex phenomenon... Nevertheless, authentic possibilities to move beyond the secular age are visible throughout the world. Unlike the "Age of Reason" when religion was marginalized, a salient feature of the 21st century is*

the prominence of religion in all spheres of interest including economics and politics... the "spiritual turn" takes the sacredness of the earth as a prerequisite."[43]

Marina Warner, professor of literature at the University at Essex, writes in her book entitled *Fantastic Metamorphoses, Other Worlds*: *Ways of Telling the Self* that "(w)ithin the Judaeo-Christian tradition, metamorphosis has marked out heterodoxy, instability, perversity, unseemliness, monstrosity."[44] She describes different forms of metamorphosis or shape-shifting, known to Western culture for at least two thousand years amongst others from Ovid's famous book *Metamorphosis*. The forms she describes are *mutating, hatching, splitting*, and *doubling*.

I came across her book when looking for reflections on other examples of human-animal relations, where of course Greek mythology is important. The many stories of Zeus who transforms himself into an animal in order to seduce goddesses or mortal women abound. One of them is the story about Leda and the Swan.[45] The most usual account according to Robert Graves is "that it was Leda herself with whom Zeus companied in the form of a swan beside the river Eurotas; that she laid an egg from which were hatched Helen, Castor and Polyceuces; and that she was consequently deified as the goddess Nemesis."[46] Nemesis was a goddess of divine retribution against those who showed arrogance before the gods.

According to Graves these stories about shape shifting are also related to general societal changes:

"Nemesis was the Moon-goddess as Nymph and, in the earliest form of the love-chase myth, she pursued the sacred king through his seasonal changes of hare, fish, bee, and mouse – or hare, fish, bird, and grain of wheat – and finally devoured him. With the victory of the patriarchal system, the chase was reversed: the goddess now fled from Zeus..."[47]

We may experience several of these forms of shape shifting due to global changes of gender orders. I think one might claim that over the last decades

43. Tu Weiming, *Cultural Diversity, Intercivilizational Dialogue, and Harmony – A Confucian Perspective*. Key note lecture at the XXIV World Congress on Philosophy of Law and Social Philosophy, Beijing China, September 2009 (Also printed in the proceedings of the IVR conference p.39) (emphasis added here).
44. Marina Warner, *Fantastic Metamorphoses, Other Worlds*, Oxford University Press, 2002, p. 35.
45. Thanks to Andreas Philippopoulos-Mihalopoulos for suggesting to me to look into the myth of Leda and the Swan.
46. Robert Graves, *Greek Myths,* Cassell & Company Ltdd., London 1958, p. 206.
47. Robert Graves, *Greek Myths,* Cassell & Company Ltdd., London 1958, p. 207.

very many women in the world have undertaken 'mutations' and have come to display a more 'masculine' femininity. This has caused anxiety but is perhaps less difficult to accept today. Maybe we will also see a number of changes of male 'gender display'[48] in the future in the form of mutations, splittings and doublings. Marina Warner claims that she intimated that;

> *"... tales of metamorphosis often arose in spaces (temporal, geographical, and mental) that were cross-roads, cross-cultural zones, points of interchange on the intricate connective tissue of communication between cultures. It is no accident that fairy tales were first written down, for example, all round the edge of the Mediterranean, in Egypt and in the great ports of Venice and Naples...it is characteristic of metamorphic writing to appear in transitional places and at the confluence of traditions and civilizations."*[49]

We do today live in a period which is in general characterized by global cultural encounters including encounters between 'male' and 'female' as well as human and non-human mental spheres – encounters which may and do cause a metamorphosis in the ways humans present themselves to others and understand themselves in relation to their surroundings. No doubt such encounters are also a challenge to individuals, collectives and cultures, including legal and normative cultures. Most likely such encounters may also lead to the "hatching" of new agendas and new understandings of future relations of complexity.[50]

6. Gender confusion and interspecies relations

There is probably no doubt that the changing gender order has been causing a lot of anxiety not least in the Western world, including in the Nordic countries. It is my hunch that the Islamophobia we have experienced over the last decade has been closely linked to a 'moral panic' about the gender order – both Muslim women and Western (secularized/Christian) women have been a

48. See the interesting analyses on gender display by Canadian sociologist Erving Goffman in his book *Gender Advertisements*. New York:Harper Colophon Books, 1976.
49. Marina Warner, *Fantastic Metamorphoses, Other Worlds*, 2002, p.17 & 18.
50. In a recent essay in the Danish newspaper Information, the Norwegian author Jan Kjærstad describes how he is longing for a ,novel machinery' driven by a new form of energy, an ,alternative causality', which he to a certain extent has found in the novels by Japanese author, Haruki Murakami. According to Kjærstad it is now relevant to speak of a 'need for a polytheistic novel, a fiction, where more gods, more cosmologies meet." Jan Kjærstad, Når virkeligheden skifter form, *Information*, 29.09.2011.

focus of many of these discussions. But changing roles of women also lead to changing roles and representations of masculinity. These changes of masculinity are often perceived as threatening.

Swiss-German masculinity researcher, Walter Hollstein is an example of the unease following gender metamorphosis. He writes with a certain disgust about the 'gender mutation' of one of the most prolific researchers in masculinity studies, the Australian professor of sociology. R.W. Connell:

'The most macabre example of the development of male self-denial is Robert Connell, sociologist, the most recognized masculinity researcher of our time, expert of the UN and author of basic books on masculinity. Connell has recently mutated into a woman and carries the female first name, Raewyn."[51].

Another gender mutated lawyer, Andrew now Alex Sharpe, quotes Derrida in his/her recent book on *Foucault's Monsters and the Challenges of Law*. Here Derrida also discusses 'the problem of animal/human hybrids.'

"The future is necessarily monstrous: the figure of the future, that is, that which can only be surprising, that for which we are not prepared... is heralded by species of monsters. A future that would not be monstrous would not be a future; it would already be a predictable, calculable, and programmable tomorrow."[52]

In a recent Nordic context it is obvious that the Norwegian mass murderer Anders Breivik is understood as a combination of a monster and a beast – the 'lone wolf' terrorist. An interesting analysis of his background was presented very shortly after the massacre by Mattias Gardell, a Swedish professor of comparative religion at Uppsala University.[53]

Gardell writes that Breivik was affected by four distinct influences: "contemporary Islamophobic ideologies, cultural conservative/neo-Confederate traditions, elements of modern White Power thinking, and anti-feminist thought".

51. Walter Hollstein, "Was vom Manne übrig bleibt – Das Problem der männlichen Identität", in www.streitbar.eu *Forum für unabhängiges Denken*, my translation, last visited 14072011
52. Quoted from Andrew N. Sharpe, *Foucault's Monsters and the Challenges of Law*, Routledge 2010, p.12
53. Mattias Gardell, The roots of Breivik's ideology: where does the romantic male warrior ideal come from today? www.opendemocracynet, 1 August 2011 (last accessed 20092011)

"Feminism, as a movement for equality and emancipation, infuriated Breivik greatly. Citing standardized cultural conservative notions, Breivik decries feminism as an ideology contrary to nature that has undermined family values and contributed to Western decadence. Born in 1979, Breivik nostalgically envisions an imaginary world of the 1950s, when men were men, women were housewives, children were well behaved, and when there were neither criminality nor Muslims in our countries.

Feminists favour multiculturalism, care for refugees, and have feminized Western men who thus have lost their ability to fight. This facilitates the Muslim effort to Islamize Europe, which Breivik like conservative authors Phyllis Chesler and Melanie Phillips believes will lead to a real (rather than imaginary) female subordination. This opens the door to the male warrior-hero's entrance...

As a white, Christian, heterosexual man from an upper middleclass family, Breivik believes that he has certain birth right privileges that are now threatened by all sorts of minorities, delusions of social equality, and the general decay of Western culture that has opened the gates of Europe to the troops of its alleged arch-enemy, Islam. Much like the radical conservative philosophers Julius Evola and the young Ernst Jünger, Breivik is convinced that Western decay can only be cured by cleansing violence."

Maybe the insecurity felt in Western culture (and beyond) created by a changed gender order may even increase in the years to come due to challenges from a combined and changed gender and species order.

The controversial novel from 1996 by Danish author, Peter Høeg, *Kvinden og aben – The Woman and the Ape* (translated 1996) describes the frustrations of a beautiful white woman, Madeleine, and her love relationship to the sympathetic ape, Erasmus. Her husband, Adam Burden, is shocked when he learns of the nature of her infidelity:

"In Adam's fantasies... Madeleine's lovers had been members of the royal family or god like figures – her infidelity had been upwardly mobile thus acting as an indirect social legup for himself."[54]

As a (hu)man being challenged by somebody not only considered below his own status but even below 'human' status is seen as a contempt, disrespect and scorn of himself and his perception of his own status as elevated.

In his book *So You Think You're Human* from 2004, the Spanish-British historian, Felipe Fernandez-Armesto, claims that "*(t)he longest-debated frontier of human identity is that between humans and other animals.*" He further claims that we are at present experiencing a paradox, which I think is also present in the indigenous myth about relations between humans and animals

54. Peter Høeg, *The Woman and the Ape*. Panther, The Harvill Press, London, 1996, p.116.

and which is expressed in the quotation with which I started this article, and which I repeat here:

> *"Over the last thirty or forty years, we have invested an enormous amount of thought, emotion, treasure, and blood in what we call human values, human rights, the defence of human dignity and of human life. Over the same period, quietly but devastatingly, science and philosophy have combined to undermine our traditional concept of humankind. In consequence, the coherence of our understanding of what it means to be human is now in peril."*

But paradox has to be accepted not resolved, writes Donald Winnicott (1896-1971), a famous British child psychiatrist.[55]

It is almost forty years ago since Christopher Stone in 1972 published his seminal book with the title question: *Should Trees Have Legal Standing? Toward Legal Rights for Natural Objects*. Today it seems that the answer to the question is increasingly affirmative. Subjects of rights are not only human or human constructions. They may be other sentient beings and other sacred beings protected by state norms, non state norms and/or 'religious-style' commandments – among others.

During the last decade Western secular academia has had to accept that God is not dead, and that there may even be more gods and goddesses in the contemporary world. Indigenous peoples did not die out with modernity, and religion was not abandoned. Mother Earth is back and we may be forced to relearn how to interact with her.

"This crisis demands that the elites of the world "adapt" to the idea that we have to change and that we cannot continue building models based on extraction and market profits... Those of us who have worked for many years with the topics of human rights, economic justice, the right to water, commerce and culture are sure that an integral focus should take on the rules of finance and marketing as well as those of culture that lies within our daily life," writes Bolivian social psychologist, researcher and activist on gender, ethnicity, water and human rights, Elizabeth Peredo Beltran.[56]

55. Donald W. Winnicott, Some Thought on the Meaning of the Word 'Democracy'. In Winnicott, *Home is Where We Come From. Essays by a Psychoanalyst.* Penguin Books. 1986.
56. Elizabeth Peredo Beltran: The Climate Crisis. A Challenge for the Human Condition and for an Ethic of Nature. http://motherearthrights.org/2009/12/20/the-climate-crisis-a-challenge-for-the-human-condition-and-for-an-ethics-of-nature/ (last accessed Oct. 10, 2011).

Very many Nordic women belong to the elites of the world. We live in times of cultural encounters, which seem to produce monsters, metamorphoses, and new relations. This is not the first time in history. The Nordic countries are in no way unique in this respect. And we are fortunate to have access to normative cultures and normative heritage which might be of inspiration, and which may open up for other ways of understanding a future monstrous world. Hopefully these coexisting normative cultures may help us to find ways towards our common futures – beyond gender and species hierarchies and accepting the paradoxes that follow from these transformations and mutations.

CHAPTER 5

Gender mainstreaming from a Danish and international perspective

By Agnete Andersen, Head of Secretariat, The Danish Ministry of Employment

1. Introduction

Gender mainstreaming, as a new concept, appeared for the first time in international texts after the United Nations Third World Conference on Women (Nairobi, 1985), in relation to the debate within the UN Commission on the Status of Women (CSW) on the role of women in development. It was seen as a means of promoting the role of women in the field of development and of integrating women's values into development work. Actually, it has developed out of necessity:

> "A governmental commitment to implement the ideas of the Nairobi Forward Looking Strategies for the Advancement of Women had as a precondition that the UN organisations dealt with these strategies in their ordinary work."

Gender mainstreaming was introduced as a gender equality tool in consequence of the fact that it is not possible to promote gender equality within all walks of life without participation from the persons who are responsible for a certain area. It implies that both women and men are to be included.

The involvement of governments needed a push forward in order to incorporate the ideas from the World Conference on Women. For the first time the UN got a plan of action on gender equality adopted unanimously by all states in the UN. It was called the Forward Looking Strategies.

At the United Nations Fourth World Conference on Women (Beijing, 1995), the strategy of gender mainstreaming was explicitly endorsed by the Platform for Action which was adopted at the end of the Conference.

The Platform for Action calls for the promotion of the policy of gender mainstreaming:

> "Governments and other actors should promote an active and visible policy of mainstreaming a gender perspective in all policies and programmes, so that, before decisions are taken, an analysis is made of the effects on women and men, respectively."

Even though it does not give any guidelines on how to develop and implement this policy, many countries have adopted a national plan for gender mainstreaming as a result of the Platform for Action.

In the EU gender mainstreaming has become part of the obligation to promote gender equality, and therefore the recast gender equality directive in matters of employment and occupation[1] has a provision on gender mainstreaming in Art. 29 in the recast directive which explicitly prescribes that public authorities have competence and a duty to mainstream gender when implementing laws, regulations, administrative provisions, policies and activities within the scope of the directive.

In the last 20 years rules have been introduced in many countries, in Denmark mainly the Gender Equality Act section 4, the Equal Treatment Act section 1 a, the Equal Pay Act section 1 b.

2. What is gender equality?

2.1. Definition of gender equality

The report on gender mainstreaming[2] from the Council of Europe begins with a definition of gender equality in recognition of the fact that gender mainstreaming is only meaningful if the concept of gender equality is defined:

> "Gender equality means an equal visibility, empowerment and participation of both sexes in all spheres of public and private life. Gender equality is the opposite of gender inequality, not of gender difference, and aims to promote the full participation of women and men in society."

1. 2006/54/EF.
2. Gender Mainstreaming. Conceptual framework, methodology and presentation of good practices, Strasbourg, May 1998, www.coe.int/T/E/Human_Rights/ Equality/02._Gender_mainstreaming/.

The prohibition against gender discrimination is a fundamental right and a decisive prerequisite to achieve gender equality. Gender equality is a broader concept than prohibition against gender discrimination because the goal for gender equality also includes structural and systemic changes.

2.1. Discussions on gender equality policy – what are the goals for gender equality policy?

Most people accept the definition of gender equality from the Council of Europe, but it is more difficult to agree on the means best suitable to promote gender equality. Everybody accepts the prohibition against gender discrimination which is legally anchored in conventions, directives and legislation as a necessary, but not sufficient tool to promote gender equality.

But it is a problem, that the work to promote gender equality is mixed up with gender mainstreaming with the result that non-experts cannot separate the two concepts. Gender mainstreaming is a tool to achieve gender equality. A meaningful use of gender mainstreaming implies of course that the goals for gender equality policy are clearly defined.

The work on gender mainstreaming is as already mentioned only meaningful if there exists a clear picture of the desirable political goals. Gender impact assessments give a picture of the facts, but the content of the initiatives to promote gender equality must be determined politically.

When a gender impact assessment of a concrete political initiative is carried out to examine the situation of women and men in relation to a proposal it is not decided what kind of gender equality is desired. Clarity is required about the gender equality policy at a concrete level.

The Danish debate on gender equality has two trends demanding the use of different means to achieve gender equality:

Protection – The starting point for this approach is that protection is the way to gender equality – the tools are legislation with demands on companies and other actors. The EU approach has to a great extent been the protection of women i.e. by prohibition against women's night work extensive maternity protection in connection with confinement. A big number of gender equality directives testify to that. The prohibition against gender discrimination has been in the centre, but also the demands on companies and other actors whose work has implications for the living conditions of women and men have called upon the interest of the EU Commission and the EU Parliament. The insurance business is one of the new areas which recently have been regulated.

Freedom – The prohibition against gender discrimination is recognised. The tools are preparation of attitudes and equal opportunities. The view is that gender equality is achieved as time goes on without doing much. Everybody must take responsibility for their position in the family, on the labour market and in society. You decide for yourself.

In Denmark the Socialdemocrats, the Socialist People's Party, the Social Liberals and the Unity List are more protection-oriented than the Liberal Party and the Conservatives.

It is commonly agreed that some protection is needed i.e. in connection to maternity. The disagreement occurs when the size of the protection is to be decided. At the same time it is commonly agreed that protection alone does not create gender equality. The individual's involvement and effort in order to create both structural and personal changes is necessary.

It is difficult to decide where to strike the balance, and one wing accuses the other wing of not to wanting gender equality, and the other wing thinks one wing wants to regulate too much.

Nordic gender equality policy supported by all the political parties has always stressed that women are to participate in the political decision making process, Therefore, the female percentage in Nordic Parliaments has been higher than in other countries from a very early stage. The idea is that it is necessary to be where decisions are made and in that way get influence on own living conditions. It gives opportunities to strike a balance between compensating initiatives (protection) or assistance to help oneself (freedom).

What is the role of gender mainstreaming in this landscape, and what is the legal perspective? Gender impact assessments are a good tool to understand women's and men's situation in society, but when the analyses of gender are available, decisions are to be taken if and to what extent tools to promote gender equality are to be used. These tools may be new legislation or change of administrative routines which demand further scrutiny in relation to the goal of gender equality policy. What is the impact of if the changes? Do the initiatives change the living conditions of men and women?

3. What is gender mainstreaming?

In 1998 the Council of Europe presented the first well worked-out definition of gender mainstreaming which still gives the best idea of what is to be achieved with gender mainstreaming:

> "Gender mainstreaming is the (re)organisation, improvement, development and evaluation of policy processes, so that a gender equality perspective is incorporated in all policies at all levels and at all stages, by the actors normally involved in policy-making."

The definition of gender mainstreaming highlights the goal of mainstreaming, the process, the objects and active subjects of mainstreaming. The objects of mainstreaming are all policies at all levels and at all stages, while the active subjects of mainstreaming are the ordinary actors. Gender mainstreaming can mean that the policy process is reorganised so that ordinary actors know how to incorporate a gender perspective. It can also mean that gender expertise is organised into the policy process by including gender expertise as a normal requirement for policy-makers.

This definition also highlights the way in which gender mainstreaming intercepts the shortcomings of specific gender equality policy. Gender mainstreaming means that gender equality is part of common policies. Gender mainstreaming implies a broader and more comprehensive definition of gender equality, giving value to differences and diversity.

In stressing the need to (re)organise, improve, develop and evaluate policy processes, gender mainstreaming makes it possible to challenge the male bias that characterises society and the structural character of gender inequality.

Mainstreaming also gets gender equality issues out of the isolation of gender equality machineries and involves more and new actors in building a balanced society. In doing so, the process of transforming gender relations in the direction of gender equality can be accelerated and strengthened.

There is little consensus about a definition of gender mainstreaming (most of the definitions speak about integrating a gender equality perspective) or on how to mainstream the gender equality perspective in practice and what this implies. All definitions focus on the broad goal of obtaining gender equality. Although the word gender equality is not necessarily mentioned, it is referred to in at least an implicit way. Equally, all definitions focus on what will be brought into the mainstream, namely a gender equality perspective or women's perspectives.

Many definitions merely describe the strategy itself, often reducing the definition to partial aspects of gender mainstreaming: they focus on the full participation of women in decision-making or on a tool, such as the screening of policy proposals from a gender perspective. In this case the definition and the goal become one and the same, gender mainstreaming is becoming the goal, it is seen as an end in itself.

Some definitions focus on the effects of gender mainstreaming and what it will lead to in the functioning and structuring of society. These definitions underline the (need for) shifts in organisational cultures and the way of working of institutions or new ways of thinking and approaching policies. These definitions are mainly found in the area of development.

3.1. Prerequisites for gender mainstreaming to be used

A necessary prerequisite to finding out how gender mainstreaming should be practiced is to carry out a gender impact assessment.

A gender impact assessment makes it possible to screen a given policy proposal to identify and assess the various impacts and effects on women and men, so that imbalances can be removed before a proposal is approved. An analysis from a gender perspective contributes to clarifying if women's and men's needs are met equitably in such a proposal.

A gender impact assessment is based on gender-segregated data within the study area.

A gender impact assessment may influence legislation, policy formulation, budgets, research, administration, and other implementation.

Seen in this broad perspective, the gender mainstreaming strategy is important in all cases where the target groups for action are to be identified. This means that any initiative that affects persons should be analysed by gender. It is quite natural that gender has a special significance as long as women's and men's living conditions are so different.

Gender has generally been discussed particularly in relation to development policies and the development of democracy. On the whole gender mainstreaming implies that the data are analysed in depth, so reactions to the effort can be predicted, politically, culturally, socially and economically.

Gender mainstreaming is to integrate gender issues into the core tasks – in employment policy, transport planning, food information, the bill in the social field, etc. Gender mainstreaming is about people and not organisational matters even if it sometimes is necessary to influence structures.

To the extent the traditional players neglect identifying their audiences, the need for gender mainstreaming strategy increases. It is not sufficient to specify in general what is needed to accomplish with the initiative. One can almost say that gender mainstreaming becomes a kind of litmus test to see if the administration or the handling of customers meets the quality standards set up.

4. Gender mainstreaming as a tool

4.1. What can gender mainstreaming be used for

Gender mainstreaming started as a multidisciplinary instrument that is legally anchored in the Equality Directives, the Act on Gender Equality, the Equal Treatment Act and the Equal Pay Act. It is a legal political issue if gender mainstreaming should be a powerful instrument that is sanctioned and enforceable.

Gender mainstreaming work is carried out from pre-formulated general policies which focus on a gender perspective, and in addition, defines the gender policy goals. The production of gender-segregated data is needed to understand who is going to be affected by specific initiatives, and therefore gender-segregated data are a crucial starting point for gender mainstreaming work. The commitment to gender mainstreaming involves knowledge of gender, and understanding of what it takes to accommodate both genders.

Gender mainstreaming contributes to creating better understanding of the characteristics of the two sexes and in this way provide new knowledge about the target groups covered by concrete action. The two sexes' different living conditions are important for their needs for and attitudes to both tangible goods and public services.

Gender mainstreaming ensures that the target groups are well defined when there is a wish to create change. People are never neuter; one must understand each group's background, situation and needs. Understanding the gender perspective is to create a better understanding of the purpose of this work.

Gender mainstreaming is used to assess how the two sexes are affected by general policies and services. At the same time they affect the demand and supply on the market in the broadest sense, not least in relation to labour market, and it leads to different positions in society.

Lack of knowledge about the importance of gender may indicate that political objectives are not achieved due to ignorance about the behavior of the persons concerned. The collection of gender-segregated data is important tools to determine who the persons concerned are. This is true both for clarification of indirect discrimination and for understanding gender mainstreaming. Knowledge about gender must be present in relation to both.

The implementation of the Act on Gender Equality implies that gender mainstreaming is institutionalised in the Department for Gender Equality. And it is done within an inter-ministerial gender mainstreaming project, with a steering group at manager level and a contact group at staff level. In collaboration with all ministries the Department for Gender Equality prepares action plans for the inter-ministerial gender mainstreaming work which all ministries are required to participate in.

Campaigns, budgets, bills or other initiatives are generally gender-neutral in their approach. It is widely known that there is a ban on gender discrimination because of sex in most walks of society. On the labour market the prohibition has been in force since 1978, and the prohibition is sanctioned.

Apparently, gender-neutral policies and decisions may have adverse consequences for equality between women and men. Not least the structural conditions on the labour market are invoked as justification for not promoting gender equality in the present situation.

If one sex is exposed to harmful effects, because action is based on the conditions for the other sex, it must be examined to what extent the damage may result in sanctions. Gender mainstreaming must be seen in a legal perspective similar to what is known from direct and indirect discrimination.

Below is presented where gender mainstreaming has been used in Denmark, particularly in the Department for Gender Equality's inter-ministerial gender mainstreaming project.

Equality Assessment of bills is an assessment of whether a bill may have different consequences for the female and the male population and an assessment of what this means for gender equality. This type of impact assessment may also be used in regulations or guidelines.

When bills are gender mainstreamed it is examined at which population group the bill is targeted. Data and statistics illustrate how the distribution of women and men, girls and boys looks in this group, and positive and negative effects of the bill are examined for these groups of people.

It is relevant to subject many bills to a gender impact assessment. Basically, the legislation is gender neutral. However, it is not the same as saying that the effect of a law may not have greater significance for one gender than for the other. Therefore, it is necessary to be aware of gender issues from the outset, and information on the consequences of the law should be included in the decision making process. Only thus is it possible to form a picture of how a bill will affect citizens.

All bills in the legislative programme must follow the steering committee's decision that they have to be tested in relation to gender equality. When bills are tested for gender relevance the ministries examine what bills in the legislative program must undergo a genuine equality assessment. The list of the bills to undergo a gender assessment is prepared by the Department for Gender Equality, and the list is published on the website of the Minister for Equality immediately after the Prime Minister publishes the total legislative programme.

Bills must be tested in particular to prevent unintended inequalities between women and men through otherwise gender neutral bills. Over time the procedure in several ministries is that a note on gender implications is prepared and presented to the Permanent Secretary, and the Permanent Secretary decides if a real equality assessment is to be carried out. The Ministry of Employment prepares a gender memo to all bills, and they are sent to Parliament when the bill is submitted.

In 2005 the Prime Minister's Office, the Ministry of Justice, the Ministry of Finance introduced a note on procedure for gender impact assessment of bills. The Steering Group at manager level has also developed a tool to analyse the relevance of each bill, and conduct a proper equality assessment.

Equality Assessment of the distribution of resources is an assessment of how financial resources are distributed between women and men, and the impact the distribution has on gender. There may be both planned and already implemented resource distributions.

The idea of equality evaluations of resource allocation is to create a higher degree of accuracy and quality in resource spending and in gender work, because it is mapped how resources are used and for whom. Adverse impacts on gender equality may be avoided at the same time as budgets may become a more accurate management tool.

The work to analyse budgets from a gender perspective may generally be done in two ways. First, one may adopt a gender angle when working with the budget; second one may bring the gender angle into play in an already approved budget.

4.2. Equality assessment of campaigns

Campaigns are a good topic in a gender mainstreaming effort, because the two sexes among other things have very different attitudes and are affected very differently by communication. Targeted communication is crucial for successful communication efforts. Therefore, the Department for Gender Equality points out in their recommendations that it is necessary to have a very careful and meticulous picture of the audience.

The communication method is crucial for reaching the target group. Women and men, girls and boys understand written texts or images differently. In the same way it must be considered which media are most appropriate to use. Knowledge must be available about how to communicate best with the target groups dependent on whether they are women or men, girls or boys in order to obtain the best result.

It should always be clarified whether a campaign has a general and universal topic. Very often it shows that women are not thought of. If the campaign however, is about sex and gender, men will not usually be thought of. In mainstream society the man is the norm, and therefore gender equality is only about women.

A communication campaign is often meant to change people's actions – for example by encouraging and guiding them to other ways of acting. Humans are women and men, girls and boys – and they are different. This means that in some situations, the effort has to be different. Both groups are encouraged to "eat healthy" or "not smoke": e.g. many women ought to eat more meat and men more fruit and vegetables to live healthier.

4.3. Gender-segregated data and statistics

It is a prerequisite in the process of gender mainstreaming to obtain knowledge, data and statistics on women's and men's conditions, needs and activities to avoid basing the work on stereotypes. The Ministry of Employment makes gender visible by publishing an annual report on men and women.

5. What is necessary if gender mainstreaming is to be used as part of operations

5.1. Development perspectives of the inter-ministerial gender mainstreaming project. A snapshot from 2011

Status after 10 years of work and 2 action plans is that the ministries have moved positively in formulating gender equality policy objectives and in relation to mainstreaming gender equality in personnel policy. But when it comes to incorporating gender in the ministries core functions in the agencies in charge, there are still major problems.

The Department for Gender Equality intends to give the whole gender mainstreaming project a communicative inspection. In addition, the Department for Gender Equality considers, how the future gender mainstreaming work should be organised and arranged when the actual action plan expires in 2011.

In May 2011the Department for Gender Equality held a camp where high-level executives and staff members from all ministries discussed gender mainstreaming a whole day. It was on this day quite clear that the department had not succeeded in selling the concept to the ministries, although the ministries and public authorities are under an obligation to comply, and it must be underlined that many ministries want to comply. Knowledge about gender mainstreaming is still limited and it is difficult for individual ministries to incorporate routines to ensure that gender mainstreaming is used when it is meaningful.

Here are some of the challenges that managers see in the work on gender mainstreaming:

- The word "gender mainstreaming" is in itself a significant barrier. It is very difficult to sell the concept/approach using a word people does not understand.
- There must be a "problem" – there must be an obvious reason for gender mainstreaming. Professionals / civil servants must be able to understand

what the problem is before they become motivated to finding a solution. It is not a good idea to mainstream gender, because you have to.
- As there is a need that gender mainstreaming is incorporated into all levels of an organisation's operations, there must be a sufficient grounding in an organisation. It must come both from below – from the individual employees who can see a definite need, and it must also come from above, from senior executive management. It should also be promoted at all other levels of management and it must be a priority in the task flow. It must be signaled that it is a priority both for the administrative and the political leadership.
- A better and more developed gender-segregated data base is a necessity in the core areas. (The tendency is that officials assume that there is not a gender-biased effect of their actions because they are designed in a gender-neutral form, but the assumption is not supported with relevant data)
- Gender mainstreaming should be integrated as early as possible in their policy decision-making. It may be too late / or not make sense to consider the gender implications when the political agreement is fixed and can not be changed. It is a problem that the gender equality aspect only is incorporated in many ministries when the agreement is concluded; the bill is drafted, etc.

Observations at the camp organised by the Department for Gender Equality illustrate perfectly why the problem with applying gender mainstreaming remains. More work must be done to create an understanding of the framework for gender mainstreaming work.

The main challenges for using gender mainstreaming as a method can be summarised as follows:

1. It is supplanted by other things that are perceived as more important
2. Fear of putting a foot wrong – mine-filled waters of political correctness
3. The very word 'mainstreaming' – what is that?
4. Lack of sanctions for lack of focus.
5. Hard to see how it makes the performance of assignment better. There must be a visible problem.
6. Lack of good examples of how to work in practice.
7. The Department for Gender Equality has no particular penetration.
8. Lack of real political support.
9. Gender mainstreaming should be used only where appropriate.
10. We are up against an ingrained culture of gender.
11. There are too many assumptions and too few statistics and facts.

12. The measurement of performance must improve – the effort must be documented.

The Department for Gender Equality was asked to provide the sufficient tools for moving forward. More specifically:

- It is necessary that the ministries experience that the Department for Gender Equality is able to provide them with the necessary assistance in their work with gender mainstreaming.
- Less 'counting'. More focus on what works in real life.
- Rolling action areas – where are the worst problems? This would allow more focused efforts.
- Gender mainstreaming is articulated as a goal in itself.
- Lack of focus on measurable value creation in the performance of tasks increases – "the power of habit".
- Associations to a period of the past ("women's liberation").

6. The Ministry of Employment

The Ministry has formulated a gender policy within its area. For the Ministry of Employment the goals are very clear:

- Disaggregate the gender-segregated labour market.
- Equal treatment.
- Reduce the pay differentials between women and men.
- Reconcile family life and working life.

Today, it is a generally accepted fact that there are differences between men and women. Men and women have different jobs, different education and different pay. Similarly, it is generally accepted that an effective employment policy is based on knowledge of the labour market and of the various groups of wage earners.

The role of the Government is to ensure that the legal framework within the equality policy and the labour market policy does not create obstacles to women and men's participation on the labour market. The overarching governmental objective is to promote occupational participation for everybody. When we look at the figures, it is clear that the effort has been successful.

The gender equality policy is seen as one of the means to achieve an efficient labour market policy.

Of course the legislation of the Ministry of Employment is gender neutral as it has been for nearly 30 years, and it is secured that all new legislation is gender neutral too. The legislation of the ministry of employment has to prevent gender discrimination on the labour market. Accordingly, an internal control has taken place for many years to make sure that the Ministry lives up to its goals.

The Ministry initiates special initiatives to reach the targets. All employees have the task to make sure that gender targets are met in the daily work with labour market policy initiatives.

6.1. Demands for data in the Ministry of Employment

The Ministry needs a profound knowledge about how gender equality influences the labour market. This knowledge is updated regularly for the benefit of the Ministry's work on gender equality on the labour market to ensure that the debate on gender equality takes place on an objective and informed basis. Every year the ministry publishes a report on Women and Men on the Labour Market which is seen as an important tool for the work on gender mainstreaming.

The units in the Ministry are responsible for establishing supplementary data within their own area, so they are able to deliver the analysis necessary for the bills in order to live up to the obligation of presenting supplementary memos on gender equality.

The data collection may therefore be divided from the following angles:

- Common surveillance – create consciousness on gender and its significance for a labour policy.
- Gender divided statistics to promote gender equality on equal pay, the gender segregated labour market and women in management.
- Gender divided statistics in all units in order to monitor their key services for the benefit of gender assessment of bills and identification of needs for gender mainstreaming of key services

6.2. Gender assessment of bills in the Ministry of Employment

Since 1995 all bills on active labour market initiatives and leave schemes have been gender assessed. Since then the arrangement has been extended to all bills in the ministry. All bills are accompanied by a memo since 2005.

The purpose of the memo is to uncover if there are relevant gender and equality aspects of the bill, and it must appear from the memo. Sometimes the bill is of greater importance for one sex than the other. The memo must contribute to avoiding unintended effects.

The memos contain the background to the bill. What is the occasion for presenting the bill? Is the bill part of an agreement in Parliament or part of the Government's policy basis?

7. The purpose of the bill. What problem is to be solved and how is the current situation changed?

The target group of the bill is especially important. You must know who is influenced by the bill, their number, the division between women and men, their age, their educational background, their connection to the labour market give a clear picture of the affected persons.

The memo must show what political interests are at play. Taking into account the different position of women and men on the labour market, it is very necessary to know how they are affected.

8, Gender mainstreaming in Great Britain and Sweden

8.1. Great Britain

Since the 1970s Great Britain has had an extensive equality legislation and The Equality and Human Rights Commission (EHRC)[3] is the current Equality Body. The EHRC is an independent, not departmental public institution, which is mainly financed by the government and whose task is to promote gender equality.

The general duty is the overall duty to eliminate discrimination and harassment and to promote equality. The general duty came into force in Great Britain in 2007. The duty applies in England, Scotland and Wales. The duty is made up of two elements, the 'general' duty and the 'specific' duties. The EHRC administers the general duty.

The gender equality duty is a legal requirement on all British public authorities, when carrying out all their functions, to have due regard to the need:

- To eliminate unlawful discrimination and harassment on the grounds of sex.
- To promote equality of opportunity between women and men.

3. www.equalityhumanrights.com

Functions include policy-making, service provision, employment matters, and statutory discretion, as well as decision-making. 'Due regard' means that authorities should give due weight to the need to promote gender equality in proportion to its relevance.

The duty requires organisations to take action on the most important gender equality issues within their functions. The promotion of equal opportunities between women and men requires public authorities to recognise that the two groups are not starting from an equal footing and identical treatment will not always be appropriate. The duty authorities also have an obligation to eliminate discrimination and harassment towards current and potential transsexual staff.

The specific duties are not an objective in themselves, but a means of meeting the general duty. The specific duties for England, Scotland and Wales are different. Full details of the legal requirements of the duty are set out in the statutory Code of Practice for England and Wales and the separate Code for Scotland.

The English specific duties require each organisation to:

- Prepare and publish a **gender equality scheme**, showing how it will meet its general and specific duties and setting out its gender equality objectives.
- In formulating its overall objectives, consider the need to include objectives to address the causes of any **gender pay gap**.
- **Gather and use information** on how the public authority's policies and practices affect gender equality in the workforce and in the delivery of services.
- **consult** stakeholders (i.e. employees, service users and others, including trade unions) and take account of relevant information in order to determine its gender equality objectives.
- **assess the impact** of its current and proposed policies and practices on gender equality.
- **implement** the actions set out in its scheme within three years, unless it is unreasonable or impracticable to do so.
- **report** against the scheme every year and **review** the scheme at least every three years.

The public authorities in England that are subject to the specific duties had published their gender equality schemes since 2007.

These duties and dates also apply to bodies in Scotland and Wales which have reserved functions.

8.2. Sweden

In 1979[4] Sweden got its first gender equality act for the labour market, which came into force in 1980. The same year the "ligestillingsombudet" (JämO) was set up. The task of the "Ombud" is to combat discrimination on the labour market. The first gender mainstreaming strategy was adopted in 1994. As a model of explanation of the lack of gender equality in Sweden reference was made to the theory on the Genus System which for the first time was presented in the act: Shared Power – Shared Responsibility in 1993[5]. The Genus System is described in Mainstreaming in a Legal Perspective[6].

In Sweden, gender mainstreaming is the main strategy used to achieve the gender equality policy objectives. Gender mainstreaming means that decisions in all walks of life are to have a clear gender perspective.

Since equality between women and men is created where everyday decisions are taken, resources are allocated and norms are established, the gender perspective must be part of day-to-day activities. The strategy has been developed in order to combat the tendency for gender equality issues to be left on the sidelines or merely ranked alongside other political issues and activities.

8.3. Gender mainstreaming in the Government Offices

Since 2004, an extensive process of change has been under way to implement gender mainstreaming in the Government Offices. The basis of this process is to make permanent changes in the established working methods. Knowledge and experience of gender mainstreaming has been collected, analysed and circulated within the framework of this process. Gender mainstreaming efforts in the Government Offices have been based on a special plan for 2004-2010. The plan has been evaluated and the Government intends to present a new platform for this work in the course of 2011.

8.4. Support to government agencies' work with gender mainstreaming

In order to support central government agencies' work on gender mainstreaming, in July 2008 the Government instructed the Swedish Secretariat for Gender Research at the University of Gothenburg to:

– further develop methods for gender mainstreaming.

4. 1979/1118.
5. 1993/94:147.
6. Andersen, Agnete and Ruth Nielsen, Gender Mainstreaming in a legal perspective, 2007.

- create a forum for exchanges of experience on gender mainstreaming.
- provide information on gender mainstreaming.
- create conditions that will provide long-term support to gender mainstreaming.

The programme has been evaluated and the results are now being processed by the Government Offices. In the course of 2011, the Government plans to present a new platform for providing support to agencies' gender mainstreaming efforts.

9. Gender mainstreaming in the ILO

The ILO has identified gender as an issue cutting across all of its programmes and activities in the world of work. To implement this strategy, in December 1999 the Director General of ILO issued a policy statement highlighting a strong and visible political commitment at the highest level of the Office.

The Action Plan is an instrument to institutionalise gender mainstreaming as a strategy of the International Labour Office, which is the Secretariat of the ILO, to promote gender equality. It also reflects gender as an issue cutting across the strategic objectives of the ILO.

In addition, the Action Plan incorporates fundamental changes in approaches and practices with a systematic focus on both women and men.

This is done through:

- Gender analysis of social and labour issues by (a) looking at the complexity of gender differentials in labour market participation, (b) understanding women's and men's constraints and opportunities in relation to knowledge and skills, conditions of work, social protection, family responsibilities, and economic and political decision-making, and (c) reviewing the different implications for women and men of the proposed solutions.
- Mechanisms to ensure gender concerns are incorporated into planning, programming, implementing, monitoring, and evaluating ILO's programmes and activities.

The Action Plan on Gender Equality and Gender Mainstreaming provides for a participatory approach to mainstreaming for gender equality in the world of work. The Action Plan covers:

- a new methodology for analysis to ensure gender concerns are incorporated in planning, programming, implementation, monitoring and evaluation.
- gender-sensitive data and gender-specific development tools and indicators.
- implementation of gender balance in its personnel policy and practices.

These measures aim to ensure that gender analysis and planning are introduced into all ILO activities, and at every level. They help to identify potentially different effects of the work of the ILO on women and men, and the provisions necessary to ensure that its activities have a positive influence on gender equality.

Mainstreaming is not about adding a "woman's component" or even a "gender equality component" into an existing activity. It goes beyond increasing women's participation; it means bringing the experience, knowledge, and interests of women and men to bear on the development agenda.

It may entail identifying the need for changes in that agenda. It may require changes in goals, strategies, and actions so that both women and men can influence, participate in, and benefit from development processes. The goal of mainstreaming gender equality is thus the transformation of unequal social and institutional structures into equal and just structures for both men and women.

Responsibility for implementing the mainstreaming strategy is system-wide, and rests at the highest levels within agencies. Other principles include:

- Adequate accountability mechanisms for monitoring progress need to be established.
- The initial identification of issues and problems across all area(s) of activity should be such that gender differences and disparities can be diagnosed.
- Assumptions that issues or problems are neutral from a gender-equality perspective should never be made.
- Gender analysis should always be carried out.
- Clear political will and allocation of adequate resources for mainstreaming, including additional financial and human resources if necessary, are important for translation of the concept into practice.
- Gender mainstreaming requires that efforts be made to broaden women's equitable participation at all levels of decision-making.

- Mainstreaming does not replace the need for targeted, women-specific policies and programmes, and positive legislation; nor does it do away with the need for gender units or focal points.

CHAPTER 6

Wage Surveys in an Academic Area: Active Measures for Equal Pay at the University of Gothenburg in Sweden 2002-2006

By Susanne Fransson, doctor of laws,
associated professor University of Gothenburg

1. Introduction

1.1. Background

This chapter presents results from a wage survey project at the University of Gothenburg in 2002-2006. By way of introduction I will present facts and figures from the Swedish labour market during the period for this study. Statistics Sweden (2005) shows that the average wage differentials between men's and women's wages were 17 per cent. The statistical differences are fairly constant and have remained more or less unchanged over the past thirteen years.[1] One reason for this is changes in the wage structure. (Löfström 2003:260). The gender pay gap in the European Union has not significantly diminished during this period and women earn on average 73 per cent of men's wages (Magnusson 2003:2). Blau and Kahn's study from the US shows disparate figures and a declining wage gap during the same period (Blau & Kahn 2000, 2003).

1. Figures for wages 2009 show that the gender pay gap has diminished to 15 percent (non-weighted figures) The Swedish National Mediation Office report 2010 ww.mi.se.

However, the statistics are non-weighted and theoretical wage discrimination can be less or more than 17 per cent. Weighted full-time wages show that women's wages in 2005 were 92 per cent of men's earnings. This, in an international perspective, small gender pay gap is found to be the result of relatively narrow dispersion of pay on the labour market as a whole. This situation is rather the result of ambitions towards social equality in more general terms than the result of a specific gender equality agenda. Nonetheless, pay issues was one decisive factor as the United Nations proclaimed Sweden to be the most gender equal country in the world in 1995.

Women in Sweden make up almost half of the labour force, but they are in general employed on different terms than men. Men in Sweden work on a more restricted sphere of the labour market and in occupations that are better paid. 52 per cent of the female workforce are employed in the public sector and 48 per cent in the private sector. When it comes to the male workforce on the other hand, are 19 per cent are occupied in the public sector and 81 per cent in the private sector. However, state employment in Sweden is not feminised; the relation is 45 per cent women and 55 per cent men. This might seem as a notable figure, however, the public sector in Sweden is dominated by the municipal sector where men are underrepresented. Here they make up 18 per cent of the workforce. The lowest average pay level is that of municipal workers, i.e. female workers.

It is really a minor part of the workforce, 16 per cent of all employed women and 14 per cent of all employed men, that work in occupations with equal sex distribution.[2] The gendered Swedish labour market consists of both horizontal and vertical gender segregation. Pay statistics are a valuable instrument to identify inequalities where men and women do equal work, i.e. 'the same job'. However, women and men usually perform different and not equal work. Hence the concept *work of equal value* is of great importance on a gendered labour market; however nobody currently knows the extent of value discrimination.[3] Comparing men's and women's wages performing work of equal value at a macro level goes beyond the method of statistics.

At a local level Swedish employers' have to deal with the concept work of equal value. The legislation demands wage surveys in order to discover, rem-

2. Women and men in Sweden: Facts and figures 2006. Statistics Sweden 2006. The statistics are built on persons of the total workforce and on whole-time equivalents. Compare with the figures in Blau & Kahn 2000.
3. Defined by England as "jobs filled mostly by women have pay levels that are lower than they would be if the jobs were filled mostly by men". England, 1992 p. 1. The concept is useful in a descriptive way but not in a legal context.

edy and prevent unwarranted wage differentials or other employment terms and conditions between men and women. In cooperation with the local union, or other representatives for the employees, these wage surveys are to be analysed from a gender perspective and an action plan for equal pay should be elaborated on by the employer in cooperation with labour representatives. This essay is reflecting experiences from the implementation of this proactive equal pay legislation on the level of a single employer, the University of Gothenburg.

1.2. Issues, focus and methodological aspects

The University of Gothenburg has about 6,000 employees and 55,000 students. In 2002 the University started to work seriously with annual wage surveys. One starting point was a work evaluation project. Some of the findings were summed up in an action plan for equal pay. In 2003-2004 the first plan was set in action. As the person responsible for the annual wage surveys 2002-2006, I have been able to closely follow the process with active measures for equal pay at the University. In every case study where you are close to the studied objects and processes, you have to be aware what an inside perspective has after all its limitations. Every researcher's guiding-star is to be critical to the object that is studied. My way of handling this issue is to analyse the process and the results from a structural perspective.

The data in this study includes for instance work evaluation between jobs that are female dominated (60/40) compared to those that are not female dominated. Groups affected are inter alia professors, lecturers, librarians, technicians, administrators, laboratory workers and cleaners. However, it should be observed that this is not a study on job evaluation. In Sweden as well as in other countries there is a lot of research done on job evaluation and equal pay, on a theoretical level as well as on an empirical level (Remick 1984, Acker 1989, Sorensen 1994, Rosenberg 2004). Since the Swedish legislation on active measures for equal pay and wage surveys is unique in a European perspective there are not many foreign studies that can be related to. In fact, in Sweden there are few academic empirical studies on wage surveys and action plans for equal pay as well. Experiences from equal pay legislation in Canada have thus had significant impact on the Swedish legislative process (Fransson et al 2000:37). However there are similarities as well as differences reflecting different labour market relations in the two countries. As this pro active Canadian legislation is relatively new, there is not much research done yet (McCaughy 2005).

In recent years, I have made two quantitative studies on wage surveys in Sweden. The first study included 531 private employers (Fransson 2003,

Fransson & Thörnqvist 2006) and in the second study there were 50 employers, 40 municipalities and 10 private employers (Fransson & Andersson 2005). The primary material for the studies comes from the Equal Opportunities Ombudsman's office monitoring employers wage surveys and action plans for equal pay. The results of the first study in 2003 showed that the implementation of the legislation had not reached any significant impact on the employer's activity for equal pay and that only some four per cent of the monitored employers found unwarranted wage differentials (Fransson 2003, Fransson & Thörnqvist 2006). In the second study the result of the implementation could be described as a step forward. Especially municipalities` wage surveys resulted in significant pay wage increases for female dominated groups (Fransson & Andersson 2005). The Ombudsman has presented facts and figures from 900 employers wage surveys examined between 2001 and 2004. The report shows adjustments in pay within at least 100 employers' activities (JämO, the Equal Opportunities Ombudsman 2005).

In this study of one single employer, the Gothenburg University, the description of data and the analysis of the implementation process has its point of departure from two main perspectives; the academic structure at the University and the interaction between the demand for adjustments in pay according to the Equal Pay Action Plan and traditional local bargaining. My focus in the analysis is on this second aspect, as I find that implementation of the legislation has a real potential to change traditional pay structures on the labour market from a gender perspective.

The revealed pay structure at the University is hierarchical with well paid male dominated groups like professors at the top, female dominated groups like administrators in the middle and female dominated groups like cleaners at the bottom. The structure is also patriarchal and as such a structure of power. My main question here is if legal demands for annual pay surveys combined with equal pay action plans can change these structures?

The second issue concerns the interaction between the result of the wage survey and the local bargaining rounds. When unwarranted pay differentials are identified, the employer has to take action according to the law. Groups like laboratory workers and technicians may then find themselves in competing positions as means for pay rises are limited. Is it possible for different union representatives to cooperate on pay adjustments (according to gender equality demands) on the one hand with representatives from other unions, and on top of that also cooperate with the employer in order to comply with the legislation? I will also focus on the employers` responsibility for the result of the proactive work for equal pay.

To sum up, my overriding empirical question is; are we actually closing the gender pay gap at the University? Finally this is a qualitative study and no general conclusions in relation to the Swedish labour market as a whole should therefore be made.

1.3. Theoretical framework

This essay is written in the field of labour law from a gender perspective. Law as a scientific concept, compared to social science, is in general lacking grand theories and analytical methods. Law as science can neither be used to explain, nor to describe why there are gender related wage differences on the labour market. Law as science is traditionally in Sweden dogmatic and mainly descriptive and with an ambition to be objective.[4] My approach to this is that even legal scientists have to be critical and not only act as lubricant in the machinery. Studying implementation of labour law, it is rather helpful to use theories and concepts so that an external perspective on law can be achieved. It is also necessary to contextualise analytical concepts; which I will now try to do.

Since 1803, there has been no legislation on wages in Sweden and since about 1890 collective agreements have filled out the absence of norms for wage setting. Wage setting became a collective matter of negotiations and agreements "the freedom of labour market parties" (Fahlbeck 2002:94). In 1965 the Swedish Confederation of Trade Unions, LO, and the Swedish Employers' Confederation, SAF, decided to eliminate direct gender based wages in central collective agreements. Collectively agreed direct discrimination between men and women performing the same job then ceased.

Historically and from a comparative perspective, the Swedish labour market is almost unique in that sense that the state left the task to regulate to the labour market parties. The Swedish system of industrial relations is from this perspective a *self-regulating system.*[5] Typically a self-regulating model involves organisations with the aim to regulate the standards of behaviour for its members. These organisations monitor and create standards and norms. This self-regulation model produces control-efficiency and legitimation (Baldwin & Cave 1999:126-133). In a Nordic context, self regulation is a

4. See Svensson E-M. (2007) 'Boundary-work in Legal Scholarship' in Gunnarsson, Svensson and Davies (eds.) *Exploiting the Limits of Law. Swedish Feminism and the Challenge to Pessimism.*
5. See Eijlander 2005. Eijlander uses three different categories of self-regulation; free or pure self-regulation, substitute or alternative self-regulation and conditioned self-regulation.

common concept that is used to describe the regulatory mode on the labour market, especially when it comes to wages (Fahlbeck 2002:94). In this respect the concept is used as an alternative for regulation.

My interpretation of the self-regulating system on the Swedish labour market is that it is fundamentally built on a conflict perspective. Matters of strength between the collective partners decide the outcome of bargaining. Strike and lock-outs are legitimate and necessary instruments in a system where the outcome is sealed by a collective agreement. Hence, the state as a legislator primarily has a role of defining procedural norms rather than normative ones. The mere part of Swedish labour law is also semi-autonomous and is an expression for the synthesis *legally conditioned self regulation* (Baldwin & Cave 1999 p.41, Witteveen 2005). The Co-Determination Act (1976) is an example of this legislative technique and the act is theoretically based on the assumption of cooperation and a balance of powers between the parties on the labour market. The empirical data in this essay relate to state employment and the Swedish public sector. When it comes to the concept of self regulation used as a descriptive tool of the regulatory model on the Swedish labour market, researchers seem to make their outline primarily from the private sector (Fahlbeck 2002). My thesis is that the public sector shows up specific features. For instance, self regulation among the collective parties developed at a much later stage compared to the private sector. In short, if we compare the characteristics for self regulation, there are at least three main differences at the collective level in a historical perspective; the autonomy of the unions, the right to bargain for collective agreements and the right to strike. Trade unions in the public sector, especially those of state employees, have not been as autonomous from the employer as unions in the private sector. The unions had no complete legal right to perform collective bargaining until 1965. Wage setting was extremely centralised and there was no room for local bargaining or individual wage setting. Until 1965 the model for regulation was nearly in line with what is labelled *command-and-control regulation*. The essence of command-and-control regulation are central rules and regulations backed up by sanctions to exercise influence and control over the citizen's behaviour (Baldwin & Cave 1999:25). Today there are very few differences in labour law regulations between the public and the private sector. Thus, the self regulation system characterizes the entire Swedish labour market.

In the last decade, agreement models have changed in Sweden. Paradoxically, the parties in the public sector have been the fastest to adopt decentralised wage setting and individual-based wages. Here, the state as an employer has shown itself to be the real frontrunner. The function of central collective agreements for state employed is rather to deliver frames and principles for local bargaining. E.g. that wage ought to be set individually and on factual grounds. The concept factual ground may be unknown to some readers. However, it is a common concept in Nordic labour law and within an EC context. When it comes to wages, the concept factual grounds indicates that pay for all employees from a single employer is related to the same norm, and that this norm is neither directly nor indirectly beneficial to either of the sexes. Clear criteria for wage setting should be a prerequisite and the formally agreed upon criteria should be applied in a consistent and systematic way. Moreover, the local parties are jointly responsible for adjusting and preventing differentials in wage and working conditions for men and women with the same job or the job of equal value.[6] Today's decentralised and individualised wage formation process has led to clauses in central collective agreements that usually make at least as rigorous demands for setting wages on factual grounds as the legislation. My conclusion is that there is an interaction between legislative demands and central collective agreements and that the pivotal link is the principle of individual and decentralized wage setting. We call it "collective individualisation". However, wage setting is still a part of the self-regulating system (Fransson & Thörnqvist 2003).

One can observe that the rules of active measures for equal pay in the Swedish legislation interact with the field for traditional self regulation. The law regulates matters of pay which exclusively belonged to the field for bargaining and collective agreements. The question is; what kind of regulative model is herebyused?

Firstly, we can notice that the Swedish legislation is mandatory. Secondly, the demands are the same for all employers. In Germany for instance, only public employers are affected by demands for equal opportunities plans. The demand for annual (until 2009) wage surveys is thus a regulative model that restricts the parties' full autonomy in the field of pay setting. One can say that legislation like the active measures for equal pay is a result of the failure of the self-regulating system as it comes to the responsibility for equal pay in relation to gender. This norm is thus not negotiable; wages ought to be set on non-gender discriminatory grounds.

My conclusion is that the regulative model is some sort of *co-regulation* (Eijlander 2005:5). Indeed one can see a mixture of regulatory instruments; basically the parliament has set up the norms in legislation from a theoretical

6. See for instance the central collective agreement for academics RALS 2004-2007 § 6:1.

harmony perspective as employers and employees are supposed to share the same objectives in relation to sex discrimination. At the same time it is clear in the preparatory works that the legislators' starting point is the self regulating system for setting pay. (Prop. 1999/2000:173, see Eijlander 2005:6, Fransson & Thörnqvist 2006).

To sum up, theoretically the framework of this article are the concepts *self regulation, command-and-control regulation* and *co-regulation*. From an overall point of view the first and the third concepts emerge from the dichotomy; conflict and harmony. I will use these concepts as descriptive and analytical tools. That means that I am starting at a structural level and then use the regulative models on my case study.

2. Legislation for equal pay in Sweden

2.1. Background

The first law for equal opportunities between men and women in Sweden came in force in 1980. The law included active measures for equality at the workplace and that appropriate measures should be summed up in an Equal Opportunities plan. Since 1994 Swedish employers also have the responsibility to make annual wage surveys from a gender perspective. The Equal Opportunities Act was amended in 2001 and the demand for analysis and corrections in pay within three years came into force. All employers were requested to make annual wage surveys and employers with ten or more employees were annually obliged to make written action plans for equal pay (section 10 and 11). The main purpose of the amended rules in 2001 was to close the gender pay gap and to avoid litigations on equal pay. The position of the local trade union was also strengthened at the same time. The local union representatives have the right to take part in the work with annual wage surveys. The legislation also gives the right to obtain information on individual wages beyond the realm of the own collective agreement including non-unionised employees wages if this is required for the gender pay assessment. This unique insight into pay structures is combined with rules of confidentiality and damages for the union representatives.[7]

In a European perspective, the Swedish legislation of active measures for equal pay and working conditions is unique. On the one hand this is some-

7. This insight into pay structure is unique in comparison with for instance legislation in Britain where employers are under no legal duty to answer questions on wages even in a single equal pay claim.

what surprising, as the European Union already in 1996 adopted a guideline for proactive and soft-law like measures concerning equal pay to be transformed in the member states' national systems.[8] Still, the Swedish legislation is unique in a European perspective from at least two aspects. Firstly, no other countries have experiences with proactive legislation in order to rectify unwarranted differentials in pay between men and women. Only Finland has adopted similar legislation as of 1 June 2005. Secondly, reports show that equal pay litigation in most EU countries has a poor record. This has been even more obvious in relation to the concept of equal pay for work of equal value. Reports from the Equal Opportunities Ombudsman show that Swedish legislation has had notable impacts on women's wages (the Equal Opportunities Ombudsman 2005).

On 1 January 2009 a new Discrimination Act entered into force and rules on equal pay and prohibition against gender wage-discrimination in the Equal Opportunities Act was transformed into the new law. Gender became one of seven protected discrimination grounds. Age and gender transgressing identity or expression became new protected grounds. A new agency; the Equality Ombudsman, which merges the four earlier Ombudsmen, was established. From a feminist point of view the Discrimination Act is a backlash. The Equal Opportunities Act stated that the primary aim of the law was to improve women's conditions and positions in working life. This statement was now expelled (Fransson & Stüber 2010:56). The Discrimination Act also can be questioned from an EC-perspective though the new legislative technique is to legislate through statements in the preparatory works.[9] Wage discrimination is no longer expressively prohibited in the law and neither the concepts equal work and work of equal value is used. In section 2:1 all aspects and conditions in working life is covered by the law, which due to the preparatory works include wage-discrimination (Fransson & Stüber 2010:189, Prop. 2007/2008:95).

2.2. In cooperation with the representatives for the employees

The starting-point for the work with wage surveys is cooperation between the employer and representatives for the employees in order to obtain and guarantee equal pay. Before the amendment of the Equal Opportunities Act in 2001, the possibility for cooperation and getting information was more restricted for employee representatives. However, the legislation does not regu-

8. A code of practice on the implementation of equal pay for work of equal value for men and women, EC-Commission 1996.
9. See the EC case 143/83 The Commission v. Denmark.

late or specify how this cooperation is to be done. In the preparatory legal work cooperation is expressed as: "something natural". There are also references to the Co-determination Act and that the forms of employee influence that are already present at the workplace ought to be suitable to use for gender pay audits (prop. 1999/2000:173: 82).

Compared to Canadian legislation the Swedish demand for cooperation for equal pay is more informal and not as regulated (McCaughy 2005). In comparison with the Co-determination Act which supports formalised routines combined with sanctions, the Equal Opportunities Act has a more informal view on cooperation between unions and employers. It should be underlined that more guidance is demanded from local parties, especially from union's representatives. It is also questioned from both sides how to achieve equal pay across the boundaries of collective agreements. In our study from 2004 one central union representative said: "*The union representatives are not used to cooperate across collective agreements' boundaries. It works in some workplaces but I think that most union representatives are strictly focused on benefits for their own members.*" A representative from an employer's organisation claimed that: "*The problem is the definition of the concept cooperation. Is it the same as reaching an understanding or*?" (Fransson & Andersson 2005). Actually the question puts the finger on the regulatory model – cooperation from a harmonic perspective. Surveying and analysing wages in cooperation with the employer and all unions at the workplace in the same room is fraught with difficulties. For instance, in the municipal sector the employer will have to cooperate with up to twenty different unions.

2.3. Mapping wages and working conditions

The purpose with mapping is to discover any differences that could be related to a gender aspect. Wage surveys ought to be made annually (until 2009) with the aim to give the employer and the unions a foundation for the local wage bargaining round. Moreover, the annual request is necessary to visualize gender related features, changes and developments and to give a base for comparison. Practically it is a question of facts and figures. Facts not only on wages but also fringe benefits, over-time pay etc. should be monitored. Other facts like age, length of services, part-time employment and temporary employment can give additional information from a gender perspective.

The legislation on active measures for equal pay also requests the employer to present and analyse regulations and practices for wage setting. The purpose in this case is to create a more conscious and systematic application of the norms used for wage setting. This means that collective norms agreed upon on central and local level and the subsequent practice should be analysed from a gender perspective.

Employers with at least ten employees were until 2009 required to show the result of the wage survey in a written annual action plan, section 11 The Equal Opportunities Act. The regulation was criticized primarily from an employer's perspective and the Swedish Government proposed that the rules should be changed. The keyword for that change was simplification of rules. From 2009 employers with at least 25 employees (former 10 employees) are required to create an action plan for equal pay, but now every third year and not on annual base, section 10 the Discrimination Act (Fransson & Stüber 2010:413). Still the action plan should include appropriate measures that are needed to be taken to reach the goal equal pay and equal working conditions. The measures should be cost-calculated and put into a time schedule. Pay adjustments should be carried out as soon as possible and at the latest within three years.

2.4. Equal wages and job evaluation

Job evaluation can be used for different aims and with different methods. The intent of the law is to force the employer to make norms visible so that a comparison from a gender perspective is possible. These norms should be used in the employer's entire activity for all employees and across different unions' (collective agreements' boarders. The law leaves it to the employer to define what activities are appropriate in each single business, as long as they are gender neutral and transparent. To define what is meant by work of equal value, there are four main criteria to be observed; knowledge and skills, responsibility, effort and working conditions. The employers are free to use these criteria in a simple way or to build computer-based and sophisticated work evaluation systems. If systematic work evaluation systems are used, it is up to the employer to choose a system of preference. In Sweden there is a variety of companies and consultants that offer these services. This has led to a debate because some employers prefer to cooperate with a consultant rather than cooperation with employee representatives, a practice that is not in line with the intent of the legislator.

Secondly the focus of the active measures for equal pay is primarily on the employer's gender structure. Thus, the employers are not required to evaluate every single employee's work tasks although an analysis often leads to closer checks of single individuals' wages. The demands of the law are about comparing men's and women's wages within groups of equal work.

When it comes to work of equal value the comparison ought to be between groups of equal value that are female dominated and groups that are not female dominated (60/40). To understand this structural and collective point of departure is crucial when coping with the active measures for equal pay. It is also of importance to bear in mind the purpose of the legislation – equal pay from a gender perspective and not egalitarian pay for every worker. On the other hand the law has its structural limits. There exist no references or guidelines on a national level supported by the labour market parties that define what jobs are equal or of equal value. Comparison within the requirements of the legislation for equal pay is limited to the workplace and to one single employer's staff. This makes sense as an employer as a legal object can never be responsible for any other employers' wage setting.[10] However, Swedish national economists often criticise legislation for being ineffective as a tool to change structural wage differentials between men and women (Thoursie 2005). Löfström has a more long-term perspective and states that: "*In the long run, however, when all companies have adjusted wages according to the demand for 'equal pay for equal work' and 'equal pay for work of equal value' structural wage differentials may also disappear*" (Löfström 2003: 270).

2.5. Unwarranted wage differentials and the concept of wage discrimination

If the employer finds out that there are unwarranted wage differentials between men and women, an analysis has to be made and the question "why?", must come to an answer. This simple question "why?" includes the entire gender discrimination concept. The legislation is methodically divided in two parts; active measures and prohibition against discrimination. In the active measures for equal pay, individual rights of the employees have been transformed to a proactive responsibility for the employer. The two parts of the law are to be seen as linked to each other. On the other hand the concepts used are not similar. To start with, the employer has to decide whether there is observed any unwarranted wage-setting or not. If so, the employer has to decide to what extent there have to be made any adjustments in pay, immediately and at the latest within three years. If the unwarranted wages are directly or indirectly discriminatory is not a relevant question as the concept of unwarranted wages is broader than the concept discriminatory wages. However, the outcome of the very few wage discrimination cases in the Swedish labour

10. See for instance the British case Lawrence v Regent Office Care Ltd (2002) IRLR 822.

court has spilled over to how unwarranted wage differentials have been treated.

2.6. The midwife cases and the market forces

The prohibition against discrimination is under the jurisdiction of the Swedish labour court. Since 1980 there have been only eleven gender wage discrimination claims in the labour court. In one and a half case the plaintiff did win her case. One explanation to the few cases is that unions have not used legislation to increase women's wages. The prohibition for wage discrimination has been seen as interference in the freedom of collective bargaining for wages. In Britain the unions have been active in bringing wage discrimination claims to the courts and more equal value cases have been heard in Britain than in the rest of the member states in the European Union (Branney, Howes & Hegewisch 1999:208).

It has also been stated that it is not possible to compare apples and pears i.e. different jobs. This question received an answer in 2001. In the second midwife case, AD 2001 no 13, the Labour Court figured out that it was possible to compare different jobs like midwifes and clinical engineers. The court came to the conclusion that the two jobs were of equal value. This was indeed a great step forward as the concept work of equal value was introduced by law in 1980 and especially in the light of the first midwife case, AD 1996 no 41, where the plaintiff had no success in relation to that concept. In this case the labour court rejected the evidence from the plaintiff and expressed that in a comparison with unlike work tasks, the court had to put up especially rigorous demands for the evidence. Thus the midwife lost the case.

However the most crucial evidence in the three latest wage discrimination cases in the labour court has been reference to market forces. In what way are market forces deemed to make up a factual ground for wage setting? Compared to British courts, the Swedish Labour Court actually does not demand any objective facts related to the circumstances in the specific case which can explain how market forces have been interacting in the specific situation.[11]

Thus, market forces are rather to be interpreted as a general explanation on grounds of national economist theory. This viewpoint is underpinned with the fact that labour market parties are autonomous from state intervention in the wage setting process. This means that collective agreements on pay are seen as a concrete expression of the existing market forces. My interpretation is

11. Clay Cross v. Fletcher 1979 I.C.R.1. Ratcliffe and others v. North Yorkshire County Council 1995 I.C.R. 841.

that the Swedish labour courts verdicts ought to be understood as a result of the self-regulative system; a system in which the Labour Court makes up an important and integrated part.

3. Wage surveys at the University of Gothenburg

3.1. Introduction

The following part of this chapter is a description and an analysis of how one single employer, the University of Gothenburg, has handled the requirements in the Equal Opportunities Act during the period 2002-2006. In a political context the government imposes state employers to serve as a model to other employers in active measures for equality on grounds like gender, sexual orientation, disability, race, ethnicity and religion.

In 2002, as a result of the amendment of the Equal Opportunities Act, the University decided to make a new wage survey and to restart the annual work with active measures for equal pay. Thus a wage survey group was formed with representatives from the University; the head of department from almost each faculty, the University's Equality Ombudsman, a statistician and with me as the project leader; all in all seven persons. The group was composed in a way that would give it a high degree of credibility.

The primary aim of the work with wage surveys at the University was to comply with the demands of the Equal Opportunities Act. A driving force not to be underestimated has been to simultaneously create a new wage policy and new methods for individual wage setting. A set of non discriminatory criteria to assess individual qualification and performance have been created and accepted by the head of the University. This qualification system is supposed to be used in the individual wage setting. In this process, on the one hand the demands of the Equal Opportunities Act were observed and on the other hand the needs for a more structured pay policy which meets the requirement of an efficient system for individual wage setting. These requirements as a whole are closely linked to different collective agreements on pay.

Wage surveys shall be undertaken in cooperation with the local unions or other representatives for the employees. At the University we made an informal agreement with the local unions and fulfilled the demand for cooperation in our own way. The local unions served as a reference group to the wage survey group and hence they did not take part in any 'decisions' made by the group. This was a tactical decision made by the unions with the aim to be free to negotiate in the local bargaining rounds without having to be responsible for the result of for instance the work evaluation. In an interview, the local union representatives stated that the cooperation model functioned in a good way (Segerpalm 2005).

Actually, all decisive decisions were taken by the employer's delegation which was formed as a control group. Finally, the head of the University makes the formal decision on the annual action plan.

3.2. The unions at the University

There are three large trade unions at the University; the Swedish Confederation of Professional Associations, SACO, the Swedish Confederation of Professional Employees, TCO (two white colour unions) and the Union of Service and Communication Employees, SEKO (a blue colour union). The union member density is high in an international perspective but it has declined during the last years and in 2002, 32 percent of employees at the University were not organized. The three unions' historical background is of importance to understand their approach to the work with active measures for equal pay at the University. As work evaluation and pay at the university has historically favoured aspects such as knowledge and skill, the academic group has always been privileged compared to other groups with back-up functions at universities. One union, SEKO, stands out as the most sceptic one towards the proactive work with active measures for equal pay. The local union leader expressed that the groups organized in SEKO, like cleaners and porters; "*had nothing to gain* by taking part in active measure-activities *for equal pay and especially not in a job evaluation system*". Thus, traditional trade union work such as bargaining from a conflict perspective was held to be the best method to raise wages for their members. Compared to the academic unions SACO and TCO, this union, SEKO, has historically had union traditions that never accepted a command-and-control model for regulation. The SEKO organizes blue collar workers who in fact are the lowest paid groups at the University. My conclusion is that the representatives from SEKO made a correct tactical analysis from a union perspective. From a purely class perspective, as Figart states, job evaluation historically was a regressive development (Figart 2000: 15). But the union's analysis lacks a gender perspective. It is true that there will be no comparison between cleaners and professors. The results of the job evaluation did not lead to any decisive changes in the hierarchic wage structure at the university. However, one thing that the union leader did not consider, is the gender perspective within the blue collar group; for instance, the comparison between the female dominated group cleaners and the male dominated group porters. The groups organized by SEKO are also the most gendered in the University's structure.

Cooperation for wage surveys goes beyond collective agreement boundaries and is characteristically different from traditional wage negotiations. Union representatives should bear in mind that the purpose of an equal pay survey is not to look after specific interests of union members as such. Instead the employer and the union representatives are supposed to take joint responsibility to fulfil the aim of the active measures; to make it possible to discover, remedy and prevent unwarranted wage differentials and employment terms due to gender for all employees, unionized as well as not unionized. In the initial stage of the wage survey project, there was some scepticism from all the union representatives. All the union representatives had difficulties in leaving the traditional role as a negotiator although cooperation was on the overall agenda. The concept work of equal value also caused some misunderstanding; however, the union representatives finally understood that the valuation was based on the demands of the job and not of the individual performance. Then they also understood that their members position (SACO) in the wage structure like professors actually was not threatened by the valuation of the cleaner's work tasks.

3.3. The demands of the librarians` unions

One female dominated group (85/15), the librarians, had distinguished themselves and had established claims in the local bargaining round according to the prohibition of wage discrimination and the demand for comparing work of equal value. Through their unions SACO and TCO, they claimed that their wages were unfair due to gender and that a comparison, within the frame of work of equal value, should be made with another female dominated group at the University, the group of junior lectures. This demand went beyond the demands of the legislation for equal pay, as the two groups both are female dominated, but the demands were clearly in line with the central collective agreement (RALS). Wages should be set on factual grounds in general. However, the librarians` claims are historically a matter of gender, which means value discrimination. One can also make a link to the concept of "crowding" – originally a theory of labour surplus from 1922 (see Löfström 2003:263). Crowding as a model to explain wage differentials on the labour market has been empirically studied for instance among members of the union SACO. The report shows that when there are 10 percent more women in a job category the pay decreases with 4 percent (SACO 2003). Other studies show that men and women gain less in relation to educational length if they are working in female dominated jobs. This thesis covers the entire Swedish labour market (Thoursie 2004:68 compare with Löfström 2003:265-68 and Blau & Kahn 2000). Historically, the librarians at the Swedish universities have been a small group of well-paid men, now the group is highly feminized. As the feminization of the occupation – the oversupply of women – has led to shrinking wages, this is an example of the crowding hypothesis.

In 2002 the librarians` unions reached a local collective agreement with the University with the content that the wage survey group should primarily evaluate and compare the work tasks of librarians and lecturers. If the evaluation was not completed at a certain date the University should pay the librarians in general a pay increase of 100 Euro per month. The valuation made clear that there was a difference between the work demands of librarians compared to those of junior lecturers. The difference in valuation points, 33 (maximum 1000), did obviously not correspond with the wage differential of 450 Euro per month. In this case there was an interaction between law and collective agreement. Hence, the librarians' unions used the valuation in the local wage negotiations and reached a general pay increase of 9,5-10 per cent in one year! However, this result did not satisfy the librarians' union representatives. They still thought that their wages were too low compared with junior lecturers (see *GU-Journalen* 2003).

In any case the "militancy" from the librarians is interesting to analyse from the model of self regulation and the model of cooperation. Tactically the librarians have used both. The demands of the librarians take its point of departure from the prohibition of wage discrimination. They have also been very active in the union reference group in the wage survey project. In this way they tactically have combined a legal strategy with traditionally union ones, which means bargaining for collective agreements. Hence, the model for self regulation is used as well as the model for cooperation. So far this has been a successful way of reaching higher wages for the librarians.

3.4. The result of the wage survey

A wage survey does not fulfil the demands of the law if it merely compiles statistics on monthly salary without reflecting a gender perspective. For instance facts like age, time of employment, part-time work, wage distribution and position are all necessary to acknowledge as indicators which can be relevant from a gender perspective.

Data of all employees including their wages and working conditions, e.g. different employment terms such as part-time, short contract, unionized and non-unionized, were collected from the University's HR database and were presented in Excel-files. We used the existing nomenclature for profession, (more than 300 different groups of work tasks) aware that in each group there can be individuals who actually do not perform the same job. Hence there can be individuals in one group that do the same job compared to individuals in another group. The result of the wage surveys made in 2003 to 2006 was that the University is a workplace with equal sex distribution, 57 per cent women compared to 43 per cent men (2005). We also found that there are no gender differences according to age and length of service and that 26 per cent of women work part-time compared to 24 per cent of the male staff (2005) compared to 21 and 17 percent in 2003. The amount of part-time work has increased, for both men and women at the University during the last five years. This we deemed as not being a gender issue but rather an employment issue. Since the year 2000 the Employment Security Act obliges the employer to employ those who have been working as supply staff totally three years within a period of five years on a permanent contract. This obligation has led to a minimalist employment approach considering the amount of working hours. This approach has led to increasing part-time employed especially among the group lecturers.

But let us return to part-time work from a gender perspective; the figure for men working part time is relatively high; however one explanation is that men's part-time work depends on the fact that they often have several employers or that they in addition run their own business. The hypothesis that men and women work part time on gender specific grounds is confirmed in the figures for receiving pay for extra work. Women working part time get more pay for extra work compared to men.

The mapping shows that there is horizontal as well as vertical gender segregation at the University. The structure is, as mentioned, hierarchal with large low valued female dominated groups at the bottom and one high valued male dominated group at the top. The most gender segregated groups are the technical and the administrative staff. Actually, men and women are not doing the same job. This horizontal phenomenon characterizes the entire Swedish labour market; the public sector as well as the private sector (Fransson 2003, Fransson & Thörnqvist 2006). In a report from the Swedish Agency of Government Employers, the wage differentials between men and women during the period 2000-2005 is analysed. Using the work task classification system BESTA the Agency came to the result that the most important explanation for wage differentials is the vertical segregation, i.e. work tasks performed by male groups are classified with a higher degree of difficulty (Swedish Agency of Government employers 2005).

Full time equivalent figures gave the result that women at the entire University in 2001 earned 83 percent of men's wages. The wage survey made in 2006 showed that this figure had increased to 85.5 percent (2005 wages). Wage dispersion within groups with equal work showed no significant gender related features. However, the statistics showed very small wage differentials between men and women with equal work. For instance, female professors earn 102 percent of male professors' wages, female senior lecturers earn 98 percent of male senior lecturers' wages and female junior lecturers earn 101 percent of male junior lecturers' wages (2005). The amount of additional pay for leadership is also increasing for women in relation to male colleagues. 47 percent of the senior lecturers are women and 63 percent of the junior lecturers are women. It ought to be mentioned that in 2005, 22 per cent of full professors were female. In an international perspective this figure is nothing to be proud of. At least the figures are better than those from the US, 16.2 per cent (Blau & Kahn 2000:89). In summer 2006, for the first time a woman took the position as the head of the university. Hence academic groups are not the most problematic ones when studying wages from a gender perspective. The glass-ceiling is broken and actually there are no wage limits (see Löfström 2003:260). These groups have successfully been represented by their unions at the university and there has been a strong commitment to adjust women's wages within academic groups in the local wage rounds during the last decade.

More problematic is the heavily feminized (circ. 90/10) administrative group where the wage gap between men and women tends to increase. Seen as a group, the wage differentials have increased with 11 percent from 2001 to 2005. One explanation is that the University has had a successful strategy in employing younger (well-educated) men for administrative work with the aim to achieve a less gender segregated administrative staff. One can discuss if it is "necessary" or not that these young men generally are better paid than their female and older colleagues.

We also collected pay data in all its different forms. The EC-court has interpreted the concept of pay in a broad manner within the scope of Article 157 (141) and each piece of wage should in a case of wage discrimination be compared separately.[12] Statistics from the University show that male employees get more over-time pay and due to the patriarchal structure they are still dominating academic and administrative leadership at the University. Equal pay is also a matter of structure and power. It has to be noticed that the gender pay gap at the University increases if we broaden the concept pay and add different kind of pay such as overtime pay and above all, additional pay for leadership assignments. In legal terms, this is not a question of direct discrimination. However, the active measures for equal pay have a more broad and structural perspective for equality between men and women. In the action

12. See C-236/98 the Equal Opportunities Ombudsman v. Örebro County Council.

plan for equal pay the employer has also to handle these structural gender related features.

3.5. The scheme design

In an organisation with a high horizontal gender segregation the comparison between different kinds of work tasks is a matter of decisive importance if the aim is to reach more equal and fair wages from a gender perspective. The legislation on active measures for equal pay draws up the necessary criteria for the employer's method to compare work tasks in a non-gender discriminatory way. These criteria are: knowledge and skills, responsibility, effort and working conditions. To make it possible to compare different kinds of work tasks, an analytical work evaluation system was created at the University by the wage survey group and with the unions as a reference group. The points of departure were the above mentioned criteria.

In a factor plan we defined the different factors for evaluation, their levels and we attached scores to each level. In connection to each sub-factor, we made a description of how each factor ought to be interpreted. For instance, the sub-factor demand for knowledge is of crucial importance, so the factor includes 8 different levels. The sub-factor demand for responsibility includes personnel, students, research and development. The different factors of the work evaluation system were also internally weighted from an academic structure as follows; high points for knowledge and low points for physical effort

As a comment, one can say that there was no intention to make a big revolution in the University's wage policy. In the project group our attempt was rather to make a soft revolution in our proposal for how to weigh the different factors in the evaluation system. This proposal was rejected by the employer's delegation. Hence the work evaluation system maintains the structure from a class and educational perspective (Figart 2000:15). Like the union leaders from SEKO said; their members had nothing to gain in a work evaluation system.

3.6. The evaluation process

It is a common misunderstanding that work evaluation is objective in itself and that the method automatically leads to pay equity. From a methodological view-point, it should be underlined that work evaluation is not objective and scientific as such (Remick 1984). The purpose is to evaluate work tasks in a systematic and non gender discriminatory way with the purpose to find out if there are any unwarranted wage differentials at the University. Work evaluation is rather a method that can reveal values and subjectivity in a structured way.

The work tasks or professions that were valued were professor, senior lecturer, junior lecturer, librarian, different kinds of administrators, laboratory worker, research laboratory worker, research-engineer, technician, IT-technician, cleaner, porter, catering assistant i.e. groups that are female or not female dominated. Compared to the study at Karlstad University the work tasks as junior lecturer as well as senior lecturer was seen as two groups where the differentials within the groups are so small that they can be classified as two equal work groups (Gonäs, Bergman & Rosenberg 2006). To have a ground for the evaluation process, general descriptions of the different work tasks were made by the project group. The most striking was that it is very easy to use subjective and estimating words even in a process of describing different kind of work tasks in general.[13] To support the group in this part of the work, the local union representatives were directly involved and also other employees at the University with special knowledge. Especially the description of the librarians work tasks was discussed and adjusted in cooperation with the librarians and the local union representatives, but unfortunately we did not reach full consensus. One Union representative stated that: "*The valuation is coloured with words that are sex discriminatory in itself. The junior lecturers' work tasks is expressed in an active manner while the librarians' work tasks are described in a passive manner*" (*GU-Journalen* 2003). Even after an adjustment the librarians thought that their work tasks were not described in a fully correct manner, so they subsequently found that the valuation had failed. Their tactical goal was to be equally valued compared to the junior lecturers.

The result of the work valuation was presented in a report. Three different methods were used to describe the result of the evaluation; an expression for working in an academic structure with high demands for legitimization. According to the first method the evaluated work tasks were divided into groups from the letter A to J within an interval of 40 points.[14] In each group the work tasks were considered being of equal value. For instance in group H, including the female dominated group administrators and the non female dominated group IT-technicians, the wage differentials were about 400 Euros per month. Comparison was also made between different groups ranged at a lower and higher level. In three female dominated groups, laboratory workers, research

13. No interviews or paper questionnaires were made with employees describing their jobs.
14. The second method had the interval 60 points which led to more comparable groups.

laboratory workers and assistant secretaries, the work tasks were ranged higher than the IT-technicians work tasks. The wages of the IT-technicians were however higher than the mentioned higher evaluated female groups.[15] In the bottom group, group J, including the work tasks of an office porter, office foreman, cleaner and catering assistant, all groups are organized in The Union of Service and Communication Employees, SEKO. The wage differentials are between 100 to 300 Euros to the advantage of the non female dominated groups.

The third method gives a more complex picture of the valuation and is useful to compare occupations without having to form fixed comparable groups. The method is more open, however, to decide whether the wage differentials are unwarranted or not. I think you need to use the first or the second method with defined groups for comparison.

4. How to handle unwarranted wage differentials

4.1. To deconstruct the gender pay structure

The wage surveys showed no significant wage differentials between men and women with equal work at an aggregated level. It is likely that there may be unwarranted wage differentials between individual men and women at the department level. However, it was deemed that such a level of detailed statistics would go far beyond what would have been an appropriate effort to comply with the demands for gender based analyses.

The work evaluation showed that there are comparable female dominated groups and non-female dominated groups who perform work of equal value. In some cases there are considerable differentials in pay between these groups. This has to be analyzed, and if the pay differentials are founded unwarranted the employer is responsible to undertake corrections and define these corrections in the action plan. The action plan has to include a cost computation and a time schedule for the pay differentials to be adjusted. This should be done as soon as possible but at the latest within three years. That's what the legislation stipulates! The way to carry out these pay adjustments is controversial. Should these adjustments be regarded as a part of the local bargaining wage scope? Or should there be a rectification separately from the ordinary wage scope? In compliance with the self-regulatory system, the local parties are supposed to carry out the wage adjustment in the local bargain-

15. Compare with the EC-case Macarthys LtD 129/79.

ing wage round (Prop. 1999/2000:173). Otherwise the employer is responsible according to the law. The question not answered within the legal framework is if the employer is obliged to give in extra money on top of what is planned to be negotiated in the bargaining rounds?

4.2. Local bargaining and equal pay at the University

In the work evaluation report, we did not analyze whether the wage differentials were unwarranted or not. In the report it is said that the University has to 'objectively' justify the wage differentials between female and non-female groups that perform work of equal value. From my point of view, this was an issue for the employer and the unions to decide upon. It would have gone beyond the mission and the mandate of the wage survey group to make such a decision. If the wage differentials are concluded as unwarranted, the next step is to decide about the remedy. In this case, the persons in charge need authorisation to make such decisions. Ultimately, the person in charge is the head of the University.

It has been stated that annual wage surveys go beyond the scope for what is necessary to guarantee equal pay in the sense of EC law and that the surveys rather cause a lot of extra work for the employer. However, the meaning with these annual wage surveys was to integrate legal obligations according to active measures with the local bargaining round, i.e. obligations according to collective agreements. The wage surveys are to be seen as a foundation for the local parties and they are also necessary to fulfil as wage surveys are part of central collective agreements such as RALS. During the local bargaining round in spring 2005, the employer and the three unions at the University came to similar agreements with the following summarized content: The result of the work evaluation shall be one part of the foundation for the local wage round. The parties agree to further cooperation with the aim to analyse wage differentials between groups with work of equal value. If there are any resisting unwarranted wage differentials when the local wage round 2005-2007 is completed, they should be adjusted outside the frame for local bargaining. The parties also stated their commitment to collaborate in matters regarding equal pay. However, it is underlined in the agreement that the employer is responsible if there are any unwarranted wage differentials left when the wage round is completed.

My comment to these agreements is that the deconstruction of the gender related pay structure is in its primary stadium. The parties have accepted the work evaluation system as a method to compare men's and women's work tasks. They have also accepted the result of the evaluation. More over, they have used the bargaining arena and the collective agreement in matters of active measures for equal pay and that is indeed a step forward. To my knowledge there are few local collective agreements concerning equal pay matters at the Swedish labour market.

However, employers and union representatives are used to negotiate on wages from a conflict perspective but they are not familiar with analyzing wage differentials due to gender. Furthermore, they are not used to cooperate on wage issues beyond collective agreement borders. Due to this date, nothing has actually happened at the bargaining arena to fulfil the agreement. The unions have been passive and so has the employer, in spite of the collective agreements and the expelled intentions from both parties.

4.3. The market forces as a legitimizing concept?

Changes on the labour market in supply and demand for labour have in some respect bearing on wage setting. This is also the case for the University as an employer. In the Enderby-case the EC-court has stated that market forces can be the explanation to different wage setting when it comes to testing the employer's evidence in a case of wage discrimination. Judicially it is as always a matter of evidence. The EC-court stated that: *"If, as the question referred seems to suggest, the national court has been able to determine precisely what proportion of the increase in pay is attributable to market forces, it must necessarily accept that the pay differential is objectively justified to the extent of that proportion. When national authorities have to apply Community law, they must apply the principle of proportionality.*

If that is not the case, it is for the national court to assess whether the role of market forces in determining the rate of pay was sufficiently significant to provide objective justification for part or all of the difference".[16] The Swedish labour court has reflected upon the market forces as a legitimate ground for wage setting in the Midwife case, AD 2001 no 13 (also in AD 2001 no 51 and no 76). In the Midwife case the comparison was made between the performed work of two midwifes and a clinical engineer. The court found their work being of equal value and the employer, the Örebro County Council stated as objective grounds for wage setting; age, different collective agreements and market forces. In this case the court referred to the Enderby case and the question is how the labour court dealt with testing the employer's evidence from the principle of proportionality. Actually the employer did not have to prove anything and certainly did not have to present any analysis about the actual situation on the market or even to define what the relevant market was.

16. See theEC- case C-127/92 Enderby v. Frenchay Health Authority, 1993 ECR I-5535.

The employer just had to show that the wage-setting had been performed on "normal" grounds – i.e. that the wages had been set as a result of some kind of negotiation and settled by a collective agreement. In the three mentioned cases the labour court found no discriminatory wages due to gender as the market forces were seen as an objective ground for wage-setting. Market forces and the existence of a collective agreement were handled as somewhat equivalent. In comparison to the EC-court's statement in the Enderby-case and British case law, the Swedish labour court seems to be very sensitive to the employer's arguments for different wage setting for female and non-female dominated groups.

In the Ratcliffe case the Court of Appeal stated that: *"If market forces' are relied upon, he (the employer) must show that these are gender-neutral if he is to succeed in establishing the defence*". The Ratcliffe case was appealed to the House of Lords which declared: *"The basic question is whether the DSO paid women less than men for work rated as equivalent. The reason they did so is certainly that they had to compete with CCG [a private company]. The fact, however, is that they did pay women less than men engaged on work rated as equivalent. The industrial tribunal found and was entitled to find that the employers had not shown that this was genuinely due to a material difference other than the difference of sex.*

The women could not have found other suitable work and were obliged to take the wages offered if they were to continue with this work. The fact that two men were employed on the same work at the same rate of pay does not detract from the conclusion that there was discrimination between the women involved and their male comparators. It means no more than that the two men were underpaid compared with other men doing jobs rated as equivalent."17

The House of Lords then stated that the wage setting was directly discriminatory to the female group as there were no possibilities for them to apply for another job.[18]

So we have to be aware that employers on the Swedish labour market can hold up the midwife case as a *carte blanche* for their wage setting practices. This brings us back to the work evaluation at the University. The wage setting of IT-technicians at the University is probably a result of the overheated market in the 1990s. However; today's issue is for how long shuffling market effects can justify wage differentials between groups with work of equal val-

17. I.C.R. 1995.833.
18. For an analysis of the case see Aileen McColgan, Equal Pay, Market Forces and CCT, Industrial Law Journal, 1995, pp. 368-371.

ue? My point of view is that every employer has to decide upon whether there is a market effect or not; and what is meant by 'the market'. It is also in the employers hand to decide if it is necessary to pay the 'market price'. The market is not in itself objective in a way that a reference to the market forces per definition legitimises unwarranted wage differentials. To justify wage differentials between men and women with work of equal value merely with reference to market effects is also contradictory to equal pay legislation (Townshed-Smith 1996). The purpose of the legislation is thus to change discriminating values on the labour market and not to strengthen them.

In February 2006 the employer's delegation at the University decided that market forces was the factual ground that explained the wage differentials between female dominated and non-female dominated groups with work of equal value. Consequently there were no unwarranted wage differentials and no adjustments had to be done. I find this decision very problematic and not quite logical. First, a work evaluation system like the system used at the University is used at a collective level for evaluating the demands of work tasks in general. It should be stressed that in this evaluation at a group level, market forces are not considered, as the evaluation process is reflecting the employer's internal values. In an individual discrimination case where we evaluate a single employee's work tasks compared to another single employee, the market factor could be an external explanation and the wage differential then might be deemed as non discriminatory.

Secondly, in 2004 the University established norms for how to handle the concept market forces in individual wage setting. Market factors that can influence the employer's individual wage setting are:

1. The employee's wage in relation to comparable jobs at a relevant market, i.e. the private sector, the municipal sector and foreign universities,
2. Actual risk that the employee will leave the university,
3. The possibilities for replacing the employee in a situation of possible loss.

All these three factors are described as external factors to be used in a situation where the employer is able to calculate the costs. To sum up my opinion is that critics ought to be stressed upon how the employer's delegations handled the result of the wage evaluation. However, this is a spill over effect of the Swedish labour court's case-law concerning the market concept as a general legitimisation for men's higher wages.

5. Closing the gender pay gap at the University – a matter of co-operation or self-regulation?

By way of introduction, I put forward some issues that are complex and internally linked to each other. They are connected in purpose with the active measures to close the gender pay gap at the University. The primary issue was whether the undertaken active measures for equal pay can change the gender structure i.e. the patriarchal structure?

The work with active measures for equal pay and equal working conditions is today highly legitimised at the University even by the trade unions. From this angle, the implementation of the legislation is successful (see Segerpalm 2005). Actually we have not yet faced any strong open resistance in the implementation process, which in one way bothers me. Research on policy changes due to equality between women and men, always points out resistance in the organization as the main problem (Pincus 2002).

The general feminization of the employed staff at the University increases and in 2006 almost 60 per cent of the employees were women. This also has to be mirrored in a structure of power; academically as well as administrative. By working with different kinds of active measures, for instance affirmative action, the amount of female academics and administrative leaders has increased. The glass-ceiling has been broken. This is in line with the general plan for equality at the University.

My main issue concerns the interaction between the results of the wage surveys, especially the work evaluation and the local bargaining. Is it possible for the union representatives to cooperate with the employer to achieve pay equity, when their member's position in the wage structure is threatened? My study shows that there are problems in cooperation on wages. The work with active measures for equal pay at the University proceeded on two parallel agendas; cooperation within the wage survey group and wage negotiations between the unions and the employer, i.e. the self-regulating model. The two agendas for wage formation are built on two different perspectives; a harmony perspective and a conflict perspective. Theoretically the grounds for wage setting should be similar; wages ought to be set on factual and objective grounds in line with the central collective agreements. However, the local unions are supposed to take responsibility for the result of the work evaluation for all the employees and not only for their members. I am not sure how to analyse the passivity at the bargaining arena after the agreements set in spring 2005. It might be, as Brian Bercusson stated that: *"In discussing the potential for collective bargaining as a mechanism for promoting gender equality it is necessary to observe that, even where collective bargaining is securely estab-*

lished and extensive, there will be areas outside the scope of joint regulation and within employer prerogative which are crucial for equal opportunities. Employers' opportunities to tackle discrimination and promote gender equality in the workplace are, therefore, potentially greater than those open to trade unions, since employers can act not only through collective bargaining but also by unilateral action in their employment strategies and human resource policies" (Bercusson 1996 p. 186).

This potential the University as an employer has not used yet. My concern that there was a risk that the market forces as a legitimizing concept would be the easy way out of any consequences, was unfortunately redeemed and the union representatives seem to make no fuzz about that. In this way, it seems as like everybody wants to keep status quo.

My conclusion is that the University and the unions have failed in cooperating for equal pay; they have also failed in bargaining for equal pay at the local level. The implementation of the law has gone so far that the employer and the unions have accepted the goal and the methods; however they are not capable of handling any kind of consequences at a collective or a structural level. My conclusion is that there is a serious will to comply with the active measures for equal pay but in case the market forces are allowed to function as a general legitimate ground for wage differentials between male and female groups doing work of equal value, the result of the wage survey and the action plan will only legitimise the existing wage structure. The University's wage adjustment strategy at a central level is then actually to make no changes in the wage structure.

Finally, we must neither underestimate small wage differentials between men and women nor small steps to narrow the gender pay gap. Nonetheless, the gender pay gap at the University has diminished with 2.5 per cent during the period when the activities in favour for equal pay have been going on. However, analysing wage from a gender perspective gives rise to a variety of new perspectives that hardly ever before have been addressed. Nonetheless, closing the gender pay gap at the University of Gothenburg takes greater demands than a project on wage surveys. It also takes two to tango.

References

Acker J. (1989) Doing Comparable Worth – Gender, Class and Pay Equity. Philadelphia: Temple University Press.

Baldwin R. & Cave M. (1999) Understanding Regulation. Theory, Strategy and Practice. Oxford: Oxford University Press.

Bercusson B. (1996) 'EC equality law in context: collective bargaining', in Hervey & O'Keefe (Eds), *Sex Equality Law in the European Union.* Chichester: John Wileys & Sons.

Blau F.D. & Kahn L.M. (2000) 'Gender Difference in Pay', *Journal of Economic Perspectives*, vol. 14, No. 4, p.p. 75-99.

Blau F.D. & Kahn L.M. (2003) 'Understanding International Differences in the Gender Pay Gap', *Journal of Labour Economics,* vol. 21 p.p. 106-144.

Branney, Howes and Hegewish (1999) Union Strategies in Pursuit of Pay Equity: the Role of UNISON, in Gregory, Sales and Hegewisch (eds), *Women, Work and Inequality*, Wiltshire: Antony Rowe Ltd.

Eijlander P. (2005) 'Possibilities and Constraints in the Use of Self-Regualtion an Co-Regulation in Legislative Policy: Experiences in the Netherlands – Lesson to Be Learned for the EU?' *Electronic Journal of Comparative Law,* vol 9.1 January 2005.

England P. (1992) Comparable Worth. Theories and evidence. New York: Aldeline de Gruyter.

European Commission, *A Code of Practise on the Implementation of Equal Pay for Work of Equal Value for Men and Women.* Luxembourg: Office for Official Publications of the European Communities, 1996.

Fahlbeck R. (2002) *Industrial Relations and Collective Labour Law: Characteristics, Principles and Basic Features.* In Wahlgren P. (eds.) Stability and Change in Nordic Labour Law. Legal Abbreviations, Scandinavian Studies in Law Volume 43.

Figart D. (2000) 'Equal Pay for Equal Work: The Role of Job Evaluation in an Evolving Social Norm', *Journal of Economic Issues* No 1 March 2000.

Fransson S. & Thörnqvist C. (2003) *Gender-specific Strategies for Industrial Action: The Swedish Case in a Historical Perspective.* In Fleming D. & Thörnqvist C. (eds), Nordic Management Labour Relations and Internationalization-Converging and Diverging Tendencies. Nord 2003:015, The Nordic Council of Ministers, p.p. 193-214.

Fransson S. (2003) Rapport om JämOs 500-granskning. www.diskrimineringslagen.se

Fransson S. & Andersson M. (2005) Rapport om samverkan och lönekartläggning JämOs 50-granskning och projekt 2004-2005. www.diskrimineringslagen.se

Fransson S. & Thörnqvist C. (2006) 'Some Notes on Workplace Equality Renewal in the Swedish labour Market', *Gender, Work and Organization, Volume 13 No 6.*

Fransson S., Johansson L. & Svenaeus L. (2000), Highlighting pay differentials between women and men, The Swedish Governments Offices. www.diskrimineringslagen.se

Fransson S. & Stüber E. (2010) Diskrimineringslagen. En kommentar. Sthlm:Norstedts Juridik.

Gonäs L., Bergman A. & Rosenberg K. (2006) 'Equal opportunity and unwarranted pay differences: a case study of gender-related pay differences in a knowledge-based society', in *Gender Divisions and Working Time in the New Economy* Perrons D. et al. (eds) Cheltenham UK: Edward Elgar.

JämO, (2005) Survey, Analysis and Action Plan for Equal Pay. An in-depth analysis on effects of the regulation of 2001. Stockholm: JämO. A report to the Swedish government. The Equal Opportunities Ombudsman November 2005. www.diskrimineringslagen.se

Löfström Å. (2003) 'Overcoming barriers to equal pay in Sweden: monitoring gender main streaming', in Magnusson L et al (eds) *Equal Pay and Gender Mainstreaming in the European Employment Strategy*, Brussels: ETUI Printshop.

Magnusson L. et al (eds) Equal Pay and Gender Mainstreaming in the European Employment Strategy, Brussels: ETUI Printshop.

McCaughey K. (2005) Rights, Resources and Remedy: Equal Pay for Work of Equal Value in Quebec and Sweden. Master's Thesis in Comparative Law, Department of law, Uppsala University.

McColgan E. (1995) *Equal Pay, Market Forces and CCT*, Industrial Law Journal, 1995, p. 368-371.

National mediation office (2003, 2004, 2005, 2010) Årsrapport, Stockholm. www.mi.se .

Pincus I. (2002), The Politics of Gender Equality Policy: A Study of Implementation and Non-Implementation in Three Swedish Municipalities, Örebro: Örebro University.

Proposition 1999/00:173.

Proposition 2007/08:95.

Remick H. (1984) Comparable Worth and Wage discrimination: technical possibilities and political realities, Philadelphia: Temple University Press.

Rosenberg K. (2004) Värdet av arbete. Arbetsvärdering som ett lönepolitiskt instrument. (The valuation of work. Work evaluation as a wage political instrument.), Göteborg: Intellecta Docusys.

SACO (2003) Akademikerrapport 2003. SACO.

Segerpalm, H (2006), *Att skapa jämställda löner. En studie om tolkning och genomförande av Jämställdhetslagens 10 § vid Stockholms universitet*, 2006. Master thesis, Stockholm University.

Sorensen E. (1994) Comparable Worth. Is It a Worthy Policy?, Princeton N.J.: Princeton University Press.

Statistics Sweden (2005) *Women and men in Sweden: Facts and Figures 2005,* Demographic Analysis and Gender Equality.

Svensson E-M. (2007) 'Boundary-work in Legal Scholarship' in Gunnarsson, Svensson and Davies (eds) *Exploiting the Limits of Law. Swedish Feminism and the Challenge to Pessimism,* Ashgate.

The Swedish Government Agency (2005) Utvecklingen av löneskillnader mellan statsanställda kvinnor och män åren 2000-2005. Dnr 0605-0396-15.

Townshed-Smith R. (1996) 'Economic Defences to Equal Pay Claims', in Hervey & O'Keefe (eds), *Sex Equality in the European Union,* Chichester: John Wiley & Sons.

Toursie A. (2004) Varför tjänar kvinnor mindre? Handbok i lönediskriminering, (Why do women earn less?) LO; Bilda Idé.

Wiiteveen W. J. (2005) 'A Self-regulation Paradox: Notes towards the Social Logic of Regulation', *Electronic Journal of Comparative Law*, vol. 9.1 January 2005 (http://www.ejcl.org/)

CHAPTER 7

Discrimination against Women in the Field of Criminal Law

Particularly on Gender-based Violence

By Trine Baumbach, associate professor, PhD, Faculty of Law, University of Copenhagen

1. Introductory remarks

In most of the European countries equality between men and women has formally been recognised for many years. In spite of this recognition, in reality, there is still a widespread gender inequality within Europe and even within the member states of the European Union. Also in the Nordic Countries, which usually boast themselves of being modern societies, a great deal of discrimination against women takes place every day.

In the field of criminal law, discrimination against women has many faces. One of the considerable problem areas is gender-based violence, particularly domestic violence. This is due to at least two reasons. Firstly, domestic violence has generally been seen and understood as a private matter in which the government should not interfere and for which it is not accountable. The home has traditionally been idealised as a place of safety and security, and the relationship between members of the family has been idealised as a respectful and supportive relationship[1] – even though it has been known since the dawn of time that this approach is far from reality in every home.

1. See Dorothy Q. Thomas and Michele E. Beasley, Domestic Violence as a Human Rights Issue, Human Rights Quarterly, 1993, p. 43 and Trine Baumbach, Vold mod

Secondly, discrimination against women is not at all identified in the field of criminal law, and what is worse there is not even an awareness that discrimination might by taking place. This is due to the fact that the wielded discrimination frequently takes place in the form of indirect discrimination or in the special form of discrimination that gender-based violence constitutes.[2] Because of very well incorporated legal maxims regarding common and specific equal treatment principles, which can best be compared to the figure "direct discrimination", and which are seen as all-encompassing regarding unequal treatment, the Danish legal culture hinders recognition of the legal figure indirect discrimination in this field, just as unacquaintance with the international approach to gender-based violence hinders the identification of this special form of discrimination and thereby hinders the legal addressing of it.[3] Consequently, gender and gender discrimination have not been reputable topics in Danish academic research in the field of criminal law. The prevalent opinion, both in Danish academic research and in Danish courts' judicial review, has been that the criminal legislation applies to both men and women and furthermore that we do not discriminate against anyone in any way. Gender issues have therefore no place in this area.

Through an analysis of selected judgments this article will show that discrimination against women takes widely place in the field of criminal law and will demonstrate how the problem can be identified and addressed. The analysis will be illustrated by a Danish example regarding murder cases in the field of domestic violence and murder. Prior to the analysis, the article will account for the various discrimination figures and examine the most important international instruments in the field. Finally the article will deal with some legal-policy remarks.

kvinder – hvor hårdt skal der straffes, Juristen 2010, p. 169 f. See also Minna Ruuskanen, The "Good Battered Woman": A Silenced Defendant, in Kevät Nousiainen et all, Responsible Selves. Women in the Nordic legal culture, 2001, p. 311 ff.

2. See further below.
3. See, regarding similar issues in the fields of collective labour law, Ruth Nielsen, The Enforcement of EU Sex Discrimination Law, in Kevät Nousiainen et all, Responsible Selves. Women in the Nordic legal culture, 2001, p. 223 ff.

2. The notion of discrimination

The concept of human rights is built upon the principle of human dignity and human freedom.[4] The prohibition against discrimination represents a democratic ideal of all human beings' equal dignity and equal rights – both as a requirement of the law's content not to be (arbitrary or unfactual) discriminatory and as a requirement of equality before the law without discrimination of any kind. Not only history, but also the state of affairs in many countries today shows that discrimination, whether it happens because of race, gender or any other illegal criterion, leads to undemocratic modes – to the detriment not only for the oppressed, but also for the society as such and especially for the welfare development in the society. The legal notion of discrimination must therefore be so broad and have so far a scope that it addresses the issues that constitute the reason for which the prohibition of discrimination was introduced in the first place.

There is both national and international general legislative consensus regarding the definition of direct and indirect discrimination. The definitions go as follows:

Direct discrimination is where one person is treated less favourable on grounds of i.a. gender than another is, has been or would be, treated in a comparable situation.

Indirect discrimination is where an apparently neutral provision, criterion or practice would put persons of i.a. one gender at a particular disadvantage compared with persons of the other gender, unless that provision, criterion or practice is objectively justified by a legitimate aim, and the means of achieving that aim are appropriate and necessary.

As it is seen from the definitions, direct discrimination is usually easy to identify because the discrimination is normally flagrantly evident, whereas indirect discrimination can be difficult to identify. This is due to the fact that indirect discrimination on the surface seems non-discriminatory. But, as the definition says, if the provision, criterion or practice actually puts, for instance, women at a particular disadvantage compared with men, the woman is

4. See i.a. the C.R. v. the United Kingdom judgment of 22 November 1995, ECHR 20190/92,http://cmiskp.echr.coe.int/tkp197/view.asp?item=1&portal=hbkm&action=html&highlight=20190/92&sessionid=72559382&skin=hudoc-en, last visited 1 September 2011 and S.W. v. the United Kingdom judgment of 22 November 1995, ECHR 20166/92, http://cmiskp.echr.coe.int/tkp197/view.asp?item=1&portal=hbkm-&action=html&highlight=20166/92&sessionid=72559494&skin=hudoc-en, last visited 1 September 2011.

discriminated against unless the provision et cetera is objectively justified by a legitimate aim, and the means of achieving that aim are appropriate and necessary. It is important to note that it is not a requirement that the discrimination was intentional in any way. It is enough that the treatment has actually had that effect.

As mentioned, to these two types of discrimination there must be added the special form of discrimination which gender-based violence constitutes. This form of discrimination is characterised by the fact that it only relates to cases where women have been exposed to violence – either because they are women or where the violence affects women disproportionately. In connection with the examination of the selected judgments below, this discrimination-figure will be characterised further.

3. International initiatives on gender-based violence

On March 5, 2010 the Commission of the European Union found it necessary to devise a Women's Charter[5] because of the widespread gender inequalities within the EU.

The Women's Charter sets out five key areas for action, of which number four goes as follows:

"Dignity, Integrity and an end to Gender-Based Violence
The full enjoyment of fundamental rights by women and girls is an inalienable, integral and indivisible part of universal human rights and is essential for the advancement of women and girls, peace, security and development. Gender-based violence, including harmful customary or traditional practices, constitutes a violation of fundamental rights, in particular human dignity, the right to life, and the right to the integrity of the person. Such violation prevents the exercise of a self-determined life.

5. Communication from the Commission. A Strengthened Commitment to Equality between Women and Men. A Women's Charter. Declaration by the European Commission on the occasion of the 2010 International Women's Day in commemoration of the 15th anniversary of the adoption of a Declaration and Platform for Action at the Beijing UN World Conference on Women and of the 30th anniversary of the UN Convention on the Elimination of All forms of Discrimination against Women. See also UN Women, In Pursuit of Justice, Ten Recommendations to make Justice Systems Work for Women, especially recommendation no. 2 "Support one-stop shops and specialized services to reduce attrition in the justice chain", no. 3 "Implement gender-sensitive law reform", and no. 6 "Train judges and monitor decisions".

We reaffirm our commitment to ensure that respect for fundamental rights is at the core of our activities. We will undertake efforts to eliminate gender inequalities in access to healthcare and in health outcomes.

Europe does not tolerate gender-based violence. We will step up efforts to eradicate all forms of violence and to provide support for those affected. We will put in place a comprehensive and effective policy framework to combat gender-based violence. We will strengthen our action to eradicate female genital mutilation and other acts of violence, including by means of criminal law, within the limits of our powers."

As it appears from the introduction to the Charter, equality between women and men is a fundamental right. In relation to the European Union the principle is consequently enshrined, inter alia, in Article 2 of the Treaty on European Union and in Article 21 of the Charter of Fundamental Rights of the European Union.[6] However, the principle reaches across the European Union and is for instance stated in the hereinafter mentioned international instruments.

With particular focus on women, and thereby on gender discrimination, the United Nations in 1979 adopted the Convention on the Elimination of All Forms of Discrimination against Women (CEDAW). In the preamble to the Convention, the States Parties referred to a number of international instruments that affirm to the principle of the inadmissibility of discrimination, among them the Universal Declaration of Human Rights adopted by the General Assembly of the United Nations in 1948, and then proclaimed that all human beings are born free and equal in dignity and rights and that everyone is entitled to all the rights and freedoms set forth in those instruments, without distinction of any kind, including distinction based on gender. In spite of that ascertainment of facts the States Parties can record that extensive discrimination against women continues to exist.

The Convention defines in Article 1 discrimination against women as "...any distinction, exclusion or restriction made on the basis of sex which has the effect or purpose of impairing or nullifying the recognition, enjoyment or exercise by women, irrespective of their marital status, on a basis of equality of men and women, of human rights and fundamental freedoms in the political, economic, social, cultural, civil or any other field."[7]

6. See further of the prohibition of discrimination in EU-law, Ruth Nielsen in Ulla Neergaard and Ruth Nielsen, EU Ret, 6 revised edition, 2010, p. 191 ff. and Ruth Nielsen, Civilretlige diskriminationsforbud, 2010.
7. See further about the CEDAW-convention Stine Jørgensen (2007), *Etniske minoritetskvinders sociale rettigheder. Arbejdsmarked, seksualitet og uddannelse,* Jurist- og Økonomforbundets Forlag, Kirsten Ketscher (2003), *Kvindekonventionen gælder i dansk ret,* in Henrik Dam et al., Jura & historie. Festskrift til Inger Dübeck som forsker, p. 439 ff. and *Kvindekonventionen CEDAW og dens placering i international og*

As the name of the Convention implies, the whole Convention is dedicated to the elimination of all forms of discrimination against women and addresses a lot of vital question through the separate articles in the Convention. However, the initial articles are of general character, whereof Article 5 is significant. Article 5 reads as follows:

> "States Parties shall take all appropriate measures:
> (a) To modify the social and cultural patterns of conduct of men and women, with a view to achieving the elimination of prejudices and customary and all other practices which are based on the idea of the inferiority or the superiority of either of the sexes or on stereotyped roles for men and women;
> ..."

As we shall see later, this article is of great importance in the combating of gender-based violence, both on the individual level as well as socially, because of the crime's special nature.

In 1992 the CEDAW-Committee[8] adopted General Recommendation No. 19 on violence against women. The Recommendation is preceded with the ascertainment *that gender-based violence is a form of discrimination* that seriously inhibits women's ability to enjoy rights and freedoms on a basis of equality with men. Under the headline "General Comments" the Committee states:

> "...
> The Convention in Article 1 defines discrimination against women. The definition of discrimination includes gender-based violence, that is, violence that is directed against a woman because she is a woman or that affects women disproportionately. It includes acts that inflict physical, mental or sexual harm or suffering, threats of such acts, coercion and other deprivations of liberty. Gender-based violence may breach specific provisions of the Convention, regardless of whether those provisions expressly mention violence.
>
> Gender-based violence, which impairs or nullifies the enjoyment by women of human rights and fundamental freedoms under general international law or under human rights conventions, is discrimination within the meaning of Article 1 of the Convention..."

As a comment inter alia to Article 5, the Committee expresses:

dansk ret, Artikelsamling, Dansk Kvindesamfund, 2007, p. 7 ff., Anne Hellum (2008), *Kvinnekonvensjonens betydning for det alminnelige kjønnsdiskrimineringsvern*, in Anne Hellum et al., Diskriminerings- og Likestillingsrett, p. 58 ff., and Trine Baumbach, Hvor er kønnet i dansk strafferet, in Eva-Maria Svensson et al.

8. Committee on the Elimination of Discrimination of Women. The Committee's mandate and the administration of the Convention are defined in Article 17 to/- 30 of the Convention.

"Traditional attitudes by which women are regarded as subordinate to men or as having stereotyped roles perpetuate widespread practices involving violence or coercion, such as family violence and abuse, forced marriage, dowry deaths, acid attacks and female circumcision. Such prejudices and practices may justify gender-based violence as a form of protection or control of women. The effect of such violence on the physical and mental integrity of women is to deprive them of the equal enjoyment, exercise and knowledge of human rights and fundamental freedoms. While this comment addresses mainly actual or threatened violence the underlying consequences of these forms of gender-based violence help to maintain women in subordinate roles and contribute to their low level of political participation and to their lower level of education, skills and work opportunities.

These attitudes also contribute to the propagation of pornography and the depiction and other commercial exploitation of women as sexual objects, rather than as individuals. This in turn contributes to gender-based violence."

The General Assembly of the United Nations has yet to concede that an effective implementation of the Convention on the Elimination of All Forms of Discrimination against Women (and thereby the General Recommendation No. 19 on violence against Women) has as a requisite the elimination of the far-reaching violence against women. Because of that acknowledgement the General Assembly in 1993 adopted the Declaration on the Elimination of Violence against Women.[9] From the preamble appears, among other things, the following:

"The general Assembly
Recognizing that violence against women is a manifestation of historically unequal power relations between men and women, which have led to domination over and discrimination against women by men and to the prevention of the full advancement of women, and that violence against women is one of the crucial social mechanisms by which women are forced into a subordinate position compared with men,

...

[is] Alarmed that opportunities for women to achieve legal, social, political and economic equality in society are limited, inter alia, by continuing and endemic violence."

In accordance with Article 1 in the Declaration, "violence against women" means "any act of gender-based violence that results in, or is likely to result in, physical, sexual or psychological harm or suffering to women, including threats of such acts, coercion or arbitrary deprivation of liberty, whether occurring in public or in private life."

The notion of "violence against women" is, according to Article 2 of the Declaration, broad and encompasses (but is not limited to);

9. General Assembly Resolution 48/104 of 20 December 1993.

(a) Physical, sexual and psychological violence occurring in the family, including battering, sexual abuse of female children in the household, dowry-related violence, marital rape, female genital mutilation and other traditional practices harmful to women, non-spousal violence and violence related to exploitation;
(b) Physical, sexual and psychological violence occurring within the general community, including rape, sexual abuse, sexual harassment and intimidation at work, in educational institutions and elsewhere, trafficking in women and forced prostitution;
(c) Physical, sexual and psychological violence perpetrated or condoned by the State, wherever it occurs.

According to Article 4, letter c and d the state should, inter alia, exercise due diligence to prevent, investigate and, in accordance with national legislation, punish acts of violence against women, whether those acts are perpetrated by the State or *by private persons*, and develop penal, civil, labour and administrative sanctions in domestic legislation to punish and redress the wrongs caused to women who are subjected to violence.

In 1995 the Declaration was followed up by the Beijing Declaration and Platform for Action.[10]

Also for the Council of Europe, violence against women gives rise to major concern. In 2000 the Council of Europe Parliamentary Assembly therefore adopted a recommendation regarding violence against women in Europe.[11] The parliamentary Assembly noted among other things that hundreds of thousands of women in Europe face physical and mental violence at home or outside. Although domestic violence is one of the most common forms of violence against women, it remains the least visible.

The last-mentioned ascertainment is from a human rights perspective and from a crime fighting point of view very important to emphasise as the present crimes differ from violence committed on the street or elsewhere given that it is usually committed in hidden surroundings and often not reported to the police by the victim due to her life situation or because of fear for reprisals from the perpetrator. A lot of the domestic violence that by chance or because of necessary medical care comes to the public authority's attention are explained away or excused with a staircase stumble or something like that.

10. See further www.un.org/womenwatch/daw/beijing/index.html. The Beijing Declaration was again followed up in 2000 by the United Nations General Assembly by the Resolution on further actions and initiatives to implement the Beijing Declaration and Platform for Action.
11. Council of Europe Parliamentary Assembly's Recommendation 1450 (2000) on violence against women in Europe.

Repeated domestic violence stretches the limits of the woman's borders, just as it is many women's bitter experience that notification to the police only increases the violence and harassment they face at home. A lot of victims feel shameful and blame themselves for the wrongdoing they have been exposed to. A large part of these victims suffer an additional kind of indignity by the "disclosure" of the crime which a police report poses. In addition, women living in an abusive relationship often become isolated and are using their energy to try to avoid or minimize the violence and thus do not have the energy to find a way out of the assault situation.

In 2002 the Council of Europe Committee of Ministers too adopted a recommendation regarding protection of women against violence.[12] In the preamble to the recommendation the Committee notices, inter alia:

> "Reaffirming that violence towards women is the result of an imbalance of power between men and women and is leading to serious discrimination against the female sex, both within society and within the family;
>
> ...
>
> Considering that violence against women runs counter to the establishment of equality and peace and constitutes a major obstacle to citizens' security and democracy in Europe;
>
> ...
>
> Considering it urgent to combat this phenomenon which affects all European societies and concerns all their members..."

The recommendation is very comprehensive and thorough. Because violence against women, in spite of all the international instruments already adopted, does not cease to exist, the Committee recommends that member states review their legislation and policies with a view to, among others things, guaranteeing women the recognition, enjoyment, exercise and protection of their human rights and fundamental freedoms, and to recognise that states have an obligation to exercise due diligence to prevent, investigate and punish acts of violence, whether those acts are perpetrated by the state or private persons and provide protection to the victims. The Committee also recommends that the governments of member states recognise that male violence against women is a major structural and societal problem, based on the unequal power relations between women and men and therefore encourage the active participation of men in actions aiming at combating violence against women. It is said in the Explanatory Memorandum of the Recommendation that violence against women needs to be understood in a social context and not as a series

12. Recommendation Rec(2002)5 of the Committee of Ministers to member States on the protection of women against violence adopted on 30 April 2002.

of individual unconnected events. Violence against women is the result of a social construction of a particular form of masculinity (aggressive masculinity) justified in traditions, habits and beliefs which permit the perpetrators to assume the right to use violence as a means of exercising their dominance and control. The Explanatory Memorandum underlines that this is not to say that men are not individually responsible for their actions – the phenomenon is just to be understood and thereby combated with the knowledge of the structurally origin of the gender-based violence.[13]

The Explanatory Memorandum's remarks fall perfectly in line with resent years' research in violent behaviour. Research has thus established that male violence against women in close relationship is a gender problem and stems from a desire to be in control of the woman and have the power over her. The violence is not random, but an active choice (and thereby not an act of passion). The act of violence is hence an act under control with direction and intention, just as it is aimed downwards in the power system. Research in violence describes the phenomenon as "the hierarchical nature of violence". The research shows that a lot of perpetrators are acting on the basis of a "rights" perspective due to a patriarchal view on the relationship between men and women.[14]

It is interesting to notice that the Committee, in its Appendix to the Recommendation in the notion of "violence against women", *includes* crimes committed in the name of honour, traditional practices harmful to women, such as forced marriages and trafficking in women for the purposes of sexual exploitation and economic exploitation and sex tourism. If these acts are committed by any form of violence, the inclusion is accurate.

In the field of criminal law the Appendix to the Recommendation recommends inter alia that the Member States should provide for appropriate measures and sanctions in national legislation, making it possible to take swift and effective action against perpetrators of violence and redress the wrong done to women who are victims of violence.[15] As we shall see later

13. See Explanatory Memorandum to Recommendation Rec(2002)5 of the Committee of Ministers to Member States on the protection of women against violence adopted on 30 April 2002, pr. 54.
14. See further Per Isdal, Meningen med volden, 2002, p. 104 ff. and Per Isdal and Marius Råkil, Volden er mannens ansvar behandling av mannlige voldsutøvere som tiltak mod kvinnemishandling, in Marius råkil (ed.), Menns vold mot kvinder. Behandlingserfaringer og kunnskapsstatus, 2002, p. 103ff.
15. Recommendation Rec(2002)5 of the Committee of Ministers to member States on the protection of women against violence adopted on 30 April 2002. Appendix to Recommendation Rec(2002)5, pr. 35.

on, the proportionality of the imposed sanction is of substantial importance in the combating of the crime and in the redressing of the victims.

A general prohibition of discrimination is set forward in Article 14 of the European Convention on Human Rights and Fundamental Freedoms. The article reads:

"Prohibition of discrimination
The enjoyment of the rights and freedoms set forth in this Convention shall be secured without discrimination on any ground such as sex, race, colour, language, religion, political or other opinion, national or social origin, association with a national minority, property, birth or other status."

Article 14 is significant, even though it is not an autonomous prohibition specialized to discrimination against women or to the topic of gender-based violence, since it by a piece of legislation is incorporated into Danish law and since there to the Convention is linked a judicial court, namely the European Court of Human Rights. Article 14 covers both direct and indirect discrimination, as those figures are generally defined. Even though the Court itself does not use the terms direct and indirect discrimination – but defines discrimination with slightly different words – the definition goes as follows:

"The Court has established in its case-law that discrimination means treating differently, without an objective and reasonable justification, person in relevantly similar situations… It has also accepted that a general policy or measure that has disproportionately prejudicial effects on a particular group may be considered discriminatory notwithstanding that it is not specifically aimed at that group.… And that discrimination potentially contrary to the Convention may result from a *de facto* situation…"[16]

Like the aforementioned general definition of the legal figure discrimination, discrimination in respect of Article 14 can be established only if the applicant has been treated differently compared to others in a relevant comparable situation.

The examination done by the European Court of Human Rights has 4 elements: (1) does the complaint of discrimination fall within the ambit or scope of a protected right in the Convention or the Protocols? This element does not require that there is a breach of (another) Convention right. On the other

16. See the Opuz v. Turkey judgment of 9 June 2009, ECHR 33401/02, pr. 183, http://cmiskp.echr.coe.int/tkp197/view.asp?item=1&portal=hbkm&action=html&highlight=33401/02&sessionid=71989751&skin=hudoc-en, last visited 1 September 2011.

hand, the complaint must fall within the ambit of the protected rights in the Convention complex since Article 14 only applies in respect of "the enjoyment of the rights and freedoms set forth in this Convention". (2) Is the alleged reason for the discrimination one of the grounds listed in Article 14? This requirement rarely gives raise to any dispute between the parties since the list of grounds is not exhaustive (compare "other status"). On the other hand, element 2 is closely linked with the next element, namely (3): Can the applicant properly compare him or her self with another group of persons which is treated more favourably? In other words, it must be shown that the applicant and the comparator group are in a relevant similar situation. People in different situations are often to be treated differently, so the applicant cannot plead discrimination unless he or she is able to show that the person in question was in a relevant similar situation as the comparator group (which has been treated more favourably). The purpose of this element is to enable the Court to determine whether the less favourable treatment is attributable to one of the prohibited grounds listed in Article 14 and not to other (lawful) factors.[17] Said otherwise, element 3 contains a causal relation between the prohibited ground and the treatment. Element 3 is again closely linked with the final element, namely (4) is the difference of treatment capable of objective and reasonable justification?[18] In the L. and V. v. Austria the Court said:

> "According to the Court's established case-law, a difference in treatment is discriminatory for the purposes of Article 14 if it "has no objective and reasonable justification", that is if it does not pursue a "legitimate aim" or if there is not a "reasonable relationship of proportionality between the means employed and the aim sought to be realised". However, the Contracting States enjoy a certain margin of appreciation in assessing whether and to what extent differences in otherwise similar situations justify a different treatment."[19]

In addition to the standard or common definition of discrimination, the European Court of Human Rights has, as we shall see below, recognised that the special form of discrimination which gender-based violence reflects, is also covered by Article 14.

17. Se further Jacobs, White and Ovey, The European Convention of Human Rights Fifth Edition 2010, p. 558 ff.
18. See further Jacobs, White and Ovey, The European Convention of Human Rights Fifth Edition 2010, p. 554 ff.
19. See the L. and V. v. Austria judgment of 9 January 2003, para 44, ECHR 39392/98 and 39829/98, http://cmiskp.echr.coe.int/tkp197/view.asp?item=12&portal=hbkm-&action= html&highlight=AUSTRIA%20%7C%2014&sessionid=72849224&skin=-hudoc-en,last visited 1 September 2011.

4. Judgments from the European Court of Human Rights

As early as in 1995 in the C.R. and S.W. v. the United Kingdom[20] judgments the European Court of Human Rights (unanimous chamber) acknowledged – even though implicit – that the domestic criminal law is not allowed to be discriminatory against women, as discrimination against women would be at variance with the fundamental objectives of the Convention, the very essence of that which is respect for human dignity and human freedom. The cases were not tried under Article 14 (but under Article 7 regarding no punishment without law) given that the cases were brought before the Court by the perpetrators and not by the victims. In spite of this, the judgments respond to the substance of the problem examined in the present article.

On the basis of the Court's judgments, the facts of the cases relevant to the discrimination issue can be set out as follows.

The applicants in both cases were men who had been convicted of rape of their wives. In one of the cases the wife had informed the applicant that she wanted a divorce, but she had not moved out of the family home or had taken any legal steps to have the matrimony terminated. In the other case the wife had also informed the applicant that she wanted a divorce, and she had, together with their child, moved out of the family home. At the material time, the state of the law in England was that a husband could not rape his wife, as she, so to speak, had accepted sexual intercourse by marrying him – a legal practice that went back to 1736. There had, however, in recent times evolved some exceptions to this legal practice, i.a. if the parties were separated at the material time, but none of these exceptions could apply in neither of the cases. The substance in the state of law had for some years before the material time been debated, but without any change in the law, though. The offence of rape was traditionally defined in common law systems as the "*unlawful* sexual intercourse with a woman without her consent by force, fear or fraud".[21]

After the material time, but before the conviction of S.W., the English Court of Appeal in the case against C.R. determined that the husband's immunity was not in force any longer. The ruling was upheld by the House of Lords, as the lawlords observed that "the common law was capable of evolving in the light of changing social, economic and cultural developments".[22] S.W. was convicted by the national courts as well.

20. See supra note 2.
21. See ibid, para. 16, respective para. 19 (my italicise).
22. See ibid, para. 15, respectively para. 12.

Both of the applicants complained that they had been convicted in breach of Article 7 of the Convention since they were convicted in respect of conduct which at the material time did not, in their opinion, constitute a criminal offence. A change in law could only take place by legislation and only ex nunc. In the opinion of the applicants, the change in law of the offence of rape constituted a reversal of the former state of the law, and not just some kind of clarification of the law. Consequently, the change in law did not satisfy a foresee ability test, and this was true even though the national courts did not create an entirely new offence or change the basic ingredients of the offence of rape, as they had extended an existing offence to include conduct that until then was excluded by the common law and therefore not punishable – but quite the contrary, lawful. Such a change in law was precisely what Article 7 of the Convention was designed to prevent.[23]

The Government's main argument was that the national Courts' interpretation of the offence of rape did not go so far as to create a new offence, rather it codified the evolution that had been on its way for quite some time. The convictions had therefore been foreseeable to the applicants. The Government emphasised that the evolution must be seen in the light of "the recognition of women's equality of status with men in marriage and outside it and of their autonomy over their own bodies".[24]

The European Court of Human Rights preceded the judgment by underlining that the guarantee enshrined in Article 7, which is an essential element of the rule of law, occupies a prominent place in the Convention's system of protection, as underlined by the fact that no derogation from it is permissible under Article 15 in time of war or other public emergency. Article 7 should therefore be construed and applied, as follows from its object and purpose, in such a way as to provide effective safeguards against arbitrary prosecution, conviction and punishment.

Besides of the prohibition laid down in Article 7 regarding the retrospective application of the criminal law, the Court has from Article 7 deduced some general principles, namely the principle of legality and the principle that the criminal law must not be extensively construed to an accused's detriment, for instance by analogy. From this last-mentioned principle it follows, according to the Court that an offence must be clearly defined in the law.[25]

23. See ibid, para 35 ff., respectively para 37 ff.
24. See ibid, para. 38, respectively para. 40.
25. From a Danish perspective it is noteworthy that the notion of "law" in the Convention is broader than the corresponding notion in § 1 in the Danish criminal law (regarding

This requirement is, however, satisfied when the individual can know from the wording of the relevant provision and, if need be, with the assistance of the national courts' interpretation of it or with appropriate legal advice, what acts and omissions will make her or him criminally liable. The fact that it is not a decided demand that law is clear or "distinct" in the proper sense of the word, is due to the fact that however clearly drafted a legal provision may be, there is an inevitable element of judicial interpretation in any system of law, including criminal law, as there will always be a need for elucidation of doubtful points and for adaptation to changing circumstances. The progressive development of the criminal law through judicial law-making is a well entrenched and necessary part of the legal tradition of all the High Contracting Parties, and the Court has confirmed and approved that.

In the case at hand the "changing circumstance" did not, however, concern factual circumstances, as is normally the case, for instance because of new technology or other new factual arrangements or conversions. On the contrary, the factual circumstances were quite the same. The change in law was caused by a changed attitude to marriage, women and self-determination.

The Court saw no reason to disagree with the national courts' conclusion in this matter (that the change in law could be caused by a changed attitude) and quoted the national courts' words regarding the husband's immunity, namely that the word "unlawful" in the definition of rape was merely surplusage and did not inhibit the national courts from "removing a common law fiction which had become anachronistic and offensive" and from declaring that "a rapist remains a rapist subject to the criminal law, irrespective of his relationship with his victim".[26] The national courts had therefore not constituted a new offence by implicating a husband in the scope of the offence of rape.

Consequently, the only remaining task of the Court was to determine whether the development of the offence of rape was foreseeable to the applicants at the material time and, if so, to determine if the national courts for other reasons had gone too far in their interpretation of the offence. In the Court's view there had been an evident evolution of the offence, which was consistent with the very essence of the offence, through judicial interpretation towards considering rape committed by husbands within the scope of the offence of rape, and this evolution had been foreseeable for the applicants. The convictions of the applicants had therefore not been at variance with the ob-

the national principle of legality), which is limited to legislation. The broader notion in the Convention is i.a. for the sake of the common law systems.

26. See supra note 2, para. 40, respectively para. 42.

ject and purpose of Article 7 because of the change in law or of other reasons. The Court ended its reasoning with the following statement:

> "What is more, the abandonment of the unacceptable idea of a husband being immune against prosecution for rape of his wife was in conformity not only with a civilised concept of marriage but also, and above all, with the fundamental objectives of the Convention, the very essence of that which is respect for human dignity and human freedom"[27]

Seen from a mere Article 7 standpoint, the judgments are not unproblematic – and the applicants did have a point in their argumentation, because if it had been the parliament, and not the courts, who had wanted to change the legal position of the rape offence, they could only have done it ex nunc. Seen from a general human rights perspective, and taking into account the overriding purpose of the human rights concept and the fact that the rights and freedoms set out in the Convention are meant to protect all human beings – and therefore in a criminal law context both perpetrators and victims – the judgments could not have had a different outcome. In addition, the common law development was not considered extensive and unexpected.

As it is seen from the exposition of the case, the Court perceived a lack of recognition of women's right to equality and autonomy over their own bodies in and outside marriage as a violation of the bedrock principle of human rights, namely the principle of human dignity and human freedom. Such a violation is in no circumstances justifiable and especially not on the basis of a law that already on the judicial time had been obsolete for many years – which the Court was quite aware of. Even though the case was not tried under Article 14 (due to the applicants' positions), the judgment is an important point of orientation with respect to discrimination in the field of criminal law.

In the M.C. v. Bulgaria judgment[28] – where the applicant was the victim of the crime – the European Court of Human Rights also assessed the case from a gender discrimination perspective even though the Court in the light of the other findings in the case did not consider it necessary to examine the complaint under Article 14 of the Convention.

27. Ibid, para 42, respectively para. 44.
28. See the M.C. v. Bulgaria judgment of 4 December 2003, ECHR 39272/98, http://cmiskp.echr.coe.int/tkp197/view.asp?item=1&portal=hbkm&action=html&highlight=39272/98&sessionid=72893866&skin=hudoc-en, last visited 1 September 2011.

This case was too a rape case although the rape was not committed in the domestic square. On the basis of the Court's judgment, the facts of the case relevant to the discrimination issue can be set out as follows:

The applicant, M.C., alleged that she had been raped twice the same night by two men (A and P) when she was only 14 years old (the age of consent for sexual intercourse in Bulgaria). The applicant met the two men at a disco. She knew both of them beforehand. They asked her if she, together with a third man, would like to go to another disco in another town. She agreed on the condition that she was driven back as she was only allowed to stay out until 11 p.m. They went in P's car. On their way back, the chauffeur decided that they should stop to have a swim at a reservoir. According to the applicant, she repealed to this suggestion, but she did not suspect the men of having anything evil in mind. The three men left the car, but immediately after P came back. He started to kiss the applicant and she asked him to stop and tried to push him back. She did not succeed as he was far too strong. Instead P had undressed her partially and had forced her to have sexual intercourse with him. In her testimony, the applicant stated: "It was my first time and it hurt a lot. I felt sick and I wanted to throw up. I started crying".[29] Besides of that, she had not had the strength to resist violently or scream.

According to P's statements, he had had sex with the applicant with her full consent.

After P had finished, he left the car and walked towards A and the third man. In A's submissions to the police he said that P had told them that he had "shagged" the applicant. Shortly afterwards, the three men returned to the car and the group drove off. None of the men had had a swim. Later that evening the applicant was taken to a private home. She claimed that A forced her to have sex with him in the house and that she cried continually both during and after the rape. According to A's statements to the police, he had sex with her with her full consent. Later, she was found by her mother and taken to a hospital where a medical examination found that her hymen had been torn recently. Besides of that she had bruises and injuries.

The police investigation lasted over a long period of time. In the end, the District Prosecution Service dismissed the case because it found that the use of force or threats had not been established beyond reasonable doubt. In particular, no resistance on the applicant's part or attempts to seek help from others had been established. The applicant appealed unsuccessfully to the re-

29. Ibid, para. 17.

gional prosecutor's office and the Chief Public Prosecutor's Office. In the regional prosecutor's decision it was i.a. stated:

> "It is true that, as can be seen from the report of the forensic psychiatric experts, the young age of the applicant and her lack of experience in life meant that she was unable to assert a stable set of convictions, namely to demonstrate firmly her unwillingness to engage in sexual contact. There can be no criminal act under Article 152 §§ 1 (2) and 3 of the Criminal Code, however, unless the applicant was coerced into having sexual intercourse by means of physical force or threats. This presupposes resistance, but there is no evidence of resistance in this particular case. P. and A. could be held criminally responsible only if they understood that they were having sexual intercourse without the applicant's consent and if they used force or made threats precisely with the aim of having sexual intercourse against the applicant's will. There is insufficient evidence to establish that the applicant demonstrated unwillingness to have sexual intercourse and that P. and A. used threats or force."[30]

The Chief Public Prosecutor reasoned his decision as follows:

> "What is decisive in the present case is that it has not been established beyond reasonable doubt that physical or psychological force was used against the applicant and that sexual intercourse took place against her will and despite her resistance. There are no traces of physical force such as bruises, torn clothing, etc. ..."
>
> It is true that it is unusual for a girl who is under age and a virgin to have sexual intercourse twice within a short space of time with two different people, but this fact alone is not sufficient to establish that a criminal act took place, in the absence of other evidence and in view of the impossibility of collecting further evidence."[31]

Under Bulgarian law, rape is defined as "sexual intercourse with a woman 1) incapable of defending herself, where she did not consent, 2) who was compelled by the use of force or threats" or "3) who was brought to a state of helplessness by the perpetrator."

The state of law concerning rape in a wide range of Council of Europe countries were accounted for in the judgment, just as several international instruments (including the CEDAW Committee's General Recommendation No. 19) and judgments were implicated.

The Court preceded its premise by determining that States have a positive obligation inherent in Articles 3 and 8 of the Convention to enact criminal-law provisions effectively punishing rape and to apply them in practice through effective investigation and prosecution.[32]

30. Ibid, para. 64.
31. Ibid, para. 65
32. Ibid, para. 148 ff.

With regard to the notion of rape, the Court, under the heading: "The modern conception of the elements of rape and its impact of the substance of member States' positive obligation to provide adequate protection", ascertained that states enjoy a wide margin of appreciation and that they are, therefore, permitted to take i.a. perceptions of the domestic culture into account. However, the Court continued immediately after by saying that the margin of appreciation is circumscribed by the Convention provisions read in the light of present day's conditions and that the Court must have regard to the changing conditions within Contracting States and respond, for example to any evolving convergence as to the standards to be achieved. The Court stated that in the last decades there has been a trend in Europe and some other parts of the world towards abandoning a formalistic definition of the offence of rape in domestic law, which previously required proof of physical force and physical resistance, towards abandoning a narrow interpretation of the offence. Firstly, it is no longer a requirement that the victim must resist physically, just as the reference to physical force has been removed in various countries. In the Court's view, it is significant that in case-law and legal theory in most European countries, lack of consent, not force, is seen as the constituent element of the offence of rape. In addition, the Member States of the Council of Europe, through the Committee of Ministers, "have agreed that penalising non-consensual sexual acts [including] cases where the victim does not show signs of resistance, is necessary for the effective protection of women against violence." The Court concluded that there is a universal trend towards regarding lack of consent as the essential element of rape and sexual abuse. The Court referred to the evolving understanding of the manner in which rape is experienced by the victim, which has shown that victims of sexual abuse (in particular, underage girls) often provide no physical resistance because of a variety of psychological factors or because they fear violence on the part of the perpetrator. The Court made it clear that "the development of law and practice in … [the rape and sexual abuse area] reflects the evolution of societies towards effective equality and respect for each individual's sexual autonomy."[33] The Court concluded its considerations regarding the "modern concept of the rape offence" by the following statement:

"In the light of the above, the Court is persuaded that any rigid approach to the prosecution of sexual offences, such as requiring proof of physical resistance in all circumstances, risks leaving certain types of rape unpunished and thus jeopardising the effective protection of the individual's sexual autonomy. In accordance with contemporary standards and trends

33. Ibid, para. 154 ff.

in that area, the member States' positive obligations under Articles 3 and 8 of the Convention must be seen as requiring the penalisation and effective prosecution of any non-consensual sexual act, including in the absence of physical resistance by the victim."[34]

The judgment shows that criminal law has a very important role to play in the fight against discrimination against women. The goal of criminal law is i.a. to protect human beings from severe violations of their physical and psychological integrity. With the Court's words in the M.C.-case:

"effective deterrence against grave acts such as rape, where fundamental values and essential aspects of private life are at stake, requires efficient criminal-law provisions."[35]

The protection of criminal law must therefore be designed in a way so it addresses the need that constituted the application of the criminal law in the first place. In that connection, women are not supposed to show resistance to be protected by the criminal law. If a woman does not consent to sexual intercourse, she is raped if the man nevertheless goes through with the act. The notion of the rape offence is therefore not – as asserted in Danish legal theory[36] – to go through with a sexual intercourse by overcoming the woman's resistance, but to go through with the act despite the lack of the woman's consent.

It is in the nature of things that the criminal law, in order to be effective, must also be applied in practice in accordance with the object and purpose of the criminalisation and the application of the law must thereby not fall back to an anachronistic view on the relationship between men and women and the woman's "duty to guard her virtue at all costs".

As shown in the M.C.-case, women do not have just a human right not to be exposed to rape and other forms of sexual abuse, women have a right to have their self-determination recognised. The right to self-determination also has reference to women's right to enter the public domain without, by doing so, having accepted sexual abuse or any other assault. In the rape-situation,

34. Ibid, para. 166. Regarding the case at hand, the Court found that the investigator and the prosecutors had had a wrong approach in the case as they had seen the case as a "date rape case" with the result had there was a presumption against rape as there was no evidence of resistance. The Court found a violation of the respondent State's positive obligation under both Article 3 and 8 of the Convention. See further para. 167 ff.
35. Ibid, para. 150.
36. See Gorm Toftegaard Nielsen, Kommenteret straffelov. Speciel del. Ninth revised edition, 2008, p. 300. See also Knud Waaben, Strafferettens specielle del, Fifth edition, 1999, p. 50

this right has the legal impact that a so called "date rape" is not to be judged on the basis of some "own fault-considerations", but only on the basis of an assessment of whether the element of the offence (actus reus) has been carried out by the perpetrator and whether this was done with the appropriate mens rea.

Recognition of women's right to self-determination encourages equality between men and women in society, simply because men have had their right to self-determination recognised all along. Recognition of women's right to self-determination must be seen as a requisite for women to be treated in accordance with the concept of human rights, which, as mentioned, has as its bedrock the principle of human dignity and human freedom. To be effective, the recognition must also take place in the field of criminal law.

On June 9, 2009 the European Court of Human Rights (unanimous chamber) gave judgment in the case of Opus v. Turkey.[37] The case concerned domestic violence, namely severe violence against the applicant and violence and murder of her mother committed by the applicant's former husband.

In the judgment the Court stated that States have a positive obligation to establish and apply effectively a system punishing all forms of domestic violence and providing sufficient safeguards for the victims and that in domestic violence cases perpetrators' rights cannot supersede victims' human rights to life and to physical and mental integrity.

With regard to the severity of the sentence the Court noticed that this must be adequate to the gravity of the offences in question, otherwise the sentence will reveal a lack of efficacy and a certain degree of tolerance to violence, without noticeable preventive or deterrent effect on the perpetrator.[38]

As something completely new and very important the Court acknowledged domestic violence as gender-based violence and recognised this kind of violence (including the murder of the applicant's mother) as a *form of discrimination against women* in violation of Article 14 in conjunction with Article 2 and 3. The Court in that connection referred to several international in-

37. The Opuz v. Turkey judgment of 9 June 2009, ECHR 33401/02, http://cmiskp.echr.coe.int/tkp197/view.asp?item=1&portal=hbkm&action=html&highlight=33401/02&sessionid=71989751&skin=hudoc-en, last visited 1 September 2011.
38. Ibid, para. 145, 147 and 170.

struments including the CEDAW Committee's General Recommendation No. 19.[39]

> "The Court's discrimination-examination in cases of domestic violence seems to be a little different than its examination in "ordinary" cases as the Court does not go through the four previously mentioned elements, but examines directly who is predominantly the victim of a certain crime (in the present case, domestic violence), the established criminal-law system in the relevant field, and how the public authorities in practise address and manage the cases: What are the public authorities' approach to the present type of cases and what is the outcome of the cases? For instance: Is domestic violence to some degree tolerated by the authorities even though it is formally criminalised, and do the perpetrators of domestic violence receive appropriate punishment within reasonable time?[40] Thus, the Court did not demand of the applicant that she could compare herself with another group of persons who had been treated more favourably, due to the fact that the crime is gender-based and a comparative group would therefore have an other character. "

The Opuz case is very important regarding discrimination in the field of criminal law, obviously, because the Court identified domestic violence as gender-based violence and as a form of discrimination against women, but also, more generally, because the case illustrates the huge ignorance regarding the discrimination-figures.

With regard to the Court's recognition of domestic violence as a form of discrimination against women, it is to be noted that even though the State, according to the judgment, has a positive obligation to establish and apply effectively a system punishing all forms of domestic violence and to provide sufficient safeguards for the victims whether domestic violence is characterised as discrimination against women or not, the recognition is in itself important. This is due to the fact that obligations for the State to prevent a violation of Article 14 in this area entails a duty for the State to combat domestic violence as a kind of special effort area – both on the practical policing level and on the valuational level, or the State will continue to violate Article 14. In other words, the State cannot only combat domestic violence as a common part of all the criminality in society with consequent risk of low priority because of resources et cetera, but must dedicate special attention to combat domestic violence. Such efforts will contribute to equality between men and women.

With regard to ignorance regarding the discrimination-figures, the respondent State (together with the legal reality in many other states) claimed

39. Ibid, para 177 ff. (particularly para. 199-202).
40. Ibid, para. 192 ff.

that since the criminal law does not have any distinction between men and women and is formulated in gender-neutral words, it applies equally to both men and women. The respondent State has thereby overlooked both the special form of discrimination that domestic violence constitutes, as we have just addressed, and the legal figure "indirect discrimination". An example from Danish case law will illustrate the harm that such ignorance produces.

5. The murder case of Denmark

Previously the state of law in Denmark in murder cases was that the original setting of the length of the sentence was 12 years of imprisonment. This sentence position applied to all types of murder. In 1993, the Supreme Court of Denmark, in a ruling regarding a husband's murder of his wife, the court decided that in cases of "domestic" murder (or murder where the parties were engaged or had been engaged or married) the length of the sentence should by default amount to only 10 years.[41] The reason for the new position in these murder-cases was that the murder was typically committed "under the influence of a particularly emotional burden".[42] This reason was given regardless of the concrete circumstances in the case. In other words, the defaults for the fixing of the sentence in domestic murder cases were independent of any aggravating or mitigating circumstances and were 2 years lower than the default in all other murder cases. According to the Supreme Court, only exceptional circumstances could depart from this original setting.

The matter of the fact was, however, that in domestic murder cases, it is almost always the woman who is the victim and the man who is the perpetrator. Roughly speaking, men are killed outside marriage where the original setting of the length of the sentence was 12 years imprisonment, while women are killed inside marriage where the original setting of the length of the sentence was 10 years. Thus, the criminal law was setting the value of women's lives lower than the value of men's lives. This was discrimination against women.[43]

The sentencing practice drew public debate among other things because of the increasing international awareness regarding domestic violence and murder, but the discrimination issue was not identified. The Danish Director of

41. See UfR 1993.742 H and UfR 1993.847 H.
42. See UfR 2009.433 H.
43. See further Trine Baumbach, Kønsligestilling i strafferetten – en overset retlig problemstilling, UfR 2009B. p. 259 ff.

Public Prosecutions (Prosecutor General) gave an account on domestic violence, murder and attempted murder and recommended a change in law.[44] Afterwards, the Supreme Court in a new domestic murder case changed the sentencing practice back to the original point of departure.[45] The facts of the case and the court's premises can be summarized as follows:

The perpetrator and the victim were cohabiting partners. During their cohabitation, the victim had been exposed to a great deal of violence from the perpetrator. Finally the victim had had enough of the violence and moved out of the shared home. This made the perpetrator threaten to kill the victim's young son – a threat that made her move back to the perpetrator. A few days later the perpetrator killed the victim.

Compared with their usual practise, the Supreme Court gave very thorough premises explaining why the sentencing practice was changed back to the original point of departure – that is 12 years imprisonment. Not the whole reasoning is convincing and the court overlooked the most important reason for the withdrawal. The main reasons the court gave for the changed point of departure is that an end to a marriage or cohabitation against one of the party's wishes today is regarded as a common life phenomenon, that the attitude regarding "domestic" murder has changed accordingly, and that the penalty for domestic violence has increased in recent years.[46]

As it is seen from the summary of the Supreme Court's premises, the court did not identify the discrimination issue. Even though the court referred to the aforementioned account on domestic violence, murder and attempted murder from the Director of Public Prosecution and the Director's remarks regarding who the victims are in these cases, namely women, the court did not uncover the gender issue. This insufficiency in the court's legal analysis can only be due to an ignorance of both the form of discrimination that domestic violence and murder constitutes and the legal figure indirect discrimination.

Thus, the court did not identify that even though the practice regarding the default of the length of the sentence in domestic murder cases apparently was gender neutral, it put persons of the womankind – who are almost always the

44. See Rigsadvokatens redegørelse om straffene i sager om samlivsrelateret vold, drab og drabsforsøg, oktober 2008, http://www.rigsadvokaten.dk/media/dokumenter/Redegorelse_om_straffenei_sager_om_samlivsrel.pdf, last visited 1 September 2011.
45. See UfR 2010.119 H.
46. As to the prohibition in Article 7 of the European Convention on Human Rights and Fundamental Freedoms, the Supreme Court noticed that the change in law did not constitute a violation of Article 7 since the change operated within the maximum penalty fixed in the murder statutory (the Danish Criminal Code § 237).

victims in these cases – at a particular disadvantage compared with men – who are almost only victim in murder cases outside marriage – given that the value of women's lives because of the lower penalty was set lower than the value of men's lives. Colloquially, the lower penalty was then also called "marital discount". To this must be added that the sentence practice was not objectively justified by a legitimate aim – the reason for the position of the length of the sentence in these cases was nearly valid and apply, if it has a substantial content at all, moreover in many murder cases also outside marriage. Finally, the means of achieving that aim were not appropriate or necessary. One can not even say that the former state of law was preventive in any way. There is no reason to believe that the Supreme Court by changing the state of law in 1993 wanted to discriminate women intentionally, but, as mentioned previously, it is not a requirement that the discrimination was intentional in any way. It is enough that the treatment actually had that effect. And it had.

6. Concluding remarks

Human rights violations which in practice typically only or mainly affects women, must be addressed by the criminal law in the same way as violations which (also) affects men. This applies both at the level of criminalization as well as at the sentencing level. Another approach to the problem constitutes discrimination against women.

Discrimination against women is not only an abuse to the particular woman who is exposed to the discriminatory treatment, but is also a charge on the welfare of the society because – with the words of the European Commission from the Women's Charter – "economic and social cohesion, sustainable growth and competitiveness, and tackling the demographic challenge depend on real equality between women and men."[47] Even though eradication of gender-based violence is not sufficient to end all discrimination against women, it is crucial to attain, since gender-based violence is one of the foundations that discrimination is built upon. In addition to the social conditions of the European societies, it cannot be stressed enough that violence against women constitutes a grave infringement of women's fundamental rights, including the right to life and the right to physical, psychological and/or sexual

47. Communication from the Commission. A Strengthened Commitment to Equality between Women and Men. A Women's Charter.

integrity, to which must be added that gender-based violence constitute discrimination against women per se and is thus an invasion on human dignity.

CHAPTER 8

The Woman's Share in the Reproductive Chain

An Illustration of a Brick in the Foundations of Women's Rights Law

By Pia Deleuran, attorney and mediator in Deleuran Law Firm[1] & Bente Holm Nielsen, MD[2]

Our focal point in this essay is the protection of the dignity of motherhood. We clarify how a superficial understanding of motherhood has consequences,

1. Pia Deleuran, born 1960 in Denmark, where she works as an attorney and mediator in Deleuran Law Firm. She has an educational background from University of Copenhagen – Faculty of Law, (1979-85) and Faculty of Humanities, (1994-1996) – Cand.jur. et art. She has been connected to Department of Psychology and Educational Studies, Roskilde University for a longer period of time 1997-2011. Her field of interest is the legal profession – i.e. understanding professions and professionals, research methods, subjectivity and sex- and gender issues as well as conflict management methods. Pia Deleuran was authorised by the Ministery of Justice as an attorney, back in 1990 and trained and certified as a mediator in the commercial, business and family-field by the mediators Henry Brown and Felicity White (1997-98). She was appointed to The Gender Equality Board, (2000-2003). Pia Deleuran has for many years been an external lecturer at University of Copenhagen in mediation and has been involved in various initiatives developing mediation. She assisted the Bar and Law Society setting up the mediation-training in Denmark in 2002, and has, since then, been involved in designing and teaching the training-courses. She gives workshops, lectures and is joining learning-settings around the world.

   She is a member of The Bar and Law Society as well as a member of The Association of Danish Law Firms "Danske Advokater" and DJØF. Projects: www.vdc123.dk www.mediationtouringexhibition.com and www.kamelkaravane.dk

which affect the prevalent perception of women in the world community as well as in Danish society. We illustrate this with an example from recent Danish legislation, namely the Act on Parental Responsibility adopted in 2007.

1. Introduction

In our opinion the Universal Declaration of Human Rights, Article 1, should rightfully begin as follows: "All human beings are born from a woman, and all are born free and equal in dignity. Rights exist to reflect this dignity with regard to gender specific characteristics."

This formulation is significant because many Danes see human rights as a kind of constitution of humanism. Our formulation of Article 1 clarifies the gender differences as well as taking gender differences into account at a fundamental level – including the impact on the laws to guide people.

The text currently begins: "All human beings are born free and equal,"[3] which ignores gender inequalities, i.e. there is no acknowledgement of the differences between women and men – even though, incredibly, such a statement has no biological foundation[4]. A similar misleading generalization can be found in the recently adopted Act on Parental Responsibility, where the same kind of superficial understanding of gender inequality is likely to have irreversible consequences. It is the intention of this article to clarify these matters.

2. Bente Holm Nielsen, MD. Born 1941. Most recently employed as academic assistant at the Danish School of Midwifery. 1989 graduated in medicine at the University of Copenhagen and historical thesis at Roskilde University. 1991 pilot project on midwifery training theory and methodology at the National School of Midwifery Department in Copenhagen. 1993-1994 taught at the Professional Midwife Diploma- (ethics). 1992-1997 PhD student at Roskilde University, enrolled at the Institute of History.
3. www.un.org/en/documents/udhr/index.shtml#a1 "All human beings are born free and equal in dignity and rights. They are endowed with reason and conscience and should act towards one another in a spirit of brotherhood".
4. From this point on, the word biology is used for concept formation associated with motherhood. The ability to distinguish between biology and genetics is weighted. See details under the heading Perspective.

2. Perspective

When the Universal Declaration of Human Rights was adopted by the United Nations in 1948 much was different from today. People had only just accepted the medical facts, already established in 1875, that a father and a mother contribute an equal number of genes (chromosomes, genome) to their offspring. Until then the belief was held that all that determined a child's qualities, for example intelligence, came from the male. But in 1875 the sperm lost its unique status and since then the two sexes have been acknowledged as equals in terms of genetic parenthood.

We don't know whether it was the chromosome equality in genetic parenthood which led the Fathers of the World Declaration to include the importance of birth in the first sentence of the World Declaration of Human Rights, but we take Article 1 as our point of departure, because to a large extent it determines what human rights are.[5]

In this article our perspective on the spirit of human rights is that people should respect one another. When the concept of birth is listed in Article 1, it follows logically that motherhood should be respected. Logically, a question like: 'Who came first – the chicken or the egg?' follows. If motherhood did not exist, no man would need the mutual respect of another. Thus the two starting points: Respect for human beings and respect for motherhood – are closely connected: Which came first – man or motherhood?

Although since 1875 it has been an established fact that the sexes have equal status at a chromosomal level, it was not until the population conference in Cairo in 1994 that women's human rights came up on a par with those of men. To this day no distinction is made, either in official documents or in everyday language, between the genetic and biological parents – despite the disparity in the reproductive roles of a mother and a father.

A linguistic awareness around the conceptualization of motherhood was awakened when egg donation was made possible. It became evident that motherhood is a triad consisting of social, genetic and biological parts. The social mother takes care of the child's upbringing – just like the social father. The genetic mother helps with the oocyte (human egg cell) that contains genes – just like the genetic father. But while the biological mother is responsible for pregnancy, childbirth and breastfeeding, because these are essential-

5. Passages in the article can be recognized from Bente Holm Nielsen "Ægproducent", in Deleuran, Pia, ed. (2007): Klienten i det omskiftelige samfund – en visuel antologi om advokatens udfordring, DJØF Publishing.

ly tied to the female body, one cannot in this perspective refer to a biological father.

There will always be problems and ethical dilemmas to be tackled when an issue involves the regulation of women's autonomy. In this case these are due to the unusual starting point which includes self-determination as well as the natural phenomenon: that women are able to become pregnant. Pregnant women's autonomy must encompass the following: 1) the gender-specific right to reproductive health (a concept drawn up by the United Nations Organization in 1984), e.g. optimal obstetrical assistance and maternity care and 2) the safe termination of pregnancy (induced abortion).[6]

The uniqueness of a pregnant woman has been described in American literature, noting that it was only after World War II, during the same historical period which created the concept of human rights, that pregnant women became part of city life[7]: "The pregnant woman, unlike all other human beings, holds two individuals in one body. This undeniable but highly anomalous phenomenon of nature refutes at least two of our culture's most powerfully held categories – the cultural idea of one individual per body, and the mathematical law that one does not equal two." In a defined period of barely one year the pregnant woman, is "the public proof of sexuality properly kept private", she is a "walking representative of nature in a culture that seeks to deny nature's power", and she "still crosses too many categories for comfort".

6. The concept of reproductive health www.who.int/topics/reproductive_health/en/ is an extension of the definition of women's health and implies that people are able to have a responsible, satisfying and safe sex life and that they have the capability to reproduce and the freedom to decide if, when and how often to do so. A consequence of the reproductive health of women can be found in Moeller, Jytte Aa., and Nielsen, Bente Holm (1997) (see note 6), namely that fertile women's lives can be divided into periods called reproductive life stages. A reproductive stage of life in a woman's life starts at the earliest before the fertilization, when she begins to think about her work-life, education and recreation in a way including the possibility of pregnancy. A reproductive stage of life lasts until the 1 year old child begins walking – even in cases of spontaneous / induced abortion or stillbirth. Choosing a full year after giving birth to be the end of reproductive life stage is related to the experience that this is as long as it takes for most women before everyday life with a toddler has become so familiar that they basically associate themselves and their own life with being a mother. Besides, the upright position and walking on two legs is specifically human.
7. Davis-Floyd, Robbie E. (1992): Birth as an American Rite of Passage, University of California Press, p. 25.

If the special situation the pregnant woman faces is that of a 2-in-1-body,[8] it is possible to talk about, at any given point in time, the existing 2-in-1-body-population in a country. However, please note that the term should not refer to individual women, e.g. a neighbour's daughter or sister, but to that group of women who in their bodies create a new corporate citizen and increase the population.[9] These thoughts continue below (under the heading Motherhood Authority). At the moment we are going on to consider whether it can be found in the concept of human rights that the 2-in-1-body-population is taken into account. In Denmark this group amounts to approximately 1% of the total population.

Within the concept of human rights, different fundamental values are to be found, including the right to life and the right to health. By comparing these values, it can be illustrated that the pregnant woman holds the right to life twice.

3. Human Rights Conventions

Since 1946, the aim of the United Nations has been to identify all the areas where women have been denied the same rights as men. In 1979, the goals were written down in The Women's Convention: Convention on the Elimination of All Forms of Discrimination against Women, namely that women – regardless of marital status – are entitled to society's benefits. Not until the population conference in Cairo in 1994 did the serious anomalies in the individual parts of the concepts of human rights become clear: between, on the one hand, women's rights and on the other hand the protection of the foetus – the latter following the preamble to The Children's Convention.[10]

8. Moeller, Jytte Aa. and Nielsen, Bente Holm (1997): Jordemoderfaglig teori og metode 1&2, gives a description of pregnancy as "procreative engineering". The description involves 2 individuals existing together in a 2-in-1-body-situation. Although "procreative engineering" is only a small part of "social engineering", it is still a prerequisite. Usually the descriptions of the procreative field primarily give knowledge about the child. However, not only the child can be the core of the midwifery profession, and midwives can not limit their activities to the child. There are two beings in a 2-in-1-body-situation. http://holmnielsen.org/jordemoderfaglig_teori_metode.htm
9. Moeller, Jytte Aa. and Nielsen, Bente Holm: Forældreansvarsloven – hvad blev der af kvindens krop? in Deleuran, Pia, ed, (2011): Temahæfte 3, Forældreansvarsloven – hvad blev der af barnets tarv? Djoef Publishing, forthcoming.
10. Convention on the Rights of the Child.

Human rights are weak when 'the right to life' is drawn into the uterus to protect the foetus. The final document from the population conference in Cairo shows that there are rights and claims that cannot be merged. This issue is only one of several contradictory issues in the concept of human rights. These contradictions cause inconsistency.

Since The Women's Convention, women, like all other people, can demand to live in peace and to be respected. But an example of inconsistency in The Women's Convention is that because of it, the female gender cannot claim something for itself in situations where women are different from men – for example as the producers of human egg cells. The Women's Convention does not protect the individual woman when she becomes a mother. On the contrary, it protects a rather vapid notion of motherhood, and therefore the name could just as well have been The Maternity Convention. That The Women's Convention resembles a Maternity Convention becomes apparent in what the UN member states (having acceded to the Convention) have undertaken to do, namely, "To ensure that family education includes a proper understanding of maternity as a social function".

The Danish Act on Parental Responsibility provides an example of how a missing focus on motherhood as a social function has consequences for the way we look at women.

4. The Danish Act on Parental Responsibility – an example of legislative sex- and gender blindness

In 2007 a new law on parental responsibility took effect in Denmark. It was an epoch-making change because the law stipulated that the legal system could force the parents to share custody of their child if no compelling grounds were proven that they should not. It was a huge experiment not based on existing knowledge but based on a wish for a better world. Through the law the citizens could be forced to cooperate in a conflicting situation they had gone to court to settle. It was explained as: "For the sake of the children". The law also gave the Courts and Regional State Administrations the authority to instruct children to live seven days alternately with each parent.

The concept "the best interest of the child" was debated by the committee that made the recommendations to the government.[11] It is in this context that

11. Report no. 1475 (2006) "Barnets perspektiv – Forældremyndighed, Barnets bopæl, Samvær, Tvangsfuldbyrdelse."

two different understandings of the concept were in competition with each other: on the one hand the child's contact with both parents, on the other hand the child's need for security and care.

That was summed up in Act's § 4 where the text reads as follows: "Decisions made pursuant to the Act will be based on the child's best interests." The interpretation of the term "child's best" is thus the very core of the law, but is not defined in terms of content – and no indication or help regarding how to interpret the concept is seen in the actual paragraph.

The meaning of "the best interests of the child" must therefore be looked for in other paragraphs in the Act and in other provisions in the associated guidelines that emphasize the child's right to both parents. In order to force people to conform with what is actually a new state ideology; accompanied by unfamiliar legal concepts such as visitation-sabotage and cooperation-harassment.[12] Concepts that, used in praxis, have a boomerang effect if one of the parents wants to protect the child against violence or abuse but cannot prove the accusation. Then this parent risks being blamed for the statement e.g. it may be considered to move the child's residence since the parent is seen as less-cooperative as the other parent.

The law was not gender mainstreamed – for whatever reason. This, despite the fact that the following description can be found on The Gender Equality Ministry's website: "As a rule, legislation is gender neutral. This is not the same as 'the effect of a law cannot have greater significance for one gender over the other'. Therefore, one should be aware of gender issues from the start, and information about the expected consequences of the law should be considered in the decision-making-process. Only thus is it possible to get a picture of how a planned bill will affect the citizens."[13]

When designing the new bill it was not taken into account that the family pattern in Denmark has changed and now includes 37 types of families as you see below. The numbers you see in the brackets tell how many families of this type live in Denmark:

1st Couples with children (448,612)
2nd Single mothers with children (110,831)
3rd Single fathers with contact to children who have visitation rights (88,562)

12. The Act: www.retsinformation.dk/Forms/R0710.aspx?id=32014. Guidelines about custody and residence: www.retsinformation.dk/Forms/R0710.aspx?id=32075 and Guidelines about visitating rights: www.retsinformation.dk/Forms/R0710.aspx?-id=32074.
13. www.lige.dk/main_varkt_lov_forside.asp

4th Couples with children and with separate children from the mother(20,355)
5th Couples with only separate children from the mother (20265)
6th Couples with only separate children of the father who has visitation rights (20153)
7th Couples with children and separate children of the father who has visitation rights (16,002)
8th Couples with separate children of the mother and separate children of the father who has visitation rights (12,189)
9th Single father with children (11,883)
10th Single father with children and children who have visitation rights(7212)
11th Single mother with children and children who have visitation rights(7061)
12th Single mother with children who have visitation rights (6465)
13th Couples with children, and with separate children of the mother and separate children of the father who has visitation rights (4099)
14th Couples with separate children of the mother who has visitation rights (2411)
15th Couples with separate children of the father (2299)
16th Couples with children and separate children of the father (1895)
17th Couples with mother's and father's separate children (1714)
18th Couples with mother's and father's separate children who have visitation rights(1668)
19th Couples with separate children of the mother and with children of the mother who has visitation rights (1538)
20th Couples with the mother's separate children and with both mother's and father's children who have visitation rights (1409)
21st Couples with children and with separate children of the mother who have visitation rights (1268)
22nd Couples with separate children of the mother and father and separate children of the father with visitation rights (1192)
23rd Couples with separate children of the father and with separate children of the father who have visitation rights (1078)
24th Couples with children, and with separate children of the mother and separate children of the mother who have visiting rights (861)
25th Couples with children, and with separate children of the father and separate children of the father who have visiting rights (678)
26th Couples with children and with separate children of the mother and the father (478)
27th Couples with children and with the mother's and father's children who have visitation rights (300)
28th Couples with children, separate children of the mother and separate children of the father who have visitation rights (239)
29th Couples with children, separate children of the mother and separate children of the mother and father who have visitation rights (238)
30th Couples with separate children of the mother and father and with separate children of the mother and father who have visitation rights (196)
31st Couples with separate children of the mother and father as separate children of the mother who have visitation rights (178)
32nd Couples with separate children of the father and separate children of the mother and father who have visitation rights (140)
33rd Couples with separate children of the father and with separate children of the mother who have visitation rights (137)

34th Couples with children, and mother's separate children and mother separate children who have visitation rights (29)
35th Couples with children, separate children of the father and separate children of the mother who have visitation rights (25)
36th Couples with children, separate children of the father and separate children of the mother and the father who have visitation rights (24)
37th Couples with children, separate children of the mother and father as separate children of the mother and father who have visitation rights (15)[14]

The figures illustrate that women, much more than men, continue to undertake work related to children's upbringing. This information was not taken into account when drafting the new bill, nor was the fact that reproduction has different impacts on women as a group than men as a group. If the law had been sex-and gender mainstreamed the politicians would have had a much more solid basis for developing the bill, using insights into family matters and dynamics between the sexes.

However, it could be that the politicians were aware that, politically, gender was an explosive topic. Already in the review of the Children Act in early 2000 the then Justice Minister Frank Jensen ordered a study from The Danish National Centre for Social Research on visitation rights for children. The background for this was the widespread perception that some fathers had contact with children, but did not honour the agreement. When the survey was available, senior researcher Mai Heide Ottosen said the following to the newspaper Politiken (26.03.2004): "It was not really because the Children Act was all about visitation rights, but there was a strong concern that the law was too wide because throughout the 90's, there was a lot of focus on the unmarried fathers' rights. There was concern that there was someone who had the right to access to the child who should not have had it."

The study concluded that some children of divorced parents are subjected to considerable strain in connection with contact with the parent not living with the child.

Thus it may seem paradoxical that children as a group, through adoption of the Parental Responsibility Act, just 3 years later were to be confronted with even more access and visitation.

14. From News from Statistics Denmark www.statistikbanken.dk/BRN12 – referred to in the newspaper Politiken 29.12.2009.

5. Sole Custody and the Obligation to give information about the Child to the Parent who has the visitation rights – another paradox

As a result of the law, the parent who does not have a share in the custody will still have the right to information about the child from institutions i.e. nurseries, schools as well as from doctors and hospitals. There is also a right to attend meetings and social activities in settings involving the child despite the fact that obtaining sole custody over a child means that the courts found compelling reasons to end the joint custody.

The parent who has sole custody can, however, apply to end the information flow to the parent who has the visiting rights, as well as having the right to stop their involvement in the child's social activities. It is only granted if you as a sole parent can prove that your child is harmed or if you have other specific reasons. The burden to apply is placed on the parent who has sole custody and the burden of proof is also placed on that person.

What happens is that even when a parent has gained sole custody of a child, that parent cannot be sure that an environment of peace and safety will be established for the child. Even disturbances around babies in nurseries can be a factor yet how the institutions are supposed to handle these kinds of conflicts is not considered in the actual settings for which § 23 creates a basis :

"Information about the child
23. (1) The parent who does not have custody has the right to request information about the child from schools, day-care facilities, the social and healthcare system, private hospitals, and private GPs and dentists. This parent also has the right to receive documents about the child if such information is available at the schools and day-care institutions. Confidential information about the holder of custody may not be passed on.

(2) The parent who does not have custody has the right to request and receive information about general social activities at the child's school or day-care institution from the school or institution in question, and is entitled to participate in these activities.

(3) The institutions, etc., mentioned in subsections (1) and (2) can refuse to give specific information or hand out documents relating to the child. They can refuse to provide information about activities and deny admission to the activities, if they consider giving the parent admission to such activities would be damaging to the child.

(4) In special cases, at the request of the holder of custody or one of the institutions mentioned in subsections (1) and (2), the regional state administration can withdraw the right of the parent who does not have custody to receive information and documents in accordance with subsection (1), or to receive information about activities and to take part in them pursuant to subsection (2). The decision will take effect from the date on which the institution, etc., is notified of the decision."

6. Awaiting the evaluation – therefore no intervention

There has been political silence on the consequences of adopting the Danish Parental Responsibility Act. In contrast, children's and women's organizations have consistently pointed to inappropriate aspects that affect especially children and women. Practically all politicians have wanted to await the evaluation of the Act that was set to take place in 2011 by political consensus. Despite the marked increase in the number of cases the decision-makers have not intervened.

Figure 1: Shows the increase in numbers of cases regarding access, residence and custody, since the new Act on Parental Responsibility came into force in 2007

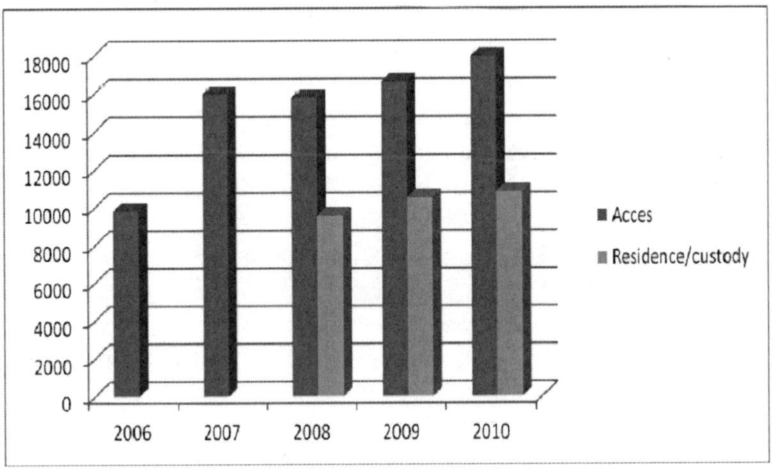

One MP – Mette Frederiksen (Social Democrat), however, has had concerns about parts of the Act. She is quoted to say the following in the newspaper Berlingske Tidende (1.10.2008) in which she continues to support the ideals of the law, but emphasizes a concern: "The result is that many children are forced into contact with a father who has subjected the child or the child's mother to assault. There are now many more cases where children have contact with a violent father, although the mother lives in a shelter. The question is whether men and women are actually always equal? In proceedings in the state administration both father and mother are negotiating "equally" about the legal claim to the children. In ordinary divorce cases it works out fine.

But in cases marked by serious conflicts, such as violence, the parties are not equal – one party has the upper hand over the other – and the decision is often made accordingly. [...]

And Mette Frederiksen continues later on in the article:

> "But I would also like to make it clear that we in parliament might have been so preoccupied with equality that we forgot thc children."

The other politicians' silence is resounding, and the National Council for Children established by the government has also been delayed in responding.

The Council was initially enthusiastic about the law when it came into force and issued in a press release on 30.9.2007, a tribute to the law. Despite current awareness of the results from the SFI – The Danish National Centre for Social Research's Survey and despite other reports on contact problems there is no trace of concern expressed by the former Chairperson of Children's Council, Chief Justice Birgitte Holmberg Pedersen, as she points out that the bill with its provisions is close to the intentions of the UN Children's Convention. She says, "Precisely because the principal goal of the law is to protect the child and its interests in divorce conflicts, there is reason to welcome it. Here we see an excellent example of UN Children's Convention being highly relevant for Danish children and the Convention being a guide to the framing of legislative and administrative procedures."

Subsequently, the statement from Children's Council is that an evaluation is necessary before it can be decided whether the law should be maintained. See for example in the newspaper Information (17.3.2010), when the chairman of the Council for Children Lisbeth Zorning Andersen points out that it is possible the law actually works, but that it is simply misinterpreted in practice by the judges, the state administration, and the child experts, and thus places the children in an extremely problematic situation.

"– I am waiting with a critical eye hoping that there will be an extremely thorough evaluation of the Parental Responsibility Act in 2011 to uncover the consequences of the legislation, says Lisbeth Zorning Andersen."

The children's organization Børns Vilkår, in connection with the evaluation of the Act, compiled a catalogue of suggestions for amendments, and various groups and networks have taken steps to demonstrate the consequences of the law.[15]

15. www.bornsvilkar.dk/~/media/BV/pdf/Forældreansvarsloven_ændringsforslag_web.ashx and www.barnetstarv.nu

7. Parental Responsibility Act, lack of care for both women and infants and toddlers.

It is no revelation that the law is concerned with infants and the toddlers. Before 1970 the law took into account the attachment between woman and infant: A child under two years could only in exceptional circumstances be removed from the mother. The Law on Marriage and dissolution, which became effective 01.01.1970 – also called the 1969-Act – repealed the provision and thereby the law – already neutral with regard to children over 2 years – became neutral as well to children under this age. Concern for the child was also prioritised as the decisive factor when deciding which parent should hold custody.

In earlier times the court could consider guilt-perspectives as a factor – but these considerations are missing in the current legislation – most find such perspectives too old-fashioned and irrelevant and difficult to consider objectively.

Also in the report from 2006 small children are singled out.[16] On pages 203-205 it is explained that the committee finds that there are opposing considerations, when the issue about access with young children is assessed. Members of the committee emphasize that there is a dilemma "with direct opposing considerations" and that this dilemma is amplified the younger the child is. The Committee is focussed on what can be done in terms of access when there is a conflict between the parents of young children, infants and toddlers. The Committee believes that the interest of the child is to have close contact with the parent who has the visiting rights as early as possible – and at the same time maintain security and stability.

Overall the concept of the visiting-rights-system is not questioned by the Committee.

The report shows that a majority of the committee members advocated that a new law should put more emphasis on the establishment of frequent access with short duration, and the parents in this regard should be made aware of the importance of making the access reliable and secure for the child despite the conflictual situation. The desire for increased visiting rights is justified by the child's needs for attachment to the parent who has the visiting rights, despite the actual conflictual situation. These members – 13 out of 15 – found that the existing system made a child's emotional attachment to the

16. See earlier note about the report.

parent who has the visiting rights difficult. They too recommended the need for cooperation between the two parents in that context.

Previously small children had been protected from being forced into access arrangements. Even though the question is loaded with sex-and-gender politics, it seems that the committee did not discuss this. It is persistently reinforced in the report and in the guidelines accompanying the law that the concept "the perspective of the child" is to be understood as the child's contact with both parents.

The minority in the committee – two persons out of the 15 – both coming from children's organisations, stated that a visitation policy which allows more frequent visits than at present will have serious developmental consequences for children aged less than 2-3 years. They referred to psychological evidence about infants that stresses how vital it is for small children to be able to depend on a strong relationship with the primary caregiver in order to have a healthy and balanced development. The two members emphasised that it is that basis and insight on which you build all initiatives concerning children, since it has been documented that separation from the primary caregiver risks causing permanent damage to the child. When the child experiences a sense of loss and there is an atmosphere of a break-up, even only a short separation from the primary caregiver can destroy their ability to bond with other people later on in life. The minority claimed that it would be contrary to the basic understanding of children, and an increase in visitation arrangements for small children would create high risk. If this were done, they claimed, it could lead to ruining the relationship with both parents on the long run. Instead the parent not being the primary caregiver should wait until the child is older to establish the contact, since a grounded and well-adjusted child will then connect much more easily with the parent with whom it did not have the daily contact. The two members also insisted that child experts were to be involved when decisions were taken about access and arrangements including small children and they pointed out that in each case the specific needs of the child have to be taken into consideration, i.e. safety, continuity and how a discordant setting could affect the child.

It is clear that no one in the committee considered the woman's position: that she is being pressured to hand over the infant to the father in a conflictual situation, and despite the fact that she is still physically bonding postnatally with the child. What impact would this have, for example, on breast feeding? No one in the committee discussed that either. Neither did anyone in the committee consider the impact an enforcement court case will have on the primary caregiver – typically the mother if the baby against the mother's will is forced to be handed over to the visiting parent having claimed the right to access, nor the impact on the mother even from the bare thread about a situation like that to occur.

On page 230 of the report from 2006, the current law in relation to the enforcement of decisions is described, and on page 239 the committee states their recommendations.

In terms of law enforcement in access cases, penalties and immediate use of force are applied. The report states that in practice a meeting at the enforcement court is arranged with the aim of settling the matter. If the meeting does not lead to a resolution of the case, the bailiff will normally impose a penalty payment and in rarer cases, force will be applied immediately. It is not discussed that the cases can be enforced without any warning of the primary caregiver, if the bailiff sees a risk of not getting the wanted result.

The Committee emphasizes that the immediate use of force to enforce the custody, residential and access, leads to a practice where children may be transported to and from a parent with physical force by strangers. It is stated that it is traumatic for a child to be transported in this manner by a bailiff – sometimes accompanied by the police. The Committee also states that immediate use of force in custody cases should continue to be an exception, and less drastic means should be tried first.

Therefore it is recommended to have a child expert present in enforcement proceedings and that there must also be an impartial person present to assist the child, for example, an employee of the municipality. The Committee approves of this and sees it to be in line with the Children's Convention, Article 12 paragraph 2. The Committee states that this contributes to a greater degree of focus on the child's perspective. It is also stated that the presence of a child expert could help in any further attempt at mediation between the parties in order to ensure that all the other less violent options for the child are exhausted. How in practice the participation of these professionals would make the situation less stressful for those involved is difficult to imagine and is not explained as such in or illustrated by any accompanying guide.

While attention to the above mentioned long-term consequences is recommended, there must be the provision in exceptional situations to implement enforcement proceedings around custody, the child's residence or access without the participation of a child expert and impartial person. This giving the enforcement courts a huge power.

The Committee recommends that enforcement courts, in cases under chapter 48 a in the Administration of Justice Act (Enforcement of children)[17], are

17. www.retsinformation.dk/Forms/r0710.aspx?id=133272#K48a

always filled with experienced jurors, as the cases are conflictual. But there has been no political agreement to support this proposal and experience from the first four years with the law states that all courts are able to follow that recommendation.

Also worth noting is that the court bailiffs who carry out enforcement in family cases also carry out other forms of enforcement. These could be to do with monetary claims, including the making of disbursements and collecting effects from debtors. There is a big difference between picking up objects from a debtor and forcing children to have contact with a parent. Bailiffs do not have any specific educational or psychological qualifications or special training in this field. The basis of Danish legal system is that judges and bailiffs are generalists rather than specialists. Despite the far-reaching consequences for those involved, it is possible for a trainee judge to be responsible for enforcement. This is not uncommon in practice.

It should be noted that there are no clauses specifically about access enforcement involving infants and small children, which means that this can happen in the same way as with other children. That the change of visiting rights allocating access with very young children will inevitably result in enforcement is not addressed, i.e. the lack of clarification of this new legal position is unfortunate because this particular group of children would previously have been given special consideration.

The committee delivered its report which was submitted for hearing. After the hearing a political agreement was made dated 26.04.2007, which stated the following in relation to access with small children:

> "The Committee is satisfied that the Bill envisages that a greater degree of access with young children is seen than is the case today. Visiting rights with minor children have a range of conflicting considerations – including that the child obtains an early close contact with the parent who has the visiting rights, while maintaining security and stability. An important prerequisite for this is that child experts are involved in the cases, which can help to give parents an understanding of the child's situation and can uncover the child and the parents' relationship.
>
> There may be good reasons to establish frequent access between parent and child in the first months of the child's life, perhaps meetings of a rather short duration, so that visits can be gradually stepped up as the child gets older. By giving the access duration of ½-1 hour the needs of the child's overall care are taken into account."[18]

18. www.familiestyrelsen.dk/fileadmin/user_upload/Foraeldremyndighed_og_samvaer/-politisk_aftale.pdf

After the act was passed, Family Affairs developed a set of guidelines in collaboration with the Psychological Society about the involvement of child experts. This shows no special consideration for the particular situation and needs of the new mother and the young child. Neither is it mentioned in the written instructions on visiting rights regarding enforcement of access in Chapter 18. In the instructions on visiting rights under the Administration of Justice Act § 536 paragraph 4,[19] the bailiff can change the scope, time and place as well as the conditions of the access during enforcement proceedings. This is a new provision, despite the provision of subsection 6, that no access enforcement should happen if there is any danger of serious mental or physical damage to the child. This was maintained despite the maxim that the law should rest on the child's perspective. Maintaining this meant that the child should be presented to the parent who holds the visiting rights if danger was the 'only' factor associated with visits.

In this situation the wellbeing of the mother is not taken into account. The impact of her recent and in all likelihood physically and mentally life-altering experience of giving birth is not considered. Attention is given to the child, but young children are not considered as a special group for attention. It will be up to the child experts in the matter to consider this special perspective. Since psychology is not an exact science, and legislation supports the ideal of two parents, it seems understandable that some child experts are not capable of withstanding the pressure to meet the expectation of the law's ideology. Some child experts may have the perception that the legal ideology about the visiting rights is also valuable also for infants and young children when there is a conflict between the parents.

That the power of child experts in these matters has a role to play for the child is laid out clearly in the ethical rules for Nordic psychologists:

> "Avoidance of abuse/harm
> The psychologist strives to avoid professional psychological information or practice being abused, and is responsible for minimising any inevitable and foreseeable damage. Psychologists do not participate in activities involving physical or mental coercion (indoctrination "brainwashing", torture) or in the threat of such coercion:
> 1) Forcing people to disclose information or admissions / confessions.
> 2) Put people under pressure to reveal, deny or modify their own or another's worldview, political, religious or ethical beliefs. The psychologist tries actively to prevent their professional expertise being used in such activities."[20]

19. www.retsinformation.dk/Forms/r0710.aspx?id=133272#K48a
20. www.psyksamtale.dk/etiske_principper_for_nordiske_psykologer_001.pdf

It cannot be denied that some child experts feel under pressure when parents are unable to co-operate on the children despite being advised to do so, and feel that the protection and safety of the child comes first.

This is likely to create ethical dilemmas for the professionals involved in some cases – and you might expect the dilemmas to be more pronounced in cases involving infants and toddlers, who cannot speak up and protect themselves, being totally dependent on the adult taking care of them.

As shown, there has been a significant increase in the number of enforcement proceedings since the law was adopted. It has not been registered in the courts how many of the actual cases involving infants and toddlers. Neither the number of businesses for the bailiffs to actually drive out and grab the child/children with or without a warning, forcing them to visitation reported in a statistical material. Neither the Court Administration nor enforcement courts were able to make this information available.

Figure 2: Shows the increase in numbers of family cases that ends in the enforcement courts

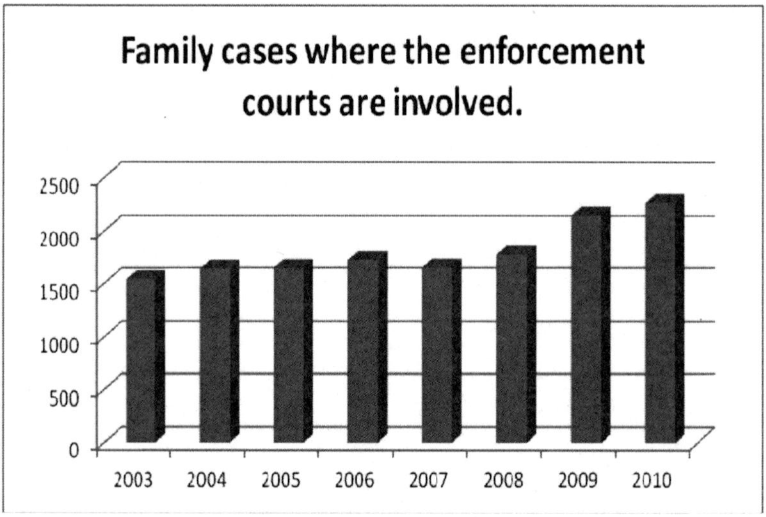

The Act on Parental Responsibility would in all probability look different if motherhood was considered worthy of protection. When there is no societal consensus that motherhood is worth protecting, the opportunities for women to be protective mothers[21] disappear. But what does it take to define motherhood as worthy of protection, without resulting in the glorifycation and oppression of women? Our proposal is an authority of motherhood which is discussed at the end of the article.

8. Human Rights in general

The constitution of humanism (human rights) demands tolerance, therefore they are at the core of the demand for democracy. Nobody can claim the right to freedom if it is a freedom that compromises the freedom of others. Democracy is an established moral and social order, which connects law and morality.

Roughly, human rights can be divided into two types: positive rights and negative rights.

Positive rights imply that there is someone who has the right and entitlement to certain benefits from another (benefits = contributions). E.g. family allowance.

However, the situation is different with negative rights. An example of a negative right is the right not to be forced into anything. It is also a negative right to be left alone. The individual citizen must be allowed to be left in peace and protected from the abuse by a state power.

Human rights protection from abuse therefore has as part of its character negative human rights. It makes good sense to use negative rights as a safeguard against abuse of the body e.g. to guard against medical experimentation and treatment trials. The rule can be found in the ECHR, art.8, § 2.

The issue in relation to The Act on Parental Responsibility is whether such rules can safeguard a population confronting an imposed ideology of parental cooperation concerning the child, and, when such efforts at cooperation fail, safeguard them from the subsequent invasion of their privacy – including resulting procedural harm if relevant findings have not been accepted. Currently there is no legal practice in this area.

21. Hanna, Mo Therese and Goldstein, Barry (2010): Domestic Violence, Abuse and Child Custody – Legal Strategies and Policy Issues, Civic Research Institute, Inc., Kingston, New Jersey. www.domesticviolenceabuseandchildcustody.com www.barnetstarv.nu/Confirmed_Mothers_were_right.pdf

Positive human rights are nothing more than claiming one's basic material needs for survival. If one compares positive human rights with a kind of consumer rights, one can easily understand the difference between having a right to drive a Mercedes and having the right not to go to bed hungry.

9. What is diffcrent, should not always be treated equally

As stated in the introduction to this article, women's and men's biology are different. Therefore it does not always make sense to talk about equality when it comes to these two groups. Biology is important in the reproductive chain and therefore for the (different) life cycles men and women have. The legal system should concern itself with this. Nowadays in many ways women are welcomed as equal members of society. Women have been granted citizenship, education, jobs and can support themselves. Something is still missing though, before it can be said that women are allowed to fully participate in society, that is, are respected for their reproductive efforts.

While it is fashionable to say that we in Denmark have a high degree of gender equality, it must be pointed out that this is not the case in the field of reproduction. The reproductive field is still an area that needs further scrutiny and attention. Already the Equal Opportunities Commission in the 1970s had a nuanced approach to gender equality, which was stated as follows:[22]

"In itself, the phrase gender equality has no meaning. It must be clarified, what the gender equality in question concerns. The reason for the requirement of equality is the perception that justice requires that all members of society should be treated equally, i.e. have the same rights and obligations. This legal approach is not new. It can be traced back to Aristotle, who believed that justice would say that what is equal, ought to be treated equally. The difficulty lies only in finding out what is equal and what is not. For Aristotle, it was obvious that slaves and free citizens were not equal and therefore had no right to be treated equally, and for the men whom in the 18th century of America formulated the idea of human freedom and equality, it was equally obvious that the claim of equality was only due to males and only white men.

Not even today does the legal system claim that absolutely all people must be treated equally. Justice demands, in many situations, different treatment of adults and children, sick and healthy, offenders and law abiding citizens, intelligent and unintelligent. So all members of society are divided into categories and the majority finds this entirely consistent with the requirement of equality, that those who belong to one category are treated differently than those belonging to the other. It is, for example obvious, that special atten-

22. Betænkning vedrørende ligestilling. Afgivet af et udvalg under kommissionen vedrørende kvindernes stilling i samfundet. Report no. 673 (1972), p. 73, 75.

tion must be paid to the sick and disabled, to ensure that they, as far as possible, are treated the same as the healthy.

So there are some qualities or characteristics, which are used to divide society members into categories that require different treatments in order to be equal, and others which should not be used this way.

E.g. the attributes of age as well as sex are assigned to the individual without fault or merit and without opportunity to rid him or herself of them. When e.g. it is determined that all individuals in a particular age group should be subject to compulsory education, no one can demand to be excused from this duty by pointing out that they should be treated as persons in another age category who are not subject to compulsory education. Compulsory education is fully consistent with requirements for equality, as long as it applies to everyone in the age group. However, this requirement does not stipulate that only 7-14 year olds and not 6-16-year-olds or any other age group should be subject to compulsory education, nor does it expound the principle that there should be compulsory education at all. Equality demands would be equally well satisfied if the demand did not exist. What matters is that if there is such a duty, it must be possible on the basis of objective characteristics to determine who should be subjected to it and who should not.

What the righteousness- or equality demand in reality says is only this: that there must be rules and that any rule should apply without exception to everyone who, according to certain objective characteristics, falls within this area. However, it offers no guidance as to what the rules should be or what features should be used or not be used when deciding which rules must be applied. Experience shows that the rules which are considered fair in one community at one time, seem to be unjust in other societies at other times. The notion of equality, as embodied in the UN Declaration of Human Rights, is therefore to be considered as a catalogue of objective characteristics which in our time, and in a community which has endorsed the declaration, it would not be fair to use as barriers between different categories of the population."

The question now is whether Woman's Law is ready to climb the ladder to the next level of objective characteristics? Did we come so far that we can do without the concept of equality when the different issues of gender in the reproductive field are yet to be addressed? We know the complexity of issues raises questions without easy solutions, but we pose them because we do not see any real societal respect for women's reproductive effort.

10. Motherhood Authority

Today gestation is socially constructed as a parenthesis in ordinary women's daily life, situated between the menstrual cycle with its amenorrhea, and the act of giving birth. The view is built on this logic: intercourse between a man and a woman can result in a child. This view is largely linked to the private sphere.

The Act on Parental Responsibility goes one step further and in the private sphere links a child with both genetic parents, regardless of their relationship with each other at the time of birth. This happens with no regard, for example, for the impact of turbulence, which will inevitably be the result in situations where a relationship with the genetic father is imposed.

Giving birth can be a life-altering experience for a woman. The work of birth-giving while the body opens and the baby comes out also opens the possibility of acquiring new dimensions of human life. Thus giving birth is a radical and profound event placing a woman at the mercy of her body. Torn out of her usual structure, she must rely on the forces of nature or the help of others to manage the situation.

She cannot give birth by means of her gender role, and contractions are not a social construct. These are facts – whether she likes it or not.[23]

An expression of logic exists about the relationship between the woman and the unborn child regarding their bodily functions. It is inspired by the women's convention: a woman's making her body available to a 2-in-1-body-situation may increase the population by another child.

This logic makes it easier to understand motherhood as a social function, providing that one defines pregnant women as the 2-in-1-body-population in the reproductive stage of life.

Basically, there will be a need for initiatives aiming at defining declarations of rights on behalf of adult women to the effect that they must be allowed to live in peace during the few times in their lives when they function differently from men because of their reproductive potential.

It could be decided – because after childbirth and about one year afterwards most women have the innate ability to satisfy the child's spontaneous demands – that this ability be granted legal status, for example as maternity authority. A practical element of maternity authority could be that it takes effect before conception (this ensures a woman's right to self-determined abortion); that it is implemented, when a couple, one of whom has given birth, does not agree on issues concerning procreation and custody. Motherhood authority as a human right could ensure peace to women who want sole custody. In other words: a negative right for the protection of woman and child, as well as the public interest in optimal reproduction. It would value and en-

23. In Denmark, the psychologist Svend Aage Madsen worked with the relationships between men and childbirths www.rigshospitalet.dk/NR/rdonlyres/676E579D-78A5-4A24-8D94-83F4E5411949/0/JMCPsyksocFaedresrelationertilderesspaedogsmaaboern.pdf

courage a general understanding of the female body as something other than a commodity.

The really big challenge is to ask whether the right to grow into existence in the human uterus in the female body and maternity authority can both be described as positive rights?

It is tempting to let the answer be influenced by compassion towards individuals' problems, because we are not accustomed to thinking objectively about motherhood. But – isn't it obvious that there should be an objective interpretation of maternity in The Women's Convention? In that case it becomes a 'good thing' in The Women's Convention, if in fact it is the objective view of motherhood The Women's Convention protects! 'A good thing' because then it is the female gender and the specific characteristics of the female body that have been found worthy of protection. How can anything other than the objective view of motherhood be considered when the requirement for governments is clearly that the state must "ensure that family education includes a proper understanding of maternity as a social function"?

As long as women give birth it lies within the reach of conventions to determine international common values and norms regarding women's specific characteristics – as natural law. It has to fall within the general principles and basic conditions that form a community. The objectivity of The Women's Convention points in this direction. Furthermore in 1948, The United Nations Universal Declaration of Human Rights based itself on natural law, in the sense that human rights were defined as objective that is the condition for each person being able to live and develop.

As a result of this background, maternity authority can be viewed positively as well as being beneficial to communities and public health. The same cannot be said about the Act on Parental Responsibility.

With this in mind, a future standard of automatic shared custody determined before birth might be prevented. Maybe human rights can be changed to become fairer to women involved in the chain of reproduction. Perhaps we can avoid a future scenario where shared custody is determined by the genetic similarity between father and child, detected using DNA profiles from a biological database, which can reveal to a man whom he has fathered.

CHAPTER 9

Balancing an individual and a structural approach towards gender equality, the question of the police hijab

By Vibeke Blaker Strand,[1] *Stipendiat, Department of Public and International Law, Oslo University*

1. The Norwegian debate regarding the police hijab

In Norway in recent years there has been much debate about whether wearing the hijab with the police uniform should be allowed. At present wearing the hijab as part of the police uniform is not allowed. This is clearly laid down in the police uniform regulations, which in paragraph 8 state that:

"Civilian clothes and effects should not be worn visibly together with the uniform effects. An exception here is civilian clothes that have been approved for both uniform and civilian use."[2]

Religious headdress has not been approved for use, and therefore is prohibited.

The debate that has taken place has been both of a political and of judicial nature. In February 2009, the Stoltenberg II government originally committed

1. I would like to thank law professor Anne Hellum for useful comments on earlier drafts of this article.
2. The Directorate of Police *Uniform Regulations for the Norwegian Police Service.*

to allowing the wearing of the hijab as part of the police uniform.[3] However, shortly afterwards, a wave of massive criticism resulted in the government back-tracking on this proposal.[4] The problem was transformed into legal form by the Equality and Anti-Discrimination Ombud (the Ombud) and the Equality and Anti-Discrimination Tribunal (the Tribunal), who subsequently became involved in the matter. Both the Ombud and the Tribunal questioned whether the uniform regulations have been formulated in a way that is in violation of Muslim police women's protection against discrimination on the grounds of religion and gender, cf. Section 4 of the Act on prohibition of discrimination based on ethnicity, religion, etc. (the Anti-discrimination Act[5]) and Section 3 of the Gender Equality Act[6].

In 2010, both the Ombud and the Tribunal concluded that the police uniform regulations are in violation of the protection against indirect discrimination on the grounds of religion and gender.[7] However, the Ministry of Justice and the Police have interpreted the anti-discrimination legislation in a different way and are of the view that there is no violation of the protection against discrimination.[8] Minister of Justice and the Police, Knut Storberget, has made it clear that the government will not change its decision not to allow the use of religious headdress as part of the police uniform. This means that there is discord between the Ombud/the Tribunal and the Ministry of Justice and the Police as regards the content of the protection against discrimination. The fact that the police uniform regulations are being upheld, despite the conclusion of the Ombud and the Tribunal, raises questions of the authority and clout of these bodies. However, this is not what this article concerns.

Common to all the legal assessments made by the Ministry, the Ombud and the Tribunal is that only the European Convention of 4 November 1950

3. The Ministry of Justice and the Police *News article entitled: The hijab as part of the police uniform* (4/2/2009), published on the Ministry's website (at www.regjeringen.no).
4. The Ministry of the Justice and the Police *Press release: The Police Uniform Regulations* (20/2/2010), published on the Ministry's website (at www.regjeringen.no).
5. Act no. 33 of 3 June 2005 relating to the prohibition against discrimination on the grounds of ethnicity, religion, etc.
6. Act no. 45 of 9 June 1978 relating to equality between the sexes.
7. See the Equality and Anti-Discrimination Ombud *Statement – the right to wear religious clothing in the police uniform regulations* (18/1/2010) and the Equality and Anti-Discrimination Tribunal, *Case no. 8/2010.*
8. The Ministry of Justice and the Police *The right to wear religious clothing in the police uniform regulations* (8/2/2010). Letter to the Equality and Anti-Discrimination Ombud.

for the Protection of Human Rights and Fundamental Freedoms (ECHR) has been drawn into the debate. Therefore, the legal assessments have been based on relatively limited human rights material. In the article I will demonstrate the significance that particularly the UN Convention of 18 December 1979 on the Elimination of All Forms of Discrimination against Women (CEDAW) and the International Covenant of 16 December 1966 on Economic, Social and Cultural Rights (ICESCR) have when dealing with the question of protection against discrimination and Muslim women's wearing of the hijab as part of the police uniform. The article draws attention to how the question of use of the hijab with the police uniform has to do with an individual's right not to be discriminated against because of gender and religion, but also involves a closer look at the state's responsibility to take steps to modify or eliminate gender discriminating structures. The case of the police hijab illustrates how an individual and a structural approach towards gender equality must sometimes be balanced against each other. In my opinion, it is this tension between an individual and a structural approach that mainly leads to the challenging considerations that raise questions regarding the use of the hijab in a Western context.

The article unfolds in seven parts. Firstly, in part 2, I give a brief overview of the protection against discrimination and its central legal elements that are of relevance when dealing with the question of hijab in the police. In part 3, I give a short presentation of how the relationship between domestic law and international human rights conventions has been regulated in Norway. Thereafter, in part 4, I elaborate on how a structural approach towards gender equality is relevant when it comes to dealing with the question of use of the hijab in the police. Both the formal reasons for women's use of the hijab and the legal norms are looked into. In part 5, I focus on an individual approach towards gender equality. Here focus is on the individuals and their motives for wearing religious headdress, and legal norms that focus on the individual'sprotection against discrimination in connection with employment are analyzed. How to balance an individual and a structural approach towards gender equality is elaborated on in part 6. Finally, in part 7, I pose some concluding comments that put the debate about the police hijab into a broader context regarding the relationship between law and politics.

2. The protection against discrimination and central legal elements

Individual's protection against discrimination is in formal legislation often expressed through provisions that prohibit direct and indirect discrimination.[9] In the Gender Equality Act Section 3 (1) it is stated that:

"Direct or indirect differential treatment of women and men is not permitted."

The Anti-discrimination Act Section 4 (1) states that:

"Direct and indirect discrimination on the basis of ethnicity, national origin, descent, skin colour, language, religion or belief is prohibited."

The police uniform regulations in Norway are formulated in a neutral way. They, however, have an effect that particularly affects Muslim women who want to use the hijab with the police uniform. This means that the question of the police hijab primarily touches upon the protection against *indirect* discrimination because of gender and religion.

Not all differential treatment that can be related directly or indirectly to gender or religion is unlawful. Only *unfair* differential treatment is unlawful and in violation of the prohibitions against discrimination. To decide in individual cases whether there has been discrimination or not, specific assessments must be made where the *justification* for the regulation or practice, which has resulted in differential treatment, is pivotal. Such assessments often take the form of specific proportionality assessments.[10] This has been codified in the following way in Section 3 (4) of the Gender Equality Act:

"In certain cases, however, indirect differential treatment is permitted if the action has an objective purpose that is independent of gender, and the means that is chosen is suitable, necessary and is not a disproportionate intervention in relation to the said purpose."

9. Prohibitions against direct and indirect discrimination are both found at the national level and in EU/EEA-law.
10. It must be noted that the right to direct discrimination is far more restricted than the right to indirect discrimination. For more details about this see Evelyn Ellis *EU anti-discrimination law* Oxford University Press (2005) p. 111 ff., Christa Tobler *Indirect discrimination* Intersentia (2005) p. 316 ff. and Mark Bell, Dagmar Schiek and Lisa Waddington *Cases, materials and text on national, supranational and international non-discrimination law* Hart Publishing (2007) p. 273 ff.

The exemption clause in Section 4 (3) of the Anti-discrimination Act is formulated in a similar way. Here it is established that the protection against direct and indirect discrimination because of, inter alia, religion can be lawful if certain conditions are met:

> "Differential treatment that is necessary in order to achieve a legitimate aim, and which does not involve a disproportionate intervention in relation to the person or persons so treated is not regarded as discrimination pursuant to the present Act."

Dealing with the question of the police hijab involves a further look at the content and scope of the prohibitions against discrimination, seen in context with the exemption clauses. In this article I want to show how international human rights conventions contain central contributions when it comes to deciding whether the police uniform regulations in Norway have an effect that constitutes discrimination against Muslim women.[11]

The protection against discrimination under the international human rights conventions has not only been formulated so that it is negatively stated that unfair differential treatment is prohibited. The conventions also contain positive obligations for the contracting states. Positive obligations mean that through the international human rights conventions there is a positive recognition and elaboration of the various active obligations that the states have in the area of discrimination. The content and scope of the prohibitions against discrimination in the Gender Equality Act and the Anti-discrimination Act cannot be determined without integrating the state's positive obligations that are rooted in the international human rights conventions.[12]

The positive obligations in the international human rights conventions include both an individual and a structural approach towards gender equality. The individual approach focuses on that women, both formally and in reality, should have the same rights and opportunities as men. Through the conventions, special focus is put on women's equal right to employment, and particular attention is paid to the special challenges that apply to minority women. The individual approach focuses, inter alia, on the state's positive obligations to take steps to secure the interests of those who face multiple forms of dis-

11. Also EU/EEA law is relevant when dealing with prohibitions against religious headdress in employment. There are however not yet any judgments from either the EU Court or the EFTA Court that looks into these issues more specifically.
12. See Anne Hellum *Kjønnet og rettens internasjonalisering* in Kritisk Juss (2002) p. 102, Vibeke Blaker Strand *Diskrimineringsvernets rekkevidde i møte med religionsutøvelse* [phd-thesis University of Oslo] (2011) para. 4.2.1.

crimination. The case of the police hijab is a typical example of how some people are vulnerable to for experiencing differential treatment on multiple grounds in the same situation, in this case both because of gender and religion.[13]

A structural approach towards issues of discrimination can consist of several elements.[14] In the case of the police hijab the structural elements anchored in the CEDAW Convention are of particular relevance. The CEDAW Convention draws attention to the state's obligation to take steps to eliminate gender discriminating structures. The obligation to take steps to eliminate gender stereotypes is especially central.[15] That the state shall eliminate stereotypical perceptions of male and female roles means that it shall take steps to change practices and attitudes that form the basis for discrimination.[16]

3. A brief overview of the status of international human rights conventions in Norwegian law

When interpreting prohibitions against direct and indirect discrimination that are formalized in the Norwegian legislation, the legislator, practitioners and legal scholars are obliged to integrate international human rights conventions. This is a consequence of the Norwegian government having ratified several international human rights conventions which have importance for the field of anti-discrimination law and of the fact that human rights conventions are given a strong formal legal status within Norwegian law.

As a starting point, it is up to the individual state how it chooses to implement human rights obligations in domestic law. In Norway, work on enhancing human rights has been in progress for the last 20 years. A special human rights committee was set up in 1989, and the committee's work formed the basis for inclusion of a special article in the Norwegian Constitution in 1994, Article 110 c, which addresses the state's duty to safeguard and respect hu-

13. Also ethnicity can play a part where women are wearing the hijab. The line between religion and ethnicity can be difficult to draw. Here I focus on gender and religion as discrimination grounds. This does not, however, mean that the ethnicity dimension is not relevant.
14. See Vibeke Blaker Strand *Diskrimineringsvernets rekkevidde i møte med religionsutøvelse* [phd-thesis University of Oslo] (2011) para. 4.2.4.
15. Cf. CEDAW Article 5 a).
16. See Stine Jørgensen *Etniske minoritetskvinders sociale rettigheder* Jurist- og Økonomforbundets Forlag (2007) p. 97 and Kirsten Ketscher *Socialret* Thomson (2008) p. 120 ff.

man rights, cf. Article 110 c (1). Further incorporation of human rights conventions in Norwegian law was to take place through the law, cf. Article 110 c (2) of the Norwegian Constitution. This incorporation took place when the Human Rights Act[17] came into force in 1999. Several conventions became part of Norwegian law through incorporation. Incorporation means that it is established in the legislation that a convention with its official wording should apply directly as Norwegian law. This means that the convention in question is made part of the national legislation without transformation.

When the Human Rights Act came into force, the European Convention of 4 November 1950 for the Protection of Human Rights and Fundamental Freedoms (ECHR), the International Covenant of 16 December 1966 on Economic, Social and Cultural Rights (ICESCR) and the International Covenant of 16 December 1966 on Civil and Political Rights (ICCPR) were incorporated through the law. It was explicitly stated in Article 2 that the three covenants should "have the force of Norwegian law insofar as they are binding for Norway". There was considerable debate about which covenants to include in the Human Rights Act.[18] In 2003 and 2009, the law was extended to also include the UN Convention of 20 November 1989 on the Rights of the Child (CRC) and the UN Convention of 18 December 1979 on the Elimination of All Forms of Discrimination against Women (CEDAW).[19] In the question of Muslim police women's protection against discrimination ECHR, ICESCR, ICCPR and CEDAW are significant.[20] In particular, CEDAW and ICESCR provide an important contribution when determining the scope and content of the protection against discrimination.

Section 3 of the Human Rights Act states that the provisions in the incorporated conventions; "shall take precedence over any other legislative provisions that conflict with them." This provision means that the conventions incorporated through the Human Rights Act have been given a special formal

17. Act no. 30 of 21 May 1999 relating to strengthening the position of human rights in Norwegian law.
18. See inter alia Anne Hellum *Hvorfor kvinnekonvensjonen bør inkorporeres gjennom menneskerettsloven* in Kritisk Juss No. 1 (2004) p. 64-66 and Hege Skjeie *Policy views on the incorporation of human rights conventions – CEDAW in Norwegian law* in Nordic human rights journal No. 2 (2009) p. 260-271.
19. Between 2005-2009 CEDAW was incorporated through the Gender Equality Act. There was no precedence provision here as in Section 3 of the Human Rights Act.
20. CRC is also important. This convention is of particular importance in the question of a pupil's right to wear religious headdress. For a further presentation of this, see Vibeke Blaker Strand *Diskrimineringsvernets rekkevidde i møte med religionsutøvelse* [phd-thesis University of Oslo] (2011) para. 6.6.4.

legal status when facing existing national legislation in the event of conflict between the norms. Former Chief Justice of the Norwegian Supreme Court, Carsten Smith, calls the conventions incorporated through the Human Rights Act semi-*constitutional*, because according to the wording of the Human Rights Act, they have a position that is "between" ordinary legislation and the Constitution.[21]

In order to determine the importance of the international human rights conventions for different legal questions, the conventions must be interpreted. For a long time, attention was primarily drawn to the practice of the European Court of Human Rights. In the UN system, there are no courts that enforce the human rights conventions, but there are committees that monitor the parties to the convention's compliance with the convention obligations. The UN conventions incorporated through the Human Rights Act are monitored by the Human Rights Committee (ICCPR), the Committee on Economic, Social and Cultural Rights (ICESCR), the Committee on the Rights of the Child (CRC) and the Committee on the Elimination of Discrimination against Women (CEDAW). The various UN committees have no authority to formulate judgements, but in accordance with the conventions, several other mechanisms have been established that allow the committees to express their views on how the conventions should be interpreted. Of particular importance is the committees' statements made in connection with individual complaints, which is the enforcement mechanism that most resembles court enforcement. Individuals are through this procedure given the opportunity to obtain the committees' assessments and views on whether the person has been subject to a violation of the convention by the state.

The Human Rights Committee and the CEDAW Committee have been authorized to deal with individual complaints. In December 2008, an additional protocol to ICESCR was adopted, which establishes an individual right to lodge a complaint.[22] The additional protocol has not yet come into force. There is also work internationally to establish an individual right to lodge a complaint under CRC, but this has not yet been adopted.

The committees also give general comments on how provisions in the conventions should be interpreted. These general comments are aimed at all

21. See inter alia Carsten Smith *Bør menneskerettighetene styrkes i vår grunnlov?* in Jussens Venner No. 4 (2006) p. 240.
22. The additional protocol was adopted and signing and ratification was allowed from 10 December 2008 through the General Assembly Resolution 63/117.

the convention parties.[23] They may be called something different according to the conventions – "general recommendations" or "general comments" – but they have the same intention: to develop and highlight the convention's material content and the states' obligations.

In addition, the committees issue comments that are directed directly towards individual states. Such comments – that are usually referred to as "concluding observations" – deal with the state's compliance with its convention obligations. The comments are given as response to periodic state reports.

Recently, the practice of the various UN committees has been increasingly drawn into and has played a key role in individual cases that have been heard by the Norwegian Supreme Court. This has been the case for committee views given in individual complaints and general recommendations. The use of such sources of law has in some cases meant that Norwegian legislation has been overturned based on Section 3 of the Human Rights Act or that individual provisions have been interpreted in a different way than would otherwise have been the case.[24] The consequence of the international human rights conventions being given a strong formal legal position is that interpretation of the conventions is essential when establishing the content of domestic law, including the content and scope of the prohibitions against discrimination.[25]

4. Use of the hijab – A structural approach towards gender equality

4.1. Legal outset

CEDAW Article 5 a) states that parties to the convention; "shall take all appropriate measures":

> "To modify the social and cultural patterns of conduct of men and women, with a view to achieving the elimination of prejudices and customary and all other practices which are

23. Manfred Nowak *U.N. Covenant on Civil and Political Rights* N.P. Engel (2005) p. 746.
24. See the Supreme Court's rulings included in Rt. 2008 p. 1764, Rt. 2009 p. 1261, Rt. 2010 p. 1313, Rt. 2011 p. 206 and Rt. 2011 p. 462.
25. What is more specifically required by the human rights source material in connection with the interpretation is further discussed in Vibeke Blaker Strand *Diskrimineringsvernets rekkevidde i møte med religionsutøvelse* [phd-thesis University of Oslo] (2011) para. 2.4.3 ff.

based on the idea of the inferiority or the superiority of either of the sexes or on stereotyped roles for men and women."

Rebecca J. Cook and Simone Cusack define the term stereotype as follows:

"a stereotype is a generalized view or preconception of attributes or characteristics possessed by, or the roles that are or should be performed by, members of a particular group (e.g., women […]). In this view, a stereotype presumes that all members of a certain social group possess particular attributes or characteristics […], or perform specified roles (e.g., women are caregivers)."[26]

When the group to which a person belongs is used to define the individual's characteristics, stereotypes often play a role. Stereotypes surface when expectations are imposed on individuals based on all the people within the group – for example the group of women or group of men – having the same characteristics or wishes. The problem with stereotypes is that the individuals' character traits, desires, abilities and talents become subordinate to the group-based characteristics that are deemed to apply to the group to which the individual belongs.

In CEDAW Article 2 f) it is stated that the convention parties shall:

"take all appropriate measures […] to modify or abolish […] customs and practices which constitute discrimination against women."

CEDAW Articles 2 f) and 5 a) necessitates a closer look at the structures that lie behind the use of the hijab. If use of the hijab can be said to be based on a gender stereotype or on a custom or practice that discriminates against women, the state's obligations under the CEDAW Article 2 f) and Article 5 a) come into play.

4.2. Actual use of the hijab

The primary formal text basis behind Muslim women and girls' use of the veil is a verse in the Qur'an that deals with *modest* behaviour for women and men's relations with the opposite sex.[27] It is therefore the interpretation of the text below, and also a few others, which are the reason why many female

26. Rebecca J. Cook and Simone Cusack *Gender stereotyping* University of Pennsylvania Press (2009) p. 9.
27. Sissel Østberg *Muslim i Norge* Universitetsforlaget (2003) p. 116 ff.

Muslims cover their hair and sometimes also much of their face.[28] The text reads:

> "Say to the believing men that they should lower their gaze and protect their modesty: that will make for greater purity for them. Allah is well acquainted with all that they do.
>
> And say to the believing women that they should lower their gaze and protect their modesty, and not display their adornments except what must ordinarily appear. Let them draw the veil (khimar)[29] over their bosoms and not display their beauty, except to their husbands, fathers, fathers-in-law, sons, stepsons, brothers, nephews, or their wives, or the slaves, or men who serve them, but have no sexual desire, or children who do not understand the women's nakedness."[30]

The text is about the modest behaviour for both women and men, but it is only women who should cover themselves. There are different views within Islam on *how much* a woman should cover herself.[31] Spokespersons for the most conservative interpretation believe that there is a religious duty for women to cover themselves completely, so that the face and hands are covered.[32] On the other hand, there are the liberal interpreters of Islam, who believe that there is no religious obligation for Muslim women to cover themselves.[33] Liberal interpreters of Islam are often keen to show the potential for new interpretation that lies in the Islamic sources, so that the interpretations are consistent with today's social, political and economic structure.[34] Howev-

28. Lena Larsen *Tekst, tolkning og sosial endring* (2004) p. 56 in Njål Høstmælingen (ed.) *Hijab i Norge* Abstract (2004), Anne Sofie Roald *Er muslimske kvinner undertrykt?* Pax (2005) p. 188.
29. *Khimar* was a piece of cloth used to cover a woman's hair, cf. Lena Larsen *Tekst, tolkning og sosial endring* (2004) s. 54 in Njål Høstmælingen (ed.) *Hijab i Norge* Abstract (2004).
30. The Qur'an 24:30-3, quoted from ibid p. 53–54.
31. Anne Sofie Roald *Er muslimske kvinner undertrykt?* Pax (2005) p. 184.
32. The most conservative interpretations as regards veiling women have been presented in Shaheen Sardar Ali *Gender and human rights in Islam and international law* Kluwer Law International (2000) p. 77.
33. Ibid p. 77.
34. See Anne Sofie Roald *Er muslimske kvinner undertrykt?* Pax (2005) p. 11, Shaheen Sardar Ali *Gender and human rights in Islam and international law* Kluwer Law International (2000) p. 3-4 and Ziba Mir-Hosseini *Islam and gender* Tauris (2000). Shaheen Sardar Ali shows how different interpretations of the Islamic text basis are expressed through the wording of fatwas on the Internet, where questions regarding the use of religious headdresses among Muslim women are often a topic of discussion. See Shaheen Sardar Ali *Behind the Cyberspace Veil: Online Fatwa on Women's Family Rights* (2011) p. 122 ff. in Anne Hellum, Shaheen Sardar Ali and Anne Grif-

er, it is essential that the different views on the scope of the practice of veiling are based on interpretations and understandings of the *same* text base.

The verse also makes a gendered distinction between the public and the private sphere. It states explicitly that women's "adornments" belong to the private sphere – to the husband or others with whom the woman typically associates – but she must not display her adornments in public. This distinction between public and private are central not only to understand the practice of veiling of Muslim women, but *in general* in order to understand how women and men's roles are usually understood in Islam.[35]

In Islam, women and men are considered equal, and both have the same opportunities of salvation.[36] At the same time, women and men are regarded as being fundamentally different, and they are considered to have different qualities.[37] This has implications for the roles they are to fill in society. The consequence – at least according to a traditional interpretation – is that women and men are given different positions on issues related to things such as inheritance, the family's structure, work and when being a witness in court cases.[38] According to a traditional interpretation, women's lives and roles are closely linked to the home and thus the private sphere, while the husband is the family breadwinner, and thus a participant in the public arena. When Muslim women enter the public domain – the men's domain – according to Islamic law they should wear a veil to be modest. When women behave modestly, men are less susceptible to temptation than would otherwise have been

fiths (red.) *From Transnational Relations to Transnational Laws* Ashgate (2011). Different interpretations are also discussed in detail in Ekaterina Yahyaoui Krivenko *Women, Islam and international law* Martinus Nijhoff Publishers (2009) p. 56 ff.

35. Shaheen Sardar Al says the following about the distinction between public and private and the use of a veil:"In the Islamic tradition veiling represents the ultimate dichotomy into the public and private spheres of life with the woman confined to the private sphere." Cf. Shaheen Sardar Ali *Gender and human rights in Islam and international law* Kluwer Law International (2000) p. 75–76.
36. Ekaterina Yahyaoui Krivenko *Women, Islam and international law* Martinus Nijhoff Publishers (2009) p. 57-58. Also see NOU 2008:1 p. 62.
37. Bouras, former leader of the Islamic Council of Norway during the period 1993–1998, words this so that women and men are created equal, but are not identical. Cf. Mohammed Bouras *Islam i Norge* Millennium (1998) p. 103.
38. Bouras uses the various qualities of the sexes to justify that the man is head of the family, that women should not work outside the home, except when she has to (that is, if she is without a breadwinner), that men inherit "two women's shares" and that two female witnesses in a trial count the same as the testimony of one man, cf. ibid p. 105–110. For further questioning of Bouras' views, see Tordis Borchgrevink *Det flerkulturelle demokratiets hodepine* (2002) p. 154–156.

the case. This makes it easier for men to preserve *their* modesty. Seen in this perspective, use of a veil implies that Muslim women are given primary responsibility for ensuring that modest behaviour is maintained in the public domain.[39] In addition to use of the veil being about the signals a woman sends out to her surroundings, use of a veil can also be about sending out positive signals about her entire family. This is because in some circumstances women are considered to have a function as the family's official moral ambassador.[40] Therefore, women and girls have a greater responsibility for family honour than boys and men, in that they are often seen as a kind of embodiment of the collective.[41]

As already mentioned, the Islamic source material is interpreted in several ways. In the discussions about how to deal with Muslim women's use of the hijab with the police uniform, however, it can not be ignored what is often seen as the formal basis for the use. Therefore, it is difficult to understand the veiling of Muslim women disconnected from certain religiously motivated patriarchal starting points, where the sexes are regarded as being fundamentally different and where women are given a special responsibility for ensuring modest behaviour in the public domain.

4.3. A closer look at the legal obligation to eliminate gender stereotypes

Is use of the hijab based on a gender stereotype, and if so, what is the content of states' obligation to eliminate gender stereotypes?

Kirsten Ketscher is of the opinion that Muslim women's use of religious headdress is based on a stereotypical perception of the role of men and women, which falls within CEDAW's provisions regarding gender stereotypes. She describes CEDAW Article 5 a) as a "prohibition against maintaining gender stereotypes as an important part of the states' obligation to ensure women's equality" and further states:

39. Mashood A. Baderin sets regulations regarding women's dress in Islam in the context of the prohibition against extra-marital sexual activity: "Due to the prohibition of adultery and fornication in Islamic law, both men and women are required to dress modestly and not to expose sensuous parts of their body seductively in public. Specifically, the Qur'an directs women to 'draw their veils over their bosoms' and not to publicly display their beauty 'except for what must ordinarily appear'." Cf. Mashood A. Baderin *International human rights and Islamic law* Oxford University Press (2003) p. 64.
40. Anne Sofie Roald *Er muslimske kvinner undertrykt?* Pax (2005) p. 139.
41. Ibid p. 139. For a description of the topics "generation differences, respect and honour" in 2nd generation Pakistanis in Norway, see Sissel Østberg *Muslim i Norge* Universitetsforlaget (2003) p. 156–163.

"Religious regulations that women must wear headscarves and other dress requirements must generally be described as an expression of gender stereotypes. The requirement that women must cover themselves reflects a particular notion of women's position in society. This is a modesty requirement that has the function of preventing women from tempting men and distracting them from their duties. This is stereotypical perceptions of women and men's sexuality. Religion maintains these perceptions."[42]

Also Rebecca J. Cook and Simone Cusack regard specific dress requirements for women to build on stereotypical notions of the roles of men and women. These stereotypes are referred to as "prescriptive stereotypes":

"Prescriptive stereotypes can often be understood through the context of sex role ideologies, which tend to have their roots in cultures, religions, and, for example, colonial histories. Cultures and religions have modesty, obedience, and chastity codes that dictate a woman's behaviour, including her sexual behaviour, dress and role in society."[43]

The content of the obligation to eliminate gender stereotypes was formulated as follows in a general recommendation from the CEDAW Committee in 2004 on temporary special measures:

"States parties' obligation is to address prevailing gender relations and the persistence of gender-based stereotypes that affect women not only through individual acts by individuals but also in law, and legal and societal structures and institutions."[44]

In the Committee's general recommendation from 2010 regarding the core obligations of states parties under Article 2 of the Convention, the Committee stated that states must:

"take steps directly aimed at eliminating customary and all other practices that prejudice and perpetuate the notion of inferiority or superiority of either of the sexes, and of stereotyped roles for men and women."[45]

Only one individual complaint that has focused on the use of religious headdress has been brought in to the CEDAW Committee, the case of *Rahim Kayhan v. Turkey*.[46] The case involved a female teacher who was fired as a

42. Kirsten Ketscher *Etnisk ligebehandlng, religionsfrihed og ligestilling mellem kvinder og mænd – set i lyset af Føtex-sagen* in Ugeskrift for Retsvæsen (2005) p. 240.
43. Rebecca J. Cook and Simone Cusack *Gender stereotyping* University of Pennsylvania Press (2009) p. 35.
44. CEDAW Committee *General recommendation No. 25* (2004) para. 7.
45. CEDAW Committee *General Recommendation No. 28* (2010) para. 9.
46. CEDAW Committee *Rahime Kayhan v Turkey, Communication No. 18/2008 (2006).*

result of wearing the hijab. The Committee rejected the case, however, because the domestic remedies were not exhausted. Therefore, there was no further elaboration of Muslim women's use of the hijab and the relationship with the state's obligation to eliminate stereotypical notions about gender's roles.[47] However, the wording of Article 2 f) and Article 5 a) and the CEDAW Committee's elaboration of the contents of the state's obligation to eliminate stereotyped notions of gender roles implies – in my opinion – that it is difficult to consider questions about wearing the hijab as part of the police uniform without taking the structural aspects of the protection against gender discrimination into account. This becomes especially clear in a public institution like the police, where there is a risk that wearing the hijab can be seen as an expression of the state legitimising the structures of and views on gender roles on which the use rests.

In September 2010, the CEDAW Committee issued its view in the case of *Karen T. Vertido v. the Philippines*.[48] The case is groundbreaking in that it was the first time in an individual complaint that it was concluded that the state had failed to fulfil its obligation to eliminate stereotypical perceptions of roles for men and women, as laid down in CEDAW 2 (f) and 5 (a). The Committee concluded that the Philippine court's approach in a rape case had, inter alia, been based on stereotypical perceptions of how a woman *should* react in such a situation, which led to a revictimization of the woman.[49]

5. Use of the hijab – An individual approach towards gender equality

5.1. Legal outset

Questions relating to the right to wear the hijab in the public domain have been looked at from different angles under the international human rights conventions. A number of cases are from the field of education and concern

47. Rebecca J. Cook and Simone Cusack *Gender stereotyping* University of Pennsylvania Press (2009) p. 146. See also Anne Hellum's contribution in this book.
48. The CEDAW Committee *Karen T. Vertido v. the Philippines, Communication No. 18/2008* (2010).
49. See para. 8.8. A breach of CEDAW Article 2 c) was also established. The committee concluded the following: "the State party has failed to fulfil its obligations and has thereby violated the rights of the author under Article 2 (c) and (f), and Article 5 (a) read in conjunction with Article 1 of the Convention and general recommendation No. 19 of the Committee [...]", jf. para. 8.9.

states' right to restrict pupils'/students' and teachers' use of religious headdress in public educational institutions. This, for instance, characterizes the practice under ECHR.[50]

While the cases under ECHR have mainly concerned the state parties' right to impose restrictions on individuals' use of religious headdress, mainly to uphold the principle of secularism, the practice under several of the UN conventions is more directed towards a positive definition of the individuals' position and opportunities for participation. Individual's right not to be subjected to discrimination on the grounds of religion or gender in connection with access to employment has a strong foundation particularly in CEDAW Article 11 on women's rights in working life, ICESCR Article 6 concerning the right to work and ICESCR Article 15 paragraph 1 letter a) regarding the right to culture, seen in connection with the prohibitions against discrimination in ICESCR Article 2 paragraph 2 and Article 3. Moreover, the state parties have special positive obligations when it comes to helping people from minority groups to integrate into society. This applies particularly to Muslim women, who are often subjected to multiple forms of discrimination. Therefore, from an individual perspective, women's formal protection against discrimination in employment due to wearing the hijab is as a starting point strong.

5.2. Actual use of the hijab

In a Norwegian secularized reality, individuals may have very different motives for wearing religious headdress. The reason for wearing a headdress need not only be found in religion. As pointed out by the Norwegian scholar Lena Larsen, individuals' use of the hijab may signal a number of different things, "moral purity, Islamic practice, social protest and feminist points of view – as well as conformity to Muslim culture."[51] Veiling as a social protest may be because individuals regard modern Western societies as having gone too far in turning women into sexual objects so that the veil signifies distance

50. Central cases that have been heard under ECHR are *Ahmet Arslan m.fl. v. Turkey* Application no. 41135/98 (23.2.2010), *Dahlab v. Switzerland* Application no. 42393/98 (15.2.2001), *Kurtulmuş v. Turkey* Application No. 65500/01 (24.1.2006), *Leyla Sahin v. Turkey* Application no. 44774/98 (10.11.2005), *Köse (Şefika) and 93 others v. Turkey* Application No. 26625/02 (24.1.2006) and *Dogru v. France* Application no. 27058/05 (4.12.2008). The cases have been fully discussed in Vibeke Blaker Strand *Diskrimineringsvernets rekkevidde i møte med religionsutøvelse* [phd-thesis University of Oslo] (2011) para. 6.6.6.2.
51. Lena Larsen *Tekst, tolkning og sosial endring* (2004) p. 52 in Njål Høstmælingen (ed.) *Hijab i Norge* Abstrakt (2004).

to a sexualized culture. From these individuals' point of view, it can be argued that the use of veil helps to strengthen women's position rather than to weaken it.[52] For practicing Muslims, the use of religious headdress often involves two key considerations at once. Their latitude is extended so that they can and want to participate in the public domain. At the same time, their status as virtuous and god-fearing women is maintained.[53] The alternative would be that women enter the public sphere to a lesser extent. Based on this perspective, the use of religious headdress is a door opener.

There have been many debates regarding the relationship between Muslim women's practice of veiling and women's oppression where the question of whether the use is based on free choice or is due to coercion have been central. In particular, accusations that use of the hijab is due to coercion led to strong counter-arguments from Muslim hijab-wearing women, who stress that the hijab is worn out of free autonomous choice.

In 2006, Kristin Engh Førde published a social anthropological study in which she looked at the use of hijab among Muslim girls in an upper secondary school in Oslo.[54] Her analysis of the relationship between on the one hand, power structures and social relations and on the other hand, individuals' motivation to wear the hijab, helps to refine this either/or approach between coercion/choice. Førde had a total of 30 respondents who were observed and given a group or in-depth interview.[55] Ten of the girls were interviewed in depth, and all of them wore the hijab. As regards the individual's motivation to wear the hijab Førde found that:

> "in practice, the religious requirement is not an invariable social norm, and that in the girls' families and groups of friends there seems to be relatively ample leeway for not wearing the hijab."

The girls mainly explained:

> "that starting to wear the hijab was an individual process involving freedom of choice, reflexivity and subjectivity.

52. Anne Sofie Roald *Er muslimske kvinner undertrykt?* Pax (2005) p. 215.
53. Berit Thorbjørnsrud Motstand mot slør / motstand med slør (2004) p. 47.
54. Kristin Engh Førde *Eget valg eller patriarkalsk tvang?* Master thesis in social anthropology, University of Oslo (2006).
55. Ibid p. 23.

> From a point of view of common sense, it can be concluded that most of the girls experience and explain the decision to wear the hijab as a 'free choice'. The action is perceived as free, that is to say, as wanted and chosen by themselves [...]."[56]

Then Førde asks: "But does 'free choice' mean the same as action uninfluenced by power?" Førde shows how thc contradiction coercion / free choice is not particularly suitable for describing the social processes and power mechanisms that influence use of the hijab.[57] She believes it is possible to see use of the hijab as both something that is individually motivated, while use is also an expression of and part of power relations.[58] As use of the hijab can also be about a woman's desire to obey Allah or to demonstrate Muslim identity, Førde shows how wearing the hijab is also about the norms of Muslim femininity and respectability.[59] Being a "respectable" or "good" girl is central here, and wearing the hijab can be understood as being about signalling an *adequate* degree of inaccessibility.[60] This is important in a Norwegian liberal society, where some may regard the public domain as something risky and potentially immoral, unlike the private sphere, which is seen as moral and safe.[61] Førde describes how being in the public domain not only has to do with Muslim women's concern for their own reputation, but is "also about a subjective bodily experience of being exposed."[62] When the hijab is worn, your body is given a boundary. Førde describes this as follows:

> "Insecurity associated with the body's natural lack of boundaries is mentioned in many of the girls' stories. [...] The idea of the female body's dangerous openness and boundlessness [...] seems to be strongly internalized and embodied in several of the girls."[63]

Hijab not only helps the girls feel safe. In practice, wearing the hijab also means that the girls do not have to be sexual objects, which several of the girls consider an advantage.[64] The hijab contributes – individually – to expand the girls' freedom. At the same time, Førde also states that:

56. Ibid p. 49.
57. Ibid p. 95.
58. Ibid p. 50.
59. Ibid p. 52.
60. Ibid p. 57 and p. 60.
61. Ibid p. 68.
62. Ibid p. 71.
63. Ibid p. 71–72.
64. Ibid p. 74.

"Many of the cultural models that motivate the girls to wear the hijab [are] linked to patriarchal power that subordinates women. These structures, which shape and limit the girls' practice, are not something they freely choose or not. In many cases, the power structures are not even acknowledged, and hardly any resistance is made. Attempts at individual rebellion usually prove to be ineffective and not least painful."[65]

Here Førde draws a line between the group-based structures that Muslim women's practice of veiling must be seen to be a part of, and the individuals' own perceptions of what wearing the hijab is all about. She shows that there is a difference between expressing individual experiences related to wearing the hijab and what wearing the hijab expresses at group level, which has also influenced and shaped the individuals. Even if veiling is a result of what a woman regards as a free choice, the practice can therefore not be entirely disconnected from the structures behind it.

5.3. A closer look at the legal obligation to protect individuals against discrimination

5.3.1. CEDAW

CEDAW Article 1 establishes a broad definition of what is regarded as; "discrimination against women", and the prohibition against discrimination includes "any distinction, exclusion or restriction made on the basis of sex which has the effect or purpose" that it violates women's human rights. As both discriminatory purposes and discriminatory effects are covered by the Convention, the dress regulations that restrict the right to wear religious headdress will fall within the Convention.

CEDAW Article 3 states that the states have undertaken to take all appropriate measures:

"to ensure the full development and advancement of women, for the purpose of guaranteeing them the exercise and enjoyment of human rights and fundamental freedoms on a basis of equality with men."

It is made clear here that state parties should take active steps to ensure that women have full development and advancement opportunities. Dress regulations restricting the right to wear religious headdress will typically challenge this positive oriented state obligation.

CEDAW Article 11 deals with the rights of women in working life, and Article 11, paragraph 1 states that the parties to the Convention must "take all

65. Ibid p. 112.

appropriate measures to eliminate discrimination against women in the field of employment [...]." This includes the right to workand access to the same employment opportunities as men, including the use of the same selection criteria for the appointment, see letter a) and letter b). The content of this provision is very relevant when dealing with dress regulations that restrict the use of religious headdress.

Although the CEDAW Committee has not yet had a hearing on the merits of any case involving the use of religious headdress, the topic has been touched on in connection with the Committee's concluding observations to state reports. In the concluding observations the Committee has also focused on the specific issues arising from multiple discrimination. It is clear that the state has a special responsibility to take active steps to ensure access to employment and educational institutions for women who are subjected to multiple forms of discrimination.[66]

The position of immigrant women in education and employment was addressed in the Committee's concluding observations to Norway in 2003. Here the Committee expressed:

> "concern about the multiple discrimination faced by migrant, refugee and minority women with respect to access to education, employment and health care and exposure to violence.
>
> The Committee urges the State party to take effective measures to eliminate discrimination against migrant, refugee and minority women and to further strengthen its efforts to combat xenophobia and racism. It also urges the State party to be proactive in its measures to prevent discrimination against these women, both within their communities and in society at large, and to increase their awareness of the availability of social services and legal remedies. The Committee recommends that the State party ensures that a gender dimension is included in legislation against ethnic discrimination."[67]

The Committee has also had particular focus on the position of minority women in its statements regarding other states' reports. Regarding the government report from Greece in 2007 the Committee stated that it:

> "remains concerned that women from ethnic minority groups, in particular Roma and Muslim women, continue to face multiple forms of discrimination with respect to access to education, employment and health care."[68]

66. Even though the article deals with employment, convention practice regarding minority women's participation in educational institutions is also relevant.
67. CEDAW-Committee *A/58/38* (2003) para. 413 and 414.
68. CEDAW Committee *CEDAW/C/GRC/CO/6* (2007) para. 17.

In the concluding observations from 2007 aimed at India, there was also special focus on the position of minority women:

> "Given the particularly disadvantaged situation of Muslim women and girls, the Committee requests the State party to provide information in its next periodic report about the action taken on the recommendations of the Sachar Committee with regard to the education of Muslim women and girls. It urges the State party to increase efforts to enable scheduled caste, scheduled tribe and Muslim women to access higher education."[69]

The relationship between the Convention's protection against discrimination and restrictions on the right to wear religious headdress has been explicitly discussed in the Committee's statements to government reports from Turkey and France. In the concluding observations to Turkey's government report from 2005, the Committee stated that it was:

> "concerned about the impact on girls and women of the ban on wearing headscarves in schools and universities."[70]

The Committee requested the Turkish authorities to:

> "monitor and assess the impact of the ban on wearing headscarves and to compile information on the number of women who have been excluded from schools and universities because of the ban."[71]

The existing French ban on pupils' wearing of so-called "conspicuous" religious signs or symbols was the topic of the CEDAW Committee's discussion of France's government report in 2008.[72] The Committee stated that it was:

> "concerned that the ban should [...] lead to a denial of the right to education of any girl and their inclusion into all facets of French society."[73]

The French authorities were requested to:

69. CEDAW Committee *CEDAW/C/IND/CO/3* (2007) para. 33.
70. CEDAW Committee *A/60/38* (2005) para. 371.
71. Ibid para. 372.
72. The content of the French legislation has been described further by Ingvill Thorson Plesner in *Freedom of religion and belief – a quest for state neutrality?* University of Oslo (2008) p. 157 ff. See also Special Rapporteur on freedom of religion or belief, Asma Jahangir *Mission to France, E/CN.4/2006/5/Add.4* (2006) para. 47 ff.
73. CEDAW Committee *CEDAW/C/FRA/CO/6* (2008) para. 20.

"continue to monitor closely the implementation of the Act so that there is no negative impact on the education of girls and their inclusion into all facets of French society. The Committee further recommends that the State party provide data in its next report on the educational achievements of migrant and immigrant girls at all levels."[74]

5.3.2. ICESCR

Restrictions on the right to wear religious headdress is a topic that also affects the provisions in ICESCR. Several provisions are relevant, and in several general recommendations, the ICESCR-Committee has shown how the different provisions should be understood in light of each other. Two provisions are particularly relevant. These are Article 6 concerning the right to work and Article 15 paragraph 1 letter a) concerning the right to culture. Both must be understood in light of the right to protection against discrimination as this is laid down in the accessory prohibitions against discrimination in ICESCR Article 2 paragraph 2 and Article 3. Article 2 paragraph 2 states that:

"The States Parties to the present Covenant undertake to guarantee that the rights enunciated in the present Covenant will be exercised without discrimination of any kind as to race, colour, sex, language, religion, political or other opinion, national or social origin, property, birth or other status."

Article 3 of the Convention states that:

"The States Parties to the present Covenant undertake to ensure the equal right of men and women to the enjoyment of all economic, social and cultural rights set forth in the present Covenant."

The following highlights the specific content of ICESCR Article 6 and Article 15 paragraph 1 letter a), understood in light of the prohibitions against discrimination in Article 2 paragraph 2 and Article 3.

The right to work is laid down in ICESCR Article 6, which states that:

"The States Parties to the present Covenant recognize the right to work, which includes the right of everyone to the opportunity to gain his living by work which he freely chooses or accepts, and will take appropriate steps to safeguard this right."

In its general recommendation from 2005 regarding the right to work, the ICESCR Committee placed particular focus on the connection between the Convention's Article 6 and the protection against discrimination in Article 2

74. Ibid para. 21.

paragraph 2 and Article 3. That the right to work should be ensured without discrimination on any ground is considered to be part of a so-called core obligation laid down in ICESCR Article 6:

"States parties have a core obligation to ensure the satisfaction of minimum essential levels of each of the rights covered by the Covenant. In the context of Article 6, this 'core obligation' encompasses the obligation to ensure non-discrimination and equal protection of employment."[75]

The Committee also states that:

"Violations of the obligation to respect the right to work include laws, policies and actions that contravene the standards laid down in Article 6 of the Covenant. In particular, any discrimination in access to the labour market or to means and entitlements for obtaining employment on the grounds of race, colour, sex, language, age, religion, political or other opinion, national or social origin, property, birth or any other situation with the aim of impairing the equal enjoyment or exercise of economic, social and cultural rights constitutes a violation of the Covenant. The principle of non-discrimination mentioned in Article 2, paragraph 2, of the Covenant is immediately applicable and is neither subject to progressive implementation nor dependent on available resources. It is directly applicable to all aspects of the right to work."[76]

It is clearly stated here that there must be no discrimination in connection with access to employment and that governments should help to ensure equal participation for all in working life.

In accordance with ICESCR Article 3, the states also have special positive duties in relation to ensuring equality between women and men. In this context, the Committee emphasizes:

"the need for a comprehensive system of protection to combat gender discrimination and to ensure equal opportunities and treatment between men and women in relation to their right to work by ensuring equal pay for work of equal value. [...]"[77]

As regards the specific implementation of ICESCR Article 3 seen in context with ICESCR Article 6, the basis is that:

"Implementing Article 3, in relation to Article 6, requires inter alia, that in law and in practice, men and women have equal access to jobs at all levels and all occupations and that vocational training and guidance programmes, in both the public and private sectors, pro-

75. ICESCR Committee *General comment No. 18* (2005) para. 31.
76. Ibid para. 33.
77. Ibid para. 13.

vide men and women with the skills, information and knowledge necessary for them to benefit equally from the right to work."[78]

In the Committee's comments from 2005 to a government report from Norway, focus was on the specific challenges that people from minority groups – particularly women – experience as regards access to employment. The Committee recommended:

"that the State party strengthens measures to combat discrimination against persons of immigrant background and ensures effective monitoring of anti-discrimination legislation."[79]

Furthermore, the Committee requested the state's authorities to:

"continue and strengthen its measures to overcome the obstacles faced by persons of immigrant background, in particular women, in accessing the labour market."[80]

Through ICESCR Article 6, seen in context with Article 2 paragraph 2 and Article 3 it is made clear that restrictions on the right to wear religious headdress touches a key individual right that has clear roots in the Convention, as well as in the Committee's general recommendations. This suggests that it will take a lot before a restriction on access to wear religious headdress, which impedes access to employment, is permitted under the Convention.

ICESCR Article 15 paragraph 1 letter a) states that:

"The States Parties to the present Covenant recognize the right of everyone to take part in cultural life."

The ICESCR Committee elaborated on the contents of the provision in its general recommendation from 2009 concerning the right to culture. A broad interpretation is used here of what is meant by "culture", so that for example "religion or belief systems, rites and ceremonies [...]" and "clothing" is included. The following is also included:

"customs and traditions through which individuals, groups of individuals and communities express their humanity and the meaning they give to their existence, and build their world view representing their encounter with the external forces affecting their lives."[81]

78. ICESCR Committee *General comment No. 16* (2005) para. 23.
79. ICESCR Committee *E/C.12/1/Add.109* (2005) para. 27.
80. Ibid para. 28.

Based on this understanding, use of religious headdress is to be seen as something that falls under the term "culture" in ICESCR Article 15 paragraph 1 letter a). When it comes to the connection between ICESCR Article 15 paragraph 1 letter a) and the Convention's protection against discrimination, the Committee states that:

> "no one shall be discriminated against because he or she chooses to belong, or not to belong, to a given cultural community or group, or to practise or not to practise a particular cultural activity."[82]

Furthermore, the ICESCR Committee emphasizes that Article 15 paragraph 1 letter a) concerns:

> "the right not to be subjected to any form of discrimination based on cultural identity, exclusion or forced assimilation, and the right of all persons to express their cultural identity freely and to exercise their cultural practices and way of life. States parties should consequently ensure that their legislation does not impair the enjoyment of these rights through direct or indirect discrimination."[83]

5.3.3. The scope of the conventions

As CEDAW contains both an individual and a structural approach to gender discrimination issues, it provides an important normative basis for dealing with questions about the scope of individuals' protection against discrimination in situations where restrictions on access to wear religious headdress are imposed. However, there is little concrete practice from the CEDAW Committee, which is suitable for shedding light on how far the individual protection against discrimination extends under the Convention.[84] The Committee's wording in its evaluation of the Turkish and French laws prohibiting the use of religious headdress in public educational institutions gave no clear answer to the question whether the legislation violates the Convention. The Committee only stated that it was concerned – and asked the authorities to closely monitor what impact the regulations have in practice. At the same time, the Committee focused on ensuring that the regulations did not lead to a:

81. ICESCR Committee *General comment No. 21* (2009) para. 13.
82. Ibid para. 22.
83. Ibid para. 49 (a).
84. See also Anne Hellum's contribution in this book.

"negative impact on the education of girls and their inclusion into all facets of French society."[85]

Here, the Committee commented on the actual position that Muslim women are put in as a result of a ban on the use of religious headdress. This must be seen in context with CEDAW's focus on what active measures the state should take to protect the interests of women and girls in general, and women and girls who are in a vulnerable position in particular. This applies especially to education and employment, which are very important arenas for the individual. There is no specific practice that is suitable for clarifying how far the individual's protection against discrimination extends under CEDAW when dealing with prohibitions against the use of religious headdress. In each individual case the individual and structural discrimination perspective will have to be weighed against each other in a way that takes the individuals' actual position into account.

ICESCR only deals with an individual approach towards discrimination issues, and the extent of individuals' protection against discrimination is closely connected to how wide the limitation clause in the Convention is to be understood. ICESCR Article 4 states that:

"The States Parties to the present Covenant recognize that, in the enjoyment of those rights provided by the State in conformity with the present Covenant, the State may subject such rights only to such limitations as are determined by law only in so far as this may be compatible with the nature of these rights and solely for the purpose of promoting the general welfare in a democratic society."

It is only the interests connected to the "general welfare" that can justify limitations on convention rights. The ICESCR Committee has emphasized that it is primarily the interests of other *individuals* that can justify restrictions on the rights under ICESCR, not for instance general control interests. This indicates that the access to restrict the use of religious headdress is narrow. The Committee stated the following in its general recommendation from 1999 concerning the right to education:

"The Committee wishes to emphasize that the Covenant's limitations clause, Article 4, is primarily intended to be protective of the rights of individuals rather than permissive of the imposition of limitations by the State. Consequently, a State party which closes a university or other educational institution on grounds such as national security or the preservation

85. CEDAW Committee *CEDAW/C/FRA/CO/6* (2008).

of public order has the burden of justifying such a serious measure in relation to each of the elements identified in Article 4."[86]

The further scope of the limitation clause has also been emphasized in other general recommendations.[87] Here it is underlined that a proportionality assessment has to be made between the strength of the infringement on rights and what is being sought to be achieved.

In the Committee's general recommendation from 2009 concerning the right to culture, the Committee stated that infringements on the right to culture had to be; "strictly necessary for the promotion of general welfare in a democratic society". To be proportionate; "the least restrictive measures must be taken when several types of limitations may be imposed."[88] This indicates a very strict proportionality assessment.

A strict proportionality assessment, seen in context with the State's positive obligations as regards safeguarding the individuals' interests in connection with access to employment and in connection with exercising culture, suggest that individuals' protection against discrimination is very strong under ICESCR. However, a narrow right of exemption exists.

6. Use of the hijab – Balancing an individual and a structural approach towards gender equality

6.1. The dilemma

From the individuals' standpoint, the hijab can be both a garment that liberates and a garment that binds. It can be a garment that provides an identity and security, or a garment that conceals an identity. It can be a garment that a woman wears to signal women's liberation or a garment that a woman is forced or compelled to wear in order to adapt to a strictly regulated pattern of gender roles. Wearing the hijab is complex and diverse.

Public authorities' rules as regards the question of veiling of Muslim women will therefore not affect Muslim women equally. If restrictions on the right to use veiling are introduced, some women probably perceive this as liberating, because then they do not have to cover themselves. Others will feel restrictions on the right to veiling as a barrier, because it is contrary to their own wishes and may mean that women no longer want to or have the

86. ICESCR Committee *General Comment No. 13* (1999) para. 42.
87. See inter alia ICESCR Committee *General Comment no. 20* (2009) para. 13
88. ICESCR Committee *General comment No. 21* (2009) para. 19.

opportunity to participate in various social arenas. For example, the current uniform regulation has the consequence that women who refuse to remove their hijab cannot work in the police.

The dilemma public authorities are facing can be described as follows: Some Muslim women feel that wearing a veil is something liberating. At the same time, use of a veil sends certain signals about affiliation with a patriarchal gender structure. The Norwegian scholar Tordis Borchgrevink has formulated the dilemma as follows:

> "The believers may judge their symbolic expressions of affiliation of no consequence to anybody but themselves, and overlook the fact that they to do not control all the sentiments and forces at play. It is in this sense that I find the *hijab* not quite innocent."[89]

Therefore, veiling of Muslim women exists in a tension between what the individuals themselves feel about its use and the patriarchal structures, which, together with other factors, form the basis for the use.

6.2. The scope of the prohibition against discrimination

Seen in light of the presented human rights material, how should the prohibitions against discrimination in the Norwegian Gender Equality Act and the Anti-discrimination Act be interpreted when it comes to the question of the police hijab? Is today's prohibition against religious headdress justified in a way that makes the regulation lawful?

In this article we have seen that wearing the hijab – from a structural perspective – must be seen in connection with a patriarchal gender role structure, where women are given particular responsibility for ensuring modest gender behaviour in the public domain. It must therefore be asked whether wearing the hijab as part of the police uniform sends signals about government acceptance and legitimization of the view on gender roles on which use of the hijab is structurally based. It may be argued that this is particularly the case if the government designs its own hijabs that fit the rest of the police uniform, because the government then would be taking active steps to contribute to the practice of veiling women. Even though such a practice may serve as a door-opener for some women, because the women have the opportunity to work as police officers, it can still mean that it sends signals to the outside world that are difficult to combine with the state's duty to eliminate gender stereotypes. The state's duty to protect individuals against discrimination and the state's

89. Tordis Borchgrevink *The Hijab debate and the liberal dilemma* in Tidsskrift for kjønnsforskning No. 2 (2007) p. 49.

duty to eliminate practices that are based on stereotypical notions of gender roles directly confront each other here. Even though individual's human rights based protection against discrimination is very strong when it comes to issues regarding minority women's access to employment, a structural approach to the protection against discrimination has in my opinion a particular relevance in a state institution like the police.

The police hold power on behalf of the community. This is partly reflected by the fact that the police are given wide powers to use force against citizens when necessary. Use of the same uniform for all people working in the police is sending out a signal of neutrality. When all the police are wearing the same clothing, individual factors relating to individual employees are set aside and the police service's profile is set to the fore. Wearing the hijab means that this neutrality is lost to some extent, because an individual standpoint is made visible. This neutrality consideration is also something that needs to be taken into account when deciding the scope of the prohibitions against discrimination.[90]

In my view, based on existing legal sources, there will be access *both to prohibit and to allow* use of the hijab with a police uniform. There are strong considerations on both sides in the legal assessment that has to be made. The sources of law can hardly be interpreted in such a way that the individual perspective on gender equality trumps the structural approach and the state's obligations in this regard. Therefore, in my view, the current ban on wearing the hijab as part of the police uniform does not violate the prohibitions against discrimination in the Gender Equality Act and the Anti-discrimination Act. However, it is also possible to amend the current police uniform regulations so that these allow for use of the hijab as part of the police uniform. This would be a political choice. If wearing the hijab as part of the police uniform is allowed, the individual's actual possibility to participate in employment would be strengthened compared with today.

90. For a more detailed discussion of the various considerations and their relevance for the problem of religious headdress, see Vibeke Blaker Strand *Diskrimineringsvernets rekkevidde i møte med religionsutøvelse* [phd-thesis University of Oslo] (2011) para. 6.9.2.

7. Concluding comments regarding the relationship between law and politics

The case of Muslim women's wearing of the hijab as part of the police uniform and a closer look at relevant legal norms has illustrated three important tasks that Scandinavian legal scholars on women's rights face in the time to come.

Firstly, the case has showed how internationalization of the legal system comes into play with full force in matters of gender equality. In practice, this creates challenges when it comes to getting an overview of all relevant sources of law. Sources of law relating to the UN covenants may for instance be less available than what is the case for judgements from the European Court of Human Rights. It can be difficult for the legislator, judges and practitioners to obtain full information about all relevant legal sources. In today's complex legal landscape, legal scholars on women's rights have a key role when it comes to integrating international sources of law into domestic law and to interpret this complex legal material.

Secondly, the example of the hijab in the police has on one side shown the extent of formalization of rights that has taken place in the field of anti-discrimination law. At the same time, the case shows that there are limits to legal norms. This is where politics begin. The internationalization of the law and formalization of rights (regardless of whether they are anchored in the EU/EEA law or in international human rights conventions) in Norway have been subject to massive debate, partly because the national legislator has been regarded as losing power at the expense of national and international courts.[91]

91. See NOU 2003:19. The majority of the committee – Øyvind Østerud, Fredrik Engelstad and Per Selle – concluded, inter alia, that affiliation with international human rights conventions involves a limitation in latitude for majority decisions in democratic institutions, and also that growing internationalization has contributed to giving the courts greater authority at the expense of the representative government. The majority regarded democracy as being in disintegration, see p. 30-32 of the report. One committee member – Hege Skjeie – did not agree with the majority's conclusion and pointed out that greater emphasis on human rights did not imply a weakening, but rather an expansion of the democracy, see ibid p. 74 ff. The last committee member – Siri Meyer – also did not agree with the majority's conclusion and gave a special statement, see ibid p. 62 ff.. The report led to great debate; see among others Morten Kinander (ed.) *Makt og rett. Om Makt- og demokratiutredningens konklusjoner om rettsliggjøring av politikken og demokratiets forvitring.* Universitetsforlaget (2005), Anne Hellum *Maktutredningens påstander om rettsliggjøring settes ut i live – en knekk for demokratiet?* in Kritisk Juss No. 2 (2004) p. 115-117 and Hege Skjeie *Poli-*

I will not go into that debate here. Given the fact that the international sources of law already have been given a strong position in domestic law, it becomes important to determine the scope of the norms, where the norms stop and where politics begin. In this way legal scholars can help to clarify what roles internationalization and formalization play in practice in the field of anti-discrimination law. The content of the norms will develop over time.

Thirdly and lastly, the case of the hijab shows that we need to look at the values that underlie the formal protection against gender discrimination. In Scandinavian countries that are less homogenous than they used to be, what should be the objective for the gender equality project? What kind of equality between the sexes do we want to achieve? A key question is: How much diversity and difference is there room for?

Religiously based views that see women and men as fundamentally different, challenge our views on what should be the goal of the gender equality project. If the goal is that no woman should ever experience to be directly or indirectly treated differently from men – regardless of what gender-subordinating practices the woman herself carries out – we risk losing some of the fundamental equality ideals that have been central for the Scandinavian equality project. Conversely, if we operate with zero tolerance for practices where women subordinate themselves in relation to men, like the hijab can be seen as an example of, the consequence will be continued exclusion of many women from key social arenas.

Legal norms guide us to a certain extent, in that both an individual and a structural approach towards gender equality should be ensured. However, the norms do not necessarily contain the solution to the value-related choices that need to be taken. Problems that are connected to less homogenous societies will continue to arise. Legal scholars on women's rights can try to put these problems into a broader legal and value oriented context. This can help highlight what underlying values are at play and what is at stake.

cy views on the incorporation of human rights conventions – CEDAW in Norwegian law in Nordisk tidsskrift for menneskerettigheter No. 2 (2009) p. 260-271.

CHAPTER 10

How do women directors make a difference to the work of corporate boards?

Evidence from Norway

By Sabina Nielsen,[1] *Associate professor, Department of International Economics and Management Copenhagen Business School & University of Technology Sydney & Morten Huse, professor, Department of Innovation and Economic Organization, Norwegian School of Management BI*

1. Introduction

The new legislation passed in Norway in 2003 required at least 40 per cent of all board members of publicly listed firms to be women. This quota law has raised vivid debate both nationally and abroad (Bernstein, 2005). The public debates in many countries present societal case and business case arguments for increasing the number of women board members. The societal case contains that corporations and corporate boards are embedded in a societal context, and shareholders must accepts that societal values can be more important than shareholder values. Hence, an increase in the number of women directors per se has often been used as effectiveness criteria relating to the so-

1. Corresponding author.

cietal case. The business case perspective, however, is concerned with the effects of women representation on firm competitiveness. Yet there is little evidence as to how forced changes in board composition have influenced the actual work of boards and whether and how women make a contribution to board processes and effectiveness.

Recent advances in the governance literature emphasize the need to open the "black box" of board behavior and explore how team processes and dynamics shape the outcomes of board work (Forbes and Milliken, 1999; Huse, 2005; Pettigrew, 1992). However, gaining access to corporate boards and being able to observe or investigate their actual work and behavior has been a significant challenge for a number of reasons (Daily, Dalton and Cannella, 2003). First, gaining access to corporate elites in general is difficult as directors have very limited time to meet with researchers or respond to survey questionnaires. Second, the confidentiality of many decisions made in the boardroom makes directors reluctant to answer any questions related to board tasks and decisions. Third, the increased scrutiny and public attention to which corporate boards have been exposed since the Enron scandals leads to a high risk of identifying and disclosing weaknesses in the board work and is a reason to avoid opening boards to public inquires. Finally, the highly sensitive nature of questions related to board diversity and women representation on boards makes it difficult to directly ask critical questions. The Value-creating board program (Huse, 2007, 2008) represents a unique effort to overcome such difficulties and analyze board work using both qualitative and quantitative inquiry over a substantial period of time.

A main part of the Value-creating board research program is questionnaire surveys with around 200 questions about actual board behavior, including board member characteristics, board working structures, board processes and board task performance. The initial surveys took place in Norway in 2003/04 and 2005/06. The surveys were sent to various samples of firms, and respondents were CEOs and board chairpersons. The 2005/2006 surveys also had responses from other board members. A total of more than 1200 respondents in 980 firms responded in 2003/04, and in 2005/06 there were more than 2350 respondents in 1230 firms. The general response rates for the various surveys were between 30 and 35 per cent. Versions of the surveys have later been conducted in other countries like Italy, the Netherlands, Belgium, Denmark, Turkey, Finland and Germany. Other parts of the Value-creating board program included projects using qualitative data collection as for example "a fly on the wall study" (see e.g. Huse, Minichilli and Schøning, 2005), a "one of the lads study" (see e.g. Huse and Zattoni, 2008) and the collection of board life stories from women directors (see e.g. Huse and Solberg,

2006). While the aim of the Value-creating board program was to investigate board effectiveness and value creation in general, a number of studies have focused particularly on women directors (Huse, Nielsen and Hagen, 2009; Huse and Solberg, 2006; Nielsen and Huse, 2010a; b; Torchia, Calabro and Huse, 2011).

Through this ambitious line of research, where we surveyed the CEOs, Chairs and board members (both men and women) of Norwegian firms over several time periods, we explain why and how women can be valuable board members and contribute to the work of corporate boards. We do not try to correlate the number of women with firm financial performance; rather we look beyond the surface into the actual dynamics and performance of corporate boards. Below we are presenting some of our most important findings.

2. The ratio of women directors and board effectiveness

In times of vivid debates about the role of women on corporate boards, we explored how the ratio and number of women on corporate boards influences board effectiveness. The work of boards is complex and multi-faceted; there is more to it than simply approving managerial decisions. As we studied the way boards conduct their work and fulfill their multiple and often contradicting tasks, we found that the impact of women directors on board effectiveness is differential, that is depends on the nature of the tasks performed. Specifically, Nielsen and Huse (2010a) found the ratio of women directors to have a positive relationship with board strategic control but no relationship with board operational control. These results suggest that while women directors do not perform operational control tasks better or worse than men, they bring specific advantages to board decision-making when it comes to board strategic tasks. It seems that women's enhanced sensitivity towards others and their consideration of the interests and perspectives of multiple parties enhance board oversight of firm strategy. In a different study, Huse, Nielsen and Hagen (2009) found that the women director ratio increased board CSR control and strategic control, whereas no association was found between the women ratio and behavioral and budget control. Together, these findings may help explain why it is difficult to establish a direct relationship between board gender composition and firm performance. To the extent that boards perform multiple tasks simultaneously and women have differential impact on some of these tasks, no overall performance differences can be detected between firms with high and low ratios of women directors. Our results are also consistent with the literature on gender differences in leadership styles (Eagly and Johnson, 1990; Eagly et al., 1995), which suggests that there are no overall differences in behavior between women and men in management positions. Rather, women directors' leadership style may be different from those of men for certain tasks and in certain situations.

3. The importance of board processes

We further set out to explore whether boards with higher numbers of women experienced different team processes and dynamics compared to boards composed entirely of men. Nielsen and Huse (2010a) assert that board processes are crucial in understanding how women directors contribute to board effectiveness and value creation. The study reveals that boards with higher percentages of women directors experience higher levels of debate. This indicates that the differences in values and perspectives brought in by women may encourage active board discussions. It seems that women often act as "the devil's advocate" and stir up discussions in the boardroom. At the same time, based on gender stereotypes, some critics argue that women may bring higher levels of conflict. To the contrary, we find that boards with higher ratios of women experience less conflict! The presence of women on board seems to reduce the confrontation among directors.

Importantly, the study's findings illustrate that board development activities and conflict are the processes or mechanisms that help explain the relationship between board gender diversity and strategic control, while board development activities mediate the relationship between women directors and operational control. Boards with high ratios of women demonstrated more frequent use of board development activities related to the introduction of working structures such as board work instructions, evaluations and development programs. These structures, in turn, enhanced board strategic and operational control. Furthermore, the study's results show that while board debate is crucial for the quality of board decision-making, increased conflict can harm board functioning. These findings points to the importance of balancing the need for constructive open debate among board members without incurring the negative effects of conflict.

In addition, these insights into the work of boards emphasize the crucial role of women directors in reducing the level of detrimental conflict in the boardroom. Prior research on gender differences suggests that women are genuinely concerned with the welfare of other people and are helpful, kind, sympathetic, interpersonally sensitive, nurturing and gentle. As a consequence, women are more likely to accept others' positions and contribute to the solution of task (cognitive) and relationship (emotional) conflict. When potential for conflict arises in the boardroom, women are better able to avoid such conflicts based on their higher sensitivity and ability to resolve interpersonal and task-related disagreements.

Nielsen and Huse's (2010a) study has important implications for practice. The study's results suggest that the number of women directors is not a critical factor determining the effectiveness of corporate boards. Rather, team processes and dynamics are crucial determinants of board effectiveness and value creation. Thus, it is not only necessary to appoint women to corporate boards, it is also essential to create favourable conditions for the board members to realize their potential. By focusing attention to board development activities and open debate while trying to minimize occurrences of conflict in the boardroom, board effectiveness can be greatly improved. Furthermore, as women directors may have differential impact on different board task, it is necessary to a priori specify the nature of the board tasks and consider how appointing women with certain qualities and characteristics can help improve the board's effectiveness in performing some of these tasks.

4. Women directors' professional experiences and personal values

How do women directors differ from their male colleagues? One of the unanswered yet intriguing questions is whether gender stereotypes are substantiated by actual differences between women and men. Some argue that gender stereotypes are not applicable to women who pursue managerial careers (Powell, 1990). Eagly and Johnson (1990) conducted a meta-analysis of studies on gender differences in leadership and found that participative leadership was used more by women than men but no gender differences existed in the use of task-oriented behavior or supportive behavior. A subsequent meta-analysis (Eagly, Karau and Makhijani, 1995) further revealed that there were no overall differences in effectiveness of male and female managers and concluded that gender per se is unlikely to be a predictor of leadership effectiveness. Hence, it is necessary to look beyond gender to determine what other characteristics determine women directors' individual behavior. Based on a review of the existing literature, we identified two types of characteristics through which women directors may exert influence on board decisions; namely women directors': (1) non-traditional professional experiences (Hillman et al., 2002; Singh, Terjesen and Vinnicombe, 2008); and (2) different values (Selby, 2000). Accordingly, we argue that the impact of women directors on board decision-making and effectiveness depends not on their gender per se but rather on the prior professional experiences and particularly the values they bring along.

4.1. Women directors' values

Prior research has shown that men and women differ ideologically, especially in terms of women's greater compassion (Beutel and Marini, 1995) and men's greater tolerance for ethical lapses and endorsement of morally nontraditional social policies (Eagly et al., 2004). A meta-analysis by Franke, Crown, and Spake (1997) revealed that men were less likely to perceive specific business practices, such as insider trading, as unethical. Hence, women joining predominantly male groups are likely to bring along different values and attitudes which will result in higher value diversity, thus increasing the level of debate and generation of alternatives in the board room. Such differences may be crucial for the board's ability to steer corporate strategy and exert control over management as a guardian of the shareholders' interests. According to this view, Adams and Ferreira (2008) found that gender diverse boards allocate more effort and are more effective in monitoring management. In addition, women directors who have different values were more likely to question the conventional wisdom and to speak up when concerned or in doubt about an issue or a particular managerial decision (Bilimoria and Huse, 1997; Huse and Solberg, 2006).

Consistently, Nielsen and Huse (2010b) demonstrated that the more different women directors' values are from those of male directors, the higher is their influence on board decision-making. A possible explanation for this relationship is that women feel strongly about their underlying values and are therefore more likely to raise their voices when issues discussed in the board are in contrast to their values. Differences in women's values are significantly associated with higher participation of women in board discussions and higher impact on issues being discussed as well as the way in which the board conducts its business. Hence, contrary to existing qualitative evidence that even if they experienced any conflict between their own beliefs and board decisions, women do not necessarily express this conflict (Bradshaw and Wicks, 2000: 201), our research shows that women are likely to act upon their different values in the boardroom. Furthermore, we demonstrate that such actions are valuable in enhancing board strategic tasks, as women directors' contribution to board decision-making leads to higher board involvement in strategy.

In another article, Huse, Nielsen and Hagen (2009), we tested for the effects of women directors' values on specific board practices and task performance. We found that when women possess different values than male directors they are likely to be more active and influential in the boardroom by influencing not only specific board decisions but also the range of issues to be discussed, which in turn influence the board's evaluation of firm organization, HR and CSR.

4.2. Women directors' backgrounds

Previous research suggests that the influence of women on the work of corporate boards may well depend on the qualifications they bring along (Peterson and Philpot, 2007). A number of empirical studies show that women directors differ from their male counterparts in terms of their prior professional experiences as they have non-traditional backgrounds (Singh et al., 2008). Women directors are more likely to come from non-business backgrounds and hold more advanced degrees (Hillman et al., 2002). Furthermore, women directors rarely hold executive positions (Ruigrok, Peck and Tacheva, 2007) and those who do are seldom in a financial or an accounting function. Rather, women executives hold positions related to the "soft" managerial issues, such as human resources, marketing, advertisement etc. (Zelechowsi and Bilimoria, 2005). Hence, women directors are likely to bring to the boardroom different backgrounds and experiences which have the potential to stimulate divergent thinking and enrich board decision-making (Burke, 1997).

According to theory, women directors who have different backgrounds offer unique perspectives that may help counter the conventional wisdom and increase consideration of a wider range of potential solutions (Milliken and Martins, 1996; Williams and O'Reilly, 1998). For instance, a woman with non-business background may be able to contribute to board decisions with state-of-the-art knowledge in technology developments (Selby, 2000). However, Nielsen and Huse (2010b) found that women with different professional backgrounds are less likely to contribute to board decision-making. Naturally, if women do not possess the relevant professional experience they are less comfortable to actively participate in board discussions. At the same time as noted above, women who have different personal values are able to exert influence on the work of boards. To sum up, the study's findings reveal that it is not the surface differences in gender per se but rather the deep-level diversity in experiences and values that really matters for women's contribution to board work. We find that the mere presence of women on corporate boards is unlikely to increase board strategic involvement. However, if women with similar (traditional) professional experiences but different values are selected, they are able to enrich board decision-making and strategic involvement.

5. Equality perception

Nielsen and Huse (2010b) recognize that the actual contribution of women directors is a function not only of their characteristics, but also of the possibilities that the board offers for women to make a difference. Equality perceptions in particular are a critical factor in determining women directors' contribution. For instance, the presence of women directors on corporate boards is highly controversial. Some studies demonstrate that despite similar competencies women do not advance to board positions at the same rates as men (Daily, Certo and Dalton, 1999; Helfat et al., 2006, Terjesen, Singh and Vinnicombe, 2008), while others question women's ability to contribute to board tasks which are predominantly male value-oriented (Burke, 2000; Schein, 1973). Burke reports that a common assumption exists among those responsible for director selection, that women lack adequate competencies for board positions. Building on stereotype threat theory (Steele, 1997; Steele and Aronson, 1995), We suggested that the perception of women directors as non equal board members can significantly reduce the potential for women to contribute to board decision-making, regardless of their values and experiences. The fear that one's behavior will confirm an existing gender stereotype has been shown to adversely affect performance (Bergeron, Block and Echtenkamp, 2006). Thus, when made salient in the context of corporate boards, gender stereotypes may limit the potential for women to exert influence and may harm women directors' contribution to the work of boards.

Nielsen and Huse's (2010b) findings have important implications for business practice. The insights that the potential contributions of women stemming from their different values are likely to be disregarded when women are not perceived as equal board members are particularly important. Understanding of such dynamics is critical to the discussions of whether or not women directors can make a difference to the work of corporate boards. If one considers only the positive cognitive effects of women characteristics without taking into consideration how women are perceived, it may be concluded that bringing in women with similar (board relevant) professional experiences and different values will enhance board decision-making. However, it is also necessary to convince the rest of the board members that women are as effective as men in their director roles in order to realize this potential. In accordance with the hypothesized gender bias, we found that male respondents are more likely to negatively evaluate women's influence on board decision-making. Furthermore, Nielsen and Huse (2010b) found a negative association between male CEO and chairperson and women's contribution to board decision-making, suggesting that the gender of the leader might be an important factor determining the level of influence of women directors. Having a female leader may make women directors more comfortable in expressing their opinions while at the same time male directors may show more respect for and openness towards views raised by women.

Interpreting the findings of this study in light of introduction of quotas for women directors in Norway, it must be noted that affirmative actions may create additional burden to women equality. The general perception that women are appointed for affirmative action reasons or to appease special interest groups (Daily et al., 2000) may increase existing prejudices and stereotypes and lead to a perception of women as less valuable board members. Furthermore, if the pool for available women directors is not large enough this may lead to appointment of female directors who lack the backgrounds necessary for competent board work, thus further reducing the potential of women directors to make valuable contributions to board decision-making. However, a recent study conducted by Elstad and Ladegård (2011), indicates that the women elected as a result of the Norwegian gender quota law do not perceive that they have less influence on board decision-making than their male counterparts, and thus do not perceive themselves as tokens.

6. Adaptive behavior and critical mass

We have above presented our observations about board effectiveness and board tasks, board processes and developmental activities, the professional experiences and personal values of the women, and the importance of equality perceptions and tokenism. If women are to make visible contributions to the boardroom they also need to bring along their alternative values. However, empirical evidence from women's experiences in the boards suggests that women during board meetings consciously avoid behaviour that would differentiate them from the men (Bradshaw and Wicks, 2000:201). Rose (2007) also argues that women are very conscious of stereotypes and consciously choose behavior that avoid fitting in with the stereotypes, and Erkut, Konrad and Kramer (2008) found that having three or more women on a board can create a critical mass where women are not seen as outsiders and are able to influence the content and process of board discussions substantially.

These observations made us in (Torchia, Calabro and Huse, 2011) test the critical mass assumption that there must be at least three women in a board before they would influence board discussions and effectiveness substantially. The test was conducted on a sample of 317 Norwegian firms on the relationship between the number of women on corporate boards and corporate innovative behavior. The data was collected during the winter 2005/2006 on firms having boards with between six and eleven members. The results suggest that attaining critical mass – going from one or two women (a few tokens) to at least three women (consistent minority) – makes it possible to enhance the level of firm innovation. Moreover, the results showed that the relationship between a critical mass of women directors and the firm level of innovation was mediated by board strategic tasks. The findings have clear implications for practice, as they indicate that the contribution of women on board is not only a matter of individual competencies and values, but also a matter of number. The findings have a direct implication for initiatives to increase the number of women on boards.

7. Conclusion

The findings from the surveys of Norwegian boards help us to better understand how women on boards contribute to firm performance, and show the importance of competencies, values, discussions, conflicts, tasks, perceptions and preparations in the boardroom regardless of gender. Norway has the highest ratio of women directors in the World, thereby making it a suitable context for investigating the influence of women directors on the work of boards. Nordic countries are particularly interesting for studying the role of women directors on corporate boards since they all share a long history of social support to gender equality. While the high ratio of women directors in Norway can be attributed to the Norwegian quota law (Hoel, 2008; Huse, 2007) similar trends toward the increase in women directors among board members can be observed in Sweden, while Finland and particularly Denmark are lagging somewhat behind (Gregoric et al., 2009). Although none of the other Nordic countries have passed legislation pertaining to the quotas of women directors on boards yet, such discussions are often raised and the "Norwegian experiment" is followed closely by policy makers in these countries. While it is still too early to evaluate the consequences of the quota law for the governance practices in Norway, it has led to an increase in the ratio of women directors serving on boards of other Norwegian firms not subject to the law (i.e. non-publicly listed firms). Moreover, public debate continues to flourish on this topic in both Norwegian and international media, leading to increased awareness of issues pertaining to gender equality in general and the role of women in upper echelons in particular.
Sections of this chapter have beend published before in the following publications

Huse, 2008. Women directors and the "black box" of board behavior. In S. Vinnicombe, V. Singh, R. Burke, D. Bilimoria, & M. Huse (Eds.), *Women on Corporate Boards of Directors. International Research and Practice:* 140-152. Cheltenham, Northampton: Edward Elgar Publishing Limited, UK.

Huse, S. Nielsen and I.M. Hagen (2009). Boards of directors, codetermination and women directors: Societal and business case CSR illustrations from Norway, *Journal of Business Ethics*, 89(4): 581-597.

Nielsen and M. Huse (2010a). The contribution of women on boards of directors: Going beyond the surface, *Corporate Governance: An International Review*, 18(2): 136-148.

Nielsen and M. Huse (2010b). Women directors' contribution to board decision making and strategic involvement: The role of equality perception, *European Management Review*, 7(1): 16-29.

References

Adams, R. B., & Ferreira, D. 2008. Women in the boardroom and their impact on governance and performance, *Working paper*, avaliable at http://ssrn.com/abstract=1107721.

Bergeron, D.M., Block, C.J. & Echtenkamp, B.A. (2006). Disabling the able: Stereotype threat and women's work performance. *Human Performance,* 19 (2): 133-158.

Bernstein, R. 2005. Men chafe as Norway ushers women into boardroom. *Wall Street Journal,* January 8.

Beutel, A.M. & Marini, M.M. 1995. Gender and values, American Sociological Review, 60: 436–448.

Bilimoria, D., & Huse, M. 1997. A qualitative comparison of the boardroom experiences of U.S. and Norwegian women corporate directors, *International Review of Women and Leadership, 3(2)*: 63-73.

Bradshaw, P., & Wicks, D. 2000. The experience of white women on corporate boards in Canada: Compliance and Non-compliance to hegemonic Masculinity In Burke, R., & Mattis, M. (Eds.). *Women on Corporate Boards of Directors: International Challenges and Opportunities*. Dordrecht: Kluwer Academic Publishers.

Burke, R. 2000. Women on corporate boards of directors: Understanding the context. In Burke, R., & Mattis, M. (Eds.). *Women on Corporate Boards of Directors: International Challenges and Opportunities.* Doordrecht: Kluwer Academic Publishers.

Burke, R. J. 1997. Women on corporate boards of directors: A needed resource. *Journal of Business Ethics, 16*: 909 – 915.

Daily, C. M., Certo, S. T., & Dalton, D. R. 1999. A decade of corporate women: Some progress in the boardroom, none in the executive suite. *Strategic Management Journal, 20*: 93-99.

Daily, C. M., Dalton, D. R., & Cannella, A. 2003. Corporate governance: Decades of dialogue and data. *Academy of Management Journal, 28*: 371-382.

Eagly, A. H., Makhijani, M.G. & Klonsky, B.G. 1992. Gender and the evaluation of leaders: A meta-analysis, Psychological Bulletin, 111: 3–22.

Eagly, A.H. & Johnson, B. T. 1990. Gender and leadership style: A meta-analysis, *Psychological Bulletin*, 108: 233–256.

Eagly, A.H. 2005. Achieving relational authenticity in leadership: Does gender matter? *Leadership Quarterly,* 16: 459-474.

Eagly, A.H., Diekman, A., Johannesen-Schmidt, M.C. & Koenig, A. M. 2004. Gender gaps in sociopolitical attitudes: A social psychological analysis, *Journal of Personality and Social Psychology*, 87: 796–816.

Eagly, A.H., Karau, S.J. & Makhijani, M. G. 1995. Gender and the effectiveness of leaders: A meta-analysis, *Psychological Bulletin*, 117: 125–145.

Elstad, B and Ladegård. 2011. Women on Corporate Boards: Key influencers or tokens, *Journal of Management and Governance*, online first.

Erkut, S., Kramer, V. W. and Konrad, A. M. (2008), Critical mass: Does the number of women on a corporate board make a difference? In: Vinnicombe, S., Singh, V., Burke, R., Bilimoria, D. and Huse, M. (eds.) Women on Corporate Boards of Directors: International Research and Practice, 350–66. Edward Elgar, Cheltenham. European Professional.

Forbes, D. P., & Milliken, F. J. 1999. Cognition and corporate governance: Understanding boards of directors as strategic decision-making groups. *Academy of Management Review,24*: 489-505.

Franke, G.R, Crown, D.F. & Spake, D.F. 1997. Gender differences in ethical perceptions of business practices: A social role theory perspective, *Journal of Applied Psychology,* 82: 920–934.

Gregoric, A., Oxelheim, L., Randøy, T., Thomsen, S. 2009. The Paths to Gender Diversity. The Nordic Case, in Gregoric, Oxelheim, Thomsen & Randøy, *Corporate governance as a source of competitiveness for Nordic firms*, Research Report, Nordic Innovation Centre, Oslo.

Helfat, C.E., Harris, D. & Wolfson, P.J. 2006. The pipeline to the top: Women and Men in the top executive ranks of U.S. corporations. *Academy of Management Perspectives,* 42-64.

Hillman, A. J., Cannella, A. A., & Harris, I. C. 2002. Women and racial minorities in boardroom: How do directors differ? *Journal of Management,* 28, 747-63.

Hoel, M. 2008. The quota story: Five years of change in Norway, in Vinnicombe, S., Singh, V., Burke, R., Bilimoria, D., & Huse, M. 2008. Women on Corporate Boards of Directors: International Research and Practice, Edward Elgar, Cheltenham.

Huse M. (ed) 2008. *The Value Creating Board: Corporate Governance and Organizational Behaviour*, Routledge, London.

Huse, M. 2005. Accountability and Creating Accountability. A Framework for Exploring Behavioural Perspectives of Corporate Governance. *British Journal of Management, 16*:65-79.

Huse, M. 2007. *Boards, Governance and Value Creation: The Human Side of Corporate Governance*, Cambridge University Press, Cambridge.

Huse, M., & Solberg, A. G. 2006. Gender related boardroom dynamics: How women make and can make contributions on corporate boards, *Women in Management Review, 21(2)*: 113-130.

Huse, M., & Zattoni, A. 2008. Trust, Firm Life Cycle and Actual Board Behavior: Evidence from 'One of the Lads' in the Board of Three Small Firms, *International Studies of Management and Organization.*

Huse, M., Minichilli, A., & Schøning, M. 2005. The Value of Process-Oriented Boardroom Dynamics, *Organizational Dynamics*, 34: 285-297.

M. Huse, S. Nielsen and I.M. Hagen (2009). Boards of directors, codetermination and women directors: Societal and business case CSR illustrations from Norway, *Journal of Business Ethics*, 89(4): 581-597.

Milliken, F. J., & Martins, L. L. 1996. Searching for common treads: Understanding the multiple effects of diversity in organizational groups. *Academy of Management Journal, 21*: 402-433.

Peterson, C.A. & Philpot, J. 2007. Women's role on U.S. Fortune 500 Boards: Directors Expertise and Committee Memberships, *Journal of Business Ethics*, 72: 177-196.

Pettigrew, A. 1992. On studying managerial elites. *Strategic Management Journal, 13*: 163-182.

Powell, G.N. 1990. One more time: Do female and male managers differ? *Academy of Management Executive,* 4 (3): 68-75.

Rose, C. 2007. Does female board representation influence firm performance? The Danish evidence, *Corporate Governance: An International Review,* 15: 404–413.

Ruigrok, W., S. Peck & S. Tacheva: 2007. Nationality and gender diversity on Swiss corporate boards, *Corporate Governance: An International Review*, 15: 546-557.

S. Nielsen and M. Huse (2010a). The contribution of women on boards of directors: Going beyond the surface, *Corporate Governance: An International Review*, 18(2): 136-148.

S. Nielsen and M. Huse (2010b). Women directors' contribution to board decision making and strategic involvement: The role of equality perception, *European Management Review*, 7(1): 16-29.

Schein, V.E. 1973. The relationship between sex role stereotypes and requisite management characteristics. *Journal of Applied Psychology,* 57: 95-105.

Selby, C.C. 2000. From male locker room to co-ed board room: A twenty-five year perspective In Burke, R. J., & Mattis, M. C. (Eds.), *Women on Corporate Boards of Directors: International Challenges and Opportunities*, 239-251. Doordrecht: Kluwer.

Singh, V., Terjesen, S. & Vinnicombe, V. 2008. Newly appointed directors in the boardroom: How do women and men differ? *European Management Journal*, 26 (1): 48-58.

Singh, V., Terjesen, S. & Vinnicombe, V. 2008. Newly appointed directors in the boardroom: How do women and men differ? *European Management Journal*, 26 (1): 48-58

Steele, C.M. 1997. A threat in the air: How stereotypes shape intellectual identity and performance, *American Psychologist,* 52(2): 613-629.

Steele, C.M., & Aronson, J. 1995. Stereotype threat and the intellectual performance of African Americans, *Journal of Personality and Social Psychology,* 69: 797-811.

Torchia, M.T., Calabrò, A. & Huse. M. 2011. Women directors on corporate boards: from tokenism to critical mass, *Journal of Business Ethics, published online 25 February 2011, doi: 10.1007/s10551-011-0815-z.*

Williams, K. Y., & O'Reilly, C. A. 1998. Demography and diversity in organizations: A review of 40 years of research. In Staw, B.M. & Cummings, L.L. (Eds.), *Research in Organizational Behavior.* Greenwich: JAI Press.

Zelekowski, D. D., & Bilimoria, D. 2005. Characteristics of women and men corporate inside directors in the US. *Corporate Governance: An International Review, 12*: 337-342.

CHAPTER 11

Women quotas on company boards in Scandinavia and EU

By Christina D. Tvarnø, Professor (mso), PhD, Law Department, Copenhagen Business School

> "Gender equality is not a 'women's issue'. It is a business issue."[1]
>
> "At the current rate of change it will take over 70 years to achieve gender-balanced boardrooms in the UK."[2]

1. Introduction

This chapter of the anthology will present the legal rules regarding women quotas on boards in public limited companies in Norway and compare these rules with the French legislation regarding women quotas. Furthermore the chapter will look at the legal status in Denmark and Great Britain. Finally the

1. Quote from Viviane Reding Vice-President of the European Commission, EU Justice Commissioner The European Commission's New Gender Equality Strategy: Towards Quotas for Women in the boardroom? European Central Bank Diversity Forum Frankfurt, 28 March 2011.
2. Lord Davies of Abersoch, CBE, Women on boards, independent review, February 24, 2011, p. 1: http://www.bis.gov.uk/assets/biscore/business-law/docs/w/11-745-women-on_-boards.pdf

   Edward Davey, the Business Minister and Lynne Featherstone, the Minister for Women, invited Lord Davies of Abersoch to undertake this review to identify the barriers preventing more women reaching the boardroom and to make recommendations regarding what government and business could do to increase the proportion of women on corporate boards.

chapter will compare the level of EU legislation in the near future in regard to legislation on women quotas.

The comparative analysis in this chapter will be carried out in order to investigate whether aspects of Norwegian and French law can be useful in regard to establishing legal rules in other countries such as Denmark and to investigate if these legal systems can generate some general principles to use in e.g. EU on the subject of a future EU harmonization by e.g. a directive.

2. The Norwegian legislation

In Scandinavia, only the Norwegian government has introduced legal instruments to ensure equal representations in boards of Directors in public limited companies. The purpose[3] of the Norwegian act on women on boards is to ensure a certain representation of both sexes in public limited companies, state-owned enterprises and state-owned subsidiaries.

> *"Three reasons for quotas*[4]
> First, sound economics! Human capital is vital! A modern, competitive economy needs the best heads and hands, regardless of gender. Modernity demands diversity!
> Secondly, a moral base! Equal opportunity for all – regardless of gender. It is about democracy and representation. Quotas may be necessary to ensure equal outputs.
> Thirdly, simply because they work! If you want radical change and want to boost the participation and representation of women in decision-making, legal measures like quotas could make a difference!"

The quote right above is an extract of a speech by Rigmor Aasrud, Norwegian Minister of the Government Administration, Reform and Church Affairs in the European Parliament.[5]

3. 2002–2003, Ot.prp. nr. 97, Om lov om endringer i lov 13. juni 1997 nr. 44 om aksjeselskaper, lov 13. juni 1997 nr. 45 om allmennaksjeselskaper og i enkelte andre lover (likestilling i styrer i statsaksjeselskaper, statsforetak, allmennaksjeselskaper mv.)
4. Rigmor Aasrud, Norwegian Minister of Government Administration, Reform and Church Affairs European Parliament. Brussels, Thursday 24 March 2011. Speech: Intervention in the Hearing: – "Quotas for Gender-Balanced Public Administration?" – hosted by the High-level Group on Gender Equality and Diversity.
5. The minister concludes, that if states *"combine equality policies with modern, gender-neutral family legislation, ample parental leave, full coverage of affordable preschool day-care facilities and flexibility in working life, then youare better prepared for future challenges in terms of demographic changes, economic competitiveness, employment and social sustainability!"* Rigmor Aasrud, Norwegian Minister of Gov-

The rules concerning public limited companies are found in § 6-11a of the Norwegian Companies Act. The Norwegian companies had the opportunity to voluntarily provide the desired representation of both genders on the board of directors by 1 July 2005. If this was not achieved, the act would come into force and ensure the desired gender balance.

§ 6-11a.[6] Demands for representation of both genders on the Board.

On the board of a public limited company both sexes shall be represented as follows:

1. If the board has two or three members, each sex must be represented.
2. If the board has four or five members, each sex must be represented by at least two.
3. If the board has six to eight members, each sex must be represented by at least three.
4. If the board has nine members, each sex must be represented by at least four, and if the board has more members, each sex must be represented by at least 40 percent.
5. The provisions of paragraphs 1 to 4 shall apply to the election of deputies.7

The corresponding rules regarding gender representation rules for state-owned enterprises can be found in § 20-6 of the act.

In 2006, the Norwegian act applied to the newly established public limited companies and from 2008 to all public limited companies. If a company fails to meet the quota it may result in penalties or in the company's dissolution.

ernment Administration, Reform and Church Affairs European Parliament. Brussels, Thursday 24 March 2011. Speech: Intervention in the Hearing: – "Quotas for Gender-Balanced Public Administration?" – hosted by the High-level Group on Gender Equality and Diversity.

6. The § 6-11a is added by legislative amendment of act of 19. dec 2003 no. 120 (ikr. 1 jan 2006 iflg. res. 9 des 2005 nr. 1429 (Tilføyd ved lov 19 des 2003 nr. 120 (ikr. 1 jan 2006 iflg. res. 9 des 2005 nr. 1429.)

7. § 6-11a. Krav om representasjon av begge kjønn i styret

   I styret i allmennaksjeselskap skal begge kjønn være representert på følgende må-te:

   1. Har styret to eller tre medlemmer, skal begge kjønn være representert

   2. Har styret fire eller fem medlemmer, skal hvert kjønn være representert med minst to

   3. Har styret seks til åtte medlemmer, skal hvert kjønn være representert med minst tre.

   4. Har styret ni medlemmer, skal hvert kjønn være representert med minst fire, og har styret flere medlemmer, skal hvert kjønn være representert med minst 40 prosent

   5. Reglerne i nr. 1 til 4 gjelder tilsvarende ved valg av varamedlemmer.

As a consequence of the act, the number of women on the boards of large companies in Norway has risen.[8]

3. A short view over Scandinavia

As mentioned above, Norway has set a quota of 40 per cent female members of public limited companies. In 2010 Iceland introduced a quota law of a minimum of 40 percent of each sex, to be achieved by 2013. The Iceland legislation is applicable to public limited companies, also state-owned, with more than 50 employees.[9] Finland has a "comply or explain" code requiring that every board should have at least one male and one female director.[10] Denmark and Sweden have also introduced corporate governance codes, which are soft law initiatives.[11]

From an economic point of view, the Norwegian legislation is interesting. Sabine Nielsen and Morten Huse have shown, that

> "*Norway has the highest number of women directors in the world... Compared to other Scandinavian countries, Norway is at the forefront of recent trends towards women representation on boards.*"[12]

This study also finds that the Nordic countries in general have a long history of prioritising gender equality. This trend is more pronounced in Sweden than in Finland. Denmark is far behind the other Nordic Countries. A Nordic study made by Trond Randøy, Lars Oxelheim and Steen Thomsen finds substantial differences in board diversity among the Scandinavian countries. There is a

8. SEC(2011) 246 final, The Gender Balance in Business Leadership, Commission Staff Working Paper, Brussels, 1.3.2011.
9. SEC(2011) 246 final, The Gender Balance in Business Leadership, COMMISSION STAFF WORKING PAPER Brussels, 1.3.2011
10. See also Lord Davies reports on women on boards, Company Law Newsletter, 2011, Sweet & Maxwell.
11. IP/11/242, Brussels, 1 March 2011.
12. Sabina Nielsen & Morten Huse, The contribution of women on boards of directors: Going beyond the surface, Corporate Governance: An international review, 2010, 18(2) pp 136.148. (The quote is on) page /p. 145. See also chapter by Sabine Nielsen in this anthology.

low fraction of women on Danish boards and Danish board members tend to be older and less diverse compared to Norway and Sweden.[13]

4. The Danish perspective

In general Danish law has no legal rules or provisions regarding women quotas in boards of public limited companies.[14] Certain sections in the Danish Equal Opportunities Act,[15] section 11, 12 and 13 apply to state government authorities, e.g. boards, representatives or similar.

According to the Danish equality Act § 11 paragraph 2, the boards of independent governmental institutions where the costs are mainly covered by public funds (state grants at a minimum of 60-70 per cent) should if possible have a balanced number of women and men.

Section 11 of the Danish Equal Opportunities Act

Subsection 1. Boards, representatives or similar collective leadership in independent governmental institutions should have an equal mix of men and women.

Subsection 2. Boards, representatives or similar collective management of independent governmental institutions, partnerships, limited companies and corporations that are not defined as part of the government, should if possible have a balanced composition of men and women. This rule applies if the funding of the private institution is mainly covered by government funds, or if the majority of the company is owned by the state.

Section 11 also includes various types of public limited companies where the majority of shares are owned by the state. If there is any doubt whether or not

13. See/cf. Trond Randøy, Lars Oxelheim and Steen Thomsen, A Nordic perspective on corporate board diversity, 2006, Nordic Innovation Center, Oslo.
14. Goran Selanec and Linda Senden, Gender Quotas and Other Positive Action Measures to Ensure Full Equality in Practice between Men and Women. The transposition of EU provisions on positive action and gender quotas in employment, in access to and supply of goods and services, and in decision-making and political bodies in 33 European countries, European Network Of Legal Experts In The Field Of Gender Equality, European Commission, Directorate-General for Justice, June 2011, Denmark by Ruth Nielsen, p. 72.
15. No 1095 of 19 September 2007. Available in Danish at: www.retsinfo.dk

a board is covered by the act, the current Minister must decide. Thus, a state-owned company should as far as possible have an equal gender balance.[16]

According to section 12, authorities or organizations recommending a member to such a board suggest both a woman and a man, or if there is to be proposed several members, suggest an equal number of women and men. Then, the relevant minister decides who will be appointed as a member. In accordance with section12, subsection 3, this does not apply if the members of the board are wholly or partly elected by direct vote.

Thus, section12 places an obligation on ministers and the authorities or organizations empowered to suggest a member for the board to propose both a woman and a man.[17] Also the competent minister has a duty to report the gender composition of the board every third year in accordance with section 13.

In regard to public limited companies in general, both public and private, the minister for gender equality in 2008 presented a Charter with the purpose

16. Section 11(1) reads: Boards; assemblies of representatives; or similar collective management bodies within the public administration should have an equal gender balance.
(2) To the extent possible: boards; assemblies of representatives; or similar collective management bodies of independent institutions; partnerships; and limited liability companies, which are not part of the public administration, should have an equal gender balance. This shall apply where the expenses relating to the independent institution are mainly covered by government funds or where the state holds a majority interest of the company.
(3) The responsible minister may decide that subsection (1) shall apply to the institutions and companies, etc. specified in subsection (2) above.
(4) The responsible minister may decide that subsection (1) or (2) shall apply to specified independent institutions, partnerships or limited liability companies where more than 50 per cent of the expenses incurred by such independent institutions are covered by government funds or where the state holds no less than a 50 per cent stake in the company, etc. The responsible minister may further decide that subsection (1) or (2) shall apply to companies carrying on activities under a concession agreement or similar public licenses.'
17. Goran Selanec and Linda Senden, Gender Quotas and Other Positive Action Measures to Ensure Full Equality in Practice between Men and Women. The transposition of EU provisions on positive action and gender quotas in employment, in access to and supply of goods and services, and in decision-making and political bodies in 33 European countries, European Network Of Legal Experts In The Field Of Gender Equality, European Commission, Directorate-General for Justice, June 2011, Denmark by Ruth Nielsen, p. 75.

of ensuring more women in top management in state owned enterprises as well as public limited companies.[18]

The purpose of the charter is to ensure more women in management on a voluntary basis. The charter has been drawn up jointly with public and private sector enterprises and institutions. The aim of the charter is among other things to ensure that women and men have equal opportunities to pursue management careers, to make sure that public and private sector deploy all talents and to create conditions for women to develop their careers through networks, mentoring programmes and other targeted initiatives.[19]

In July 2011 there were a total of 115 participating companies and public authorities submitted to the charter. The largest group is the public authorities, such as universities. The Danish charter requires enterprises to develop targets for the number of women in management, the percentage of women at selected executive levels to be achieved within a set time, or the proportion of women in talent pools or in the management pipeline. Companies must submit progress reports every two years.[20]

5. The French legislation

The legal basis for the regulation on women quotas in France can be found in the French constitution, Article 1, which provides that all legal acts and statutes shall promote equal access for women and men to elective offices and posts as well as to professional and social positions;

La Constitution du 4 octobre 1958[21]
Article 1
La France est une République indivisible, laïque, démocratique et sociale. Elle assure l'égalité devant la loi de tous les citoyens sans distinction d'origine, de race ou de religion. Elle respecte toutes les croyances. Son organisation est décentralisée.

La loi favorise l'égal accès des femmes et des hommes aux mandats électoraux et fonctions électives, ainsi qu'aux responsabilités professionnelles et sociales.

18. The Charter can be found at http://www.kvinderiledelse.dk/charter.asp
19. See/cf. http://www.kvinderiledelse.dk
20. SEC(2011)246 final, Commission Staff Working Paper, The Gender Balance in Business Leadership, Brussels, 1.3.2011.
21. Á jour de la révision constitutionnelle du 23 juillet 2008.

The French legislation on women quotas was adopted in January 2011.[22] Provisions apply to public limited companies including state-owned enterprises. The purpose of the provisions is to improve the representation of women on company boards. The provisions impose a type of quota of women on boards of public limited companies.[23]

Article L.225-17[24] du code de commerce
La société anonyme est administrée par un conseil d'administration composé de trois membres au moins. Les statuts fixent le nombre maximum des membres du conseil, qui ne peut dépasser dix-huit.

Le conseil d'administration est composé en recherchant une représentation équilibrée des femmes et des hommes.

Toutefois, en cas de décès, de démission ou de révocation du président du conseil d'administration et si le conseil n'a pu le remplacer par un de ses membres, il peut nommer, sous réserve des dispositions de l'article L. 225-24, un administrateur supplémentaire qui est appelé aux fonctions de président.

According to article L225-17 of the Commercial Code, a limited company must be managed by a board composed of at least three members and maximum eighteen, and the company is managed by a board composed of at least three members with a balanced representation of women and men. Thus, the second sentence in article L225-17 sets the general rule for equality between men and women.

22. The bill was initiated by Jean-François Copé, Secretary General of the ruling party Union for a Popular Movement (UPM), and fellow party member and MP Marie-Jo Zimmermann. The law has been adopted by the ruling party and backed by the opposition, which felt it did not go far enough. See Sarah Mongourdin-Denoix, HERA, April 14 2011, at http://www.eurofound.europa.eu/eiro/2011/01/articles/fr1101031i.htm
23. Goran Selanec and Linda Senden, Gender Quotas and Other Positive Action Measures to Ensure Full Equality in Practice between Men and Women. The transposition of EU provisions on positive action and gender quotas in employment, in access to and supply of goods and services, and in decision-making and political bodies in 33 European countries(, European Network Of Legal Experts In The Field Of Gender Equality, European Commission, Directorate-General for Justice, June 2011, France by Sylvaine Laulom, p. 97.
24. Modifié par Loi n° 2011-103 du 27 janvier 2011 relative à la représentation équilibrée des femmes et des hommes au sein des conseils d'administration et de surveillance et à l'égalité professionnelle publiée au Journal Officiel du 28 janvier 2011 – art. 1.

The general rule is specified in article L225-18-1, a new provision in the code de commerce.[25]

L225-18-1 du code de commerce26
Article 1
La proportion des administrateurs de chaque sexe ne peut être inférieure à 40 % dans les sociétés dont les actions sont admises aux négociations sur un marché réglementé et, à l'issue de la plus prochaine assemblée générale ayant à statuer sur des nominations, dans les sociétés qui, pour le troisième exercice consécutif, emploient un nombre moyen d'au moins cinq cents salariés permanents et présentent un montant net de chiffre d'affaires ou un total de bilan d'au moins 50 millions d'euros. Dans ces mêmes sociétés, lorsque le conseil d'administration est composé au plus de huit membres, l'écart entre le nombre des administrateurs de chaque sexe ne peut être supérieur à deux.

Toute nomination intervenue en violation du premier alinéa et n'ayant pas pour effet de remédier à l'irrégularité de la composition du conseil est nulle. Cette nullité n'entraîne pas celle des délibérations auxquelles a pris part l'administrateur irrégulièrement nommé.

According to the French Commercial Code Article 225-18-1, the board must consist of 40 percent of each gender in listed companies and in public limited companies with 500 permanent employees and with a net sales or total assets of €50 million Euros in the previous three consecutive years. If the Board consists of eight members, the gap between the number of female and male members cannot be more than two. There are indications that some companies are already taking positive steps to pre-empt this requirement.[27] Currently, the share of women on boards is approx. 12 per cent, having increased from 8 percent in 2008 to 12 percent in 2010.[28]

The act grants businesses six years to ensure that 40 percent of boardroom posts are filled by women. The French firms governed by the act must ensure that a figure of 20 per cent is reached within three years. The largest French companies will be affected by the law and it is estimated that about 2.000 companies could be affected by the French law. [29] The law also covers public

25. Texte Adopté N° 592, Petite Loi, Assemblée Nationale, Constitution Du 4 Octobre 1958, Treizième Législature, Session Ordinaire De 2010-2011, 13 Janvier 2011.
26. Créé par LOI n°2011-103 du 27 Janvier 2011.
27. See SEC(2011)246 final, Commission Staff Working Paper, The Gender Balance in Business Leadership, Brussels, 1.3.2011.
28. See also Lord Davies' reports regarding women on boards, Company Law Newsletter, 2011, Sweet & Maxwell.
29. See also Lord Davies' reports on women on boards, Company Law Newsletter, 2011, Sweet & Maxwell and Goran Selanec and Linda Senden, Gender Quotas and Other Positive Action Measures to Ensure Full Equality in Practice between Men and

companies regulated by commercial law, such as industrial and state-owned companies. If these thresholds are not reached, the directors will not receive wages.[30] The law initially provided that any decisions made by a board not fulfilling the quota would be invalid, but this clause was withdrawn from the final version of the text. However, any nomination to a board that fails to respect the quotas is automatically invalid.[31]

In January 2011 a first motion was made to set up quotas for women in top management in the public sector regarding public services. The proposal was made by Georges Tron, Secretary of Public Affairs. The aim of this motion was to reach a 40 percent female participation in top management in public services within four to five years and the proposal is a consequence of the act from the 27 of January 2011.[32]

6. Great Britain and Lord Davies of Abersoch

The British Company Act has no legal history in setting up requirements to the member of the board. As an exception to this general rule, section 157 of

Women. The transposition of EU provisions on positive action and gender quotas in employment, in access to and supply of goods and services, and in decision-making and political bodies in 33 European countries, European Network Of Legal Experts In The Field Of Gender Equality, European Commission, Directorate-General for Justice, June 2011, France by Sylvaine Laulom, p. 97.

30. Spain introduced an Equality Law in 2007that requires companies and publicly listed firms with more than 250 employees to apply a minimum 40 per cent board room quota for women. The law encourages large companies to bring in women on boards until each gender are represented with least 40 % by 2015. Spain has no penalty for failing to reach the 40 %. However, it will be taken into account in public procurement situations when public contractsare awarded. After the introduction of the law the percentage of women on the boards of the largest listed companies has raised from 4 % in 2006 to 10 % in 2010. See SEC(2011)246 final, Commission Staff Working Paper, The Gender Balance in Business Leadership, Brussels, 1.3.2011.
31. See also Sarah Mongourdin-Denoix, HERA, April 14th 2011, retrieved from: http://www.eurofound.europa.eu/eiro/2011/01/articles/fr1101031i.htm
32. Goran Selanec and Linda Senden, Gender Quotas and Other Positive Action Measures to Ensure Full Equality in Practice between Men and Women. The transposition of EU provisions on positive action and gender quotas in employment, in access to and supply of goods and services, and in decision-making and political bodies in 33 European countries, European Network Of Legal Experts In The Field Of Gender Equality, European Commission, Directorate-General for Justice, June 2011, France by Sylvaine Laulom, p. 101

the Companies Act from 2006 requires directors to be at least 16 years old.[33] The British company law has no requirement as to gender diversity on the boards of companies, but other developments regarding regulation of the top management of the company is implemented in the 2006 Company Act and 2008 company law.[34]

The British Company Law has no legislative requirement for a minimum proportion of women on boards. However, it is recognised that the majority of directors and board members in public limited companies are males.

Lord Davies of Abersoch investigated the importance of women on boards by examining the current situation using the number of women on FTSE[35] 350 corporate boards and by consulting with a wide range of stakeholders, interested parties and commentators including senior business figures, women business leaders, entrepreneurs, executive search firms, investors, women's networks and women who are just below senior executive level. The analysis was supported by experts drawn from the business world and academia.

Research has, according to the report, shown, that:[36]

> "... strong stock market growth among European companies is most likely to occur where there are a higher proportion of women in senior management teams. Companies with more women on their boards were found to outperform their rivals with a 42% higher return in sales, 66% higher return on invested capital and 53% higher return on equity."

The report also states that:[37]

33. This rule derives from *Re Cardiff Savings Bank (the Marquis of Bute's Case)* [1892] 2 Ch 100. See also Lord Davies' reports on women on boards, Company Law Newsletter, 2011, Sweet & Maxwell.
34. In accordance with the Company Act 2006 section 154, a private company must have at least one director and a public company must have at least two directors and section 155 requires, that in both types of company at least one director must be a natural person. See also new developments in the Companies Regulations 2008 (SI 2008/3229) in Table A and the Listing Rules Ch.9 Annex 1 (Model Code) para.16). See also Lord Davies reports on women on boards, Company Law Newsletter, 2011, 2011 Sweet & Maxwell.
35. Finansial Times Stock Exchange group of companies.
36. Lord Davies of Abersoch, CBE, Women on boards, independent review, February 24, 2011, p. 7: http://www.bis.gov.uk/assets/biscore/business-law/docs/w/11-745-women-on-boards.pdf
37. Lord Davis referrers to data from: Women Matter: gender diversity, a corporate performance driver, McKinsey & Company, 2007. The Bottom Line- Corporate Perfor-

- In 2009 only 12.2% of directors of FTSE 100 companies were women.
- The boards of FTSE 250 companies the proportion was merely 7.3%.
- By 2010 these figures had increased to 12.5% for FTSE 100 and 7.8% of FTSE 250.

Lord Davies of Abersoch emphasizes, like Rigmor Aasrud the Norwegian Minister of Government Administration, the economic benefits of the amount of women on boards:

> "The boardroom is where strategic decisions are made, governance applied and risk overseen. It is therefore imperative that boards are made up of competent, high calibre individuals who together offer a mix of skills, experiences and backgrounds. Board appointments must always be made on merit with the best qualified person getting the job. But given the long record of women achieving the highest qualifications and leadership positions in many walks of life, the poor representation of women on boards, relative to their male counterparts, has raised questions about whether board recruitment is in practice based on skills, experience and performance."

Also, studies show that businesses with more women at the top outperform companies which have only men in the management and on the board. An analysis shows that companies with women on boards have an operating income which is higher than companies without women on boards.[38]

7. EU – quotas from an economic perspective

From a macroeconomic perspective, the increase in women's participation in the labour market has accounted for a quarter of annual economic growth since 1995.[39] Several studies suggest there could be a positive correlation between the percentage of women in senior positions and company perfor-

mance and Women's Representation on Boards, Lois Joy, Nancy M Carter, Harvey M Wagener, Sriram Narayanan, Catalyst, 2007, Female FTSE Report, 2009, Cranfield School of Management, Government Equalities Office, conducted by Ipsos MORi, sample of 1,071 adults in Great Britain aged 16+. 20-24 February 2010, published 11 March 2010.

38. Lord Davies' reports on women on boards, Company Law Newsletter, 2011, 2011 Sweet & Maxwell.
39. See both OECD (2008) Gender and sustainable development. Maximising the economic, social and environmental role of women and SEC(2011)246 final, Commission Staff Working Paper, The Gender Balance in Business Leadership, Brussels, 1.3.2011, p. 7.

mance. Studies show that women who are members of company boards may also have a positive impact on financial reporting, auditing and the organisation of internal controls.[40]

The European Commission calculated the number of women on the boards of listed companies. The figures show that member states with a functioning legal binding regulation regarding women quotas have the highest amount of female board members, see tables below.[41] Furthermore, the average amount of educated women is higher than the average amount of men, which indicates that the material of well-educated potential members of boards should include more females than is currently the case.

Table 1[42]

Women and men on the boards of the largest listed companies (2010)

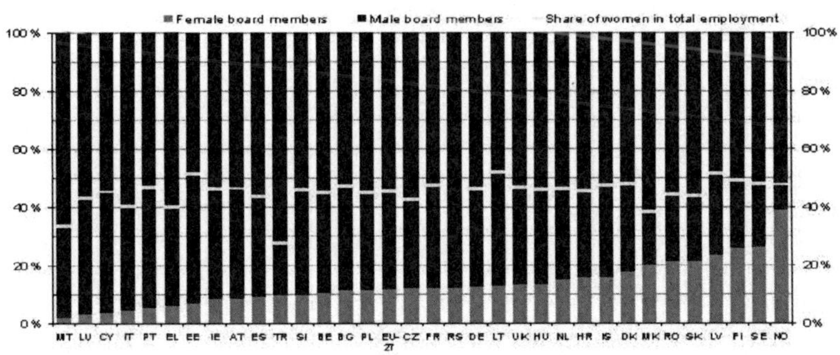

Source: European Commission, Database on women and men in decision-making.

40. SEC(2011)246 final, Commission Staff Working Paper, The Gender Balance in Business Leadership, Brussels, 1.3.2011, p. 8. See also Nielsen & Morten Huse, The contribution of women on boards of directors – going beyond the surface, (2010).
41. SEC(2011)246 final, Commission Staff Working Paper, The Gender Balance in Business Leadership, Brussels, 1.3.2011.
42. SEC(2011)246 final, p. 5.

Table 2[43] *Sex distribution of tertiary graduates for EU Member States in 2007*

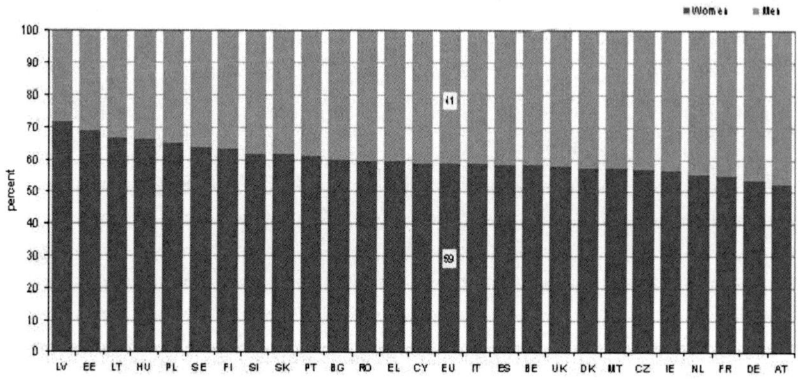

Source: Eurostat, Education statistics.
Note: LU: no data available. The EU-27 value is calculated on the basis of all countries except LU.

At the beginning of this chapter two quotations appeared:

"Gender equality is not a 'women's issue'. It is a business issue."[44]

and

"At the current rate of change it will take over 70 years to achieve gender-balanced boardrooms in the UK."[45]

43. Paolo Turchetti & Eric Gere, Population and social conditions, Education in Europe, Key statistics 2007, 37/2009, Eurostat Education statistics.
44. Viviane Reding Vice-President of the European Commission, EU Justice Commissioner The European Commission's New Gender Equality Strategy: Towards Quotas for Women in the boardroom? European Central Bank Diversity Forum Frankfurt, 28 March 2011.
45. Lord Davies of Abersoch, CBE, Women on boards, independent review, February 24, 2011, p. 1: http://www.bis.gov.uk/assets/biscore/business-law/docs/w/11-745-women-on-boards.pdf Edward Davey, the Business Minister and Lynne Featherstone, the Minister for Women, invited Lord Davies of Abersoch to undertake this review to identify the barriers preventing more women reaching the boardroom and to make recommendations regarding what government and business could do to increase the proportion of women on corporate boards.

The figures above support these statements; the issue speaks for itself and the market cannot solve this problem within the next 70 years – at least – and finally that it is not a women's issue. It is an issue which concerns serious business.

8. EU – quotas from a business law perspective

In March 2011, EU Justice Commissioner Viviane Reding made a pledge called the: 'Women on the Board Pledge for Europe'. The pledge represents, similar to the Danish initiative, a voluntary commitment to increase the number of women present on corporate boards to 30 per cent by 2015 and to 40 percent by 2020.[46]

Equality in decision-making, equal economic independence, equal pay for equal work and work of equal value, dignity, integrity, an end to gender-based violence, as well as gender equality in external action[47] are all areas in both the Women's Charter[48] and the European Commission's Strategy for Equality between Women and Men (2010-2015).[49] In both documents, the Commission has reaffirmed its commitment to working for an increase of the percentage of women in positions of responsibility.

The question is, whether a pledge and a strategy are enough? The figures describing the national legislations show that legally binding rules are effective in Norway.

An interesting question regarding the future situation on women quotas could be whether or not EU will suggest harmonized rules demanding equal opportunity between men and women on corporate boards in EU in general.

Ruth Nielsen discusses the influence of the Treaty of Lisbon on equal opportunity"[50] and she is analyzing whether the treaty can be seen as a codification of natural law in recent times, because the gender equality as a legal field has moved from case law[51] and soft law[52] to be a part of primary law in the

46. MEMO/11/124, Brussels, 1 March 2011.
47. SEC(2011)246 final, Commission Staff Working Paper, The Gender Balance in Business Leadership, Brussels, 1.3.2011.
48. COM(2010) 78 final
49. COM(2010) 491 final.
50. Ruth Nielsen, Lissabon-Traktatens betydning for ligestillingsområdet (EU- og Menneskeret, juni 2011, pp. 145-152.
51. At that time it was only the case law of the Court of Justice that obliged the Union to respect fundamental rights. See the first decision from the ECJ: Defrenne II-case: 43/75, 1976, s. 455.

EU-Treaty's Articles 2, 3(3) and 6 and Article 8 in the Treaty of the Function of the European Union.

According to Article 6 TEU, the Charter of Fundamental Rights of the European Union has become legally binding which leads to a substantial reinforcement of European Union governance by the rule of law. Thus, the Charter is a legally-binding instrument and the fundamental rights also are binding upon the EU institutions and bodies.[53] Article 157(4) TFEU allows the Member States to take positive action to achieve equal opportunities in practice between men and women in their working life.

In addition, Article 8 TFEU describes, that: "In all its activities, the Union shall aim to eliminate inequalities and to promote equality between men and women."

In COM (2011) 160 the Commission pointed out; "that despite a general trend towards more equality in society and on the labour market, progress in eliminating gender inequalities remains slow,"[54] and found among other things that action should be taken regarding equality in management, but despite the figures shown in the two tables above, the Commission does not suggest any legally binding rules.

Neither the treaties nor the charter will prevent the implementation of an EU directive stating a set of rules concerning equal representation in corporate boards. A provision demanding the same amount of female and male representatives would not be in conflict with the EU law and would thus not be discriminating against men. Neither will a rule demanding 40 percent women and 40 percent men, while the remaining 20 percent can be either of the two genders similar to the Norwegian rules.

The European Parliament agreed upon a motion report[55] based among other factors upon the EU Commissions support for efforts to increase women's presence on boards of directors, with a target of 30% female membership by 2015 and 40% by 2020 as a voluntary initiative.

The European Parliament stated that;

52. European Union Charter of Fundamental Rights, 7 December 2000. According to TEU Article 6 EU must recognize that the rights, freedoms and principles set out in the Charter of Fundamental Rights have the same legal value as the Treaties.
53. COM(2011) 160 final, Report from the Commission to the European Parliament, the Council, the European Economic and Social Committee and the Committee of the Regions, 2010 Report on the Application of the EU Charter of Fundamental Rights, Brussels, 30.3.2011, SEC(2011) 396 final.
54. COM(2011)160, p. 9.
55. European Parliament REPORT, 9 June 2011 regarding women and business leadership, (2010/2115(INI)).

"Given the poor results of efforts so far and the slow pace of change, some form of kick start is required, wider discussions with the business world in each country, and at European level, need to begin in order to break the current deadlock."[56]

The European Parliament also mentions that quotas could be considered, given that they have proved their effectiveness already. This must be considered today's status of the EU's development in relation to gender quotas. If introducing a legally binding set of rules such as legal action must among other things be based on a clear strategy for bringing in the binding legislation, provision for releasing the necessary financial resources and a clear political will.[57]

9. A comparative business law perspective

The implemented legislations on gender quota have become an example for other countries and can be an example for the rest of EU and Scandinavia. Norway and France have implemented similar legal provisions within their Company law and their Commercial law.

Spain, Iceland and the Netherlands also introduced legal rules regarding women quotas, but the Netherlands has not set a target date for compliance and the rules only require that the action performed by the company is explained in an annual report. Spain has set 2015 as the target date for compliance. Quotas for state owned enterprises are discussed in Belgium, Canada and Italy.[58]

The Norwegian objective behind the provisions was that the government regarded the low proportion of female board members as problematic and found that it was necessary to intervene. The aim of the law was to benefit from the use of both genders' resources and potential and by demanding a more equal distribution of the genders to ensure higher competition.[59]

The Norwegian Government introduced a provision allowing the public limited companies to voluntarily ensuring that the quota-demand was ful-

56. See the European Parliament REPORT, 9 June 2011 on women and business leadership, (2010/2115(INI)), EXPLANATORY STATEMENT.
57. Ibid.
58. See also Rohini Pande and Deanna Ford, Gender Quotas and Female Leadership: A Review, Background Paper for the World Development Report on Gender, April 7, 2011, p. 10.
59. Charlotte Karlberg, Kvinnors representation i bolagsstyrelser. En jämförelse mellem Norge och Sverige, Uppsats VT 2006, p. 9.

filled. The act gave the companies a grace period until 2008 to reach the target. Companies covered by the law, which after this grace period did not live up to the general provision, should be forced into dissolution.[60]

The provision in Norway and France are similar. When comparing the implementation of the provisions with the statistics in figure 1 above it, it is apparent that Norway is the only country with a degree of almost 40per cent women on boards. The figures regarding France have not yet reached the same amount, but the provisions are relatively new compared to Norway. France aims to follow a tight schedule with two deadlines (20 percent target to be reached in 2013 and 40 percent target to be reached in 2016), and plans to nullify all board appointments in violation of the quota.[61]

10. Closing remarks

Several different legal solutions and soft law initiatives have been implemented regarding the promotion of the number of women on company boards in both Scandinavia and several EU member states.

One statement springs to mind after analyzing the legal provisions and soft law initiatives in these countries and the material from EU. In regard as to the title in the beginning some changes should be made here at the end of the chapter.

It is a misunderstanding that it is all about women quotas. Instead it is all about equal quotas for both men and women. The legal rules regard equal treatment for women *and* men.

From a business law perspective both genders are ensured 40 per cent each of the representations on company boards, why the title of the chapter should in fact be changed into:

"Gender quotas on company boards in Scandinavian and EU."

The Norwegian legislation resulted in an increase in female members from 15.9 percent in 2004 to 37 percent in 2007 and finally a 40 per cent share of

60. Rohini Pande and Deanna Ford, Gender Quotas and Female Leadership: A Review, Background Paper for the World Development Report on Gender, April 7, 2011, p. 15.
61. Rohini Pande and Deanna Ford, Gender Quotas and Female Leadership: A Review, Background Paper for the World Development Report on Gender, April 7, 2011, p. 10.

women in 2008.[62] The EU statistics in section 7 above show the same development.

The quotas not only increase female representation but ensure a more equal representation of both genders.

The chapter has presented some of the legal provisions regarding quotas in company boards. Norway and France have introduced legally binding rules, Denmark, Great Britain and EU has not despite the statistics.

An interesting part of the comparative analysis was observing whether the existing Norwegian provisions will be used as general principles to apply to other countries and in EU. Already, the Norwegian provisions have become an example for other countries' legislative efforts.

62. See Rohini Pande and Deanna Ford, Gender Quotas and Female Leadership: A Review, Background Paper for the World Development Report on Gender, April 7, 2011, p. 10, Villiers, Achieving Gender Balance in the boardroom, Legal studies, 2010, issue 30, p. 533-557 and Hoel, The quota story: Five years of change in Norway, Women on Corporate Boards of Directors, International research and practice, eds. Vinnicombe, Singh, Burke, Bilimorie and Huse, Edvard Elgar, 2008.